The Post River flowed northward, snaking its way between spiraling mountains on either side. I descended into the canyon for a closer look. The weather was my friend today. A light breeze out of the west gave me a margin of safety with no down drifts. Right at the confluence of a fast-running creek and the Post River, I could see a gravel bar that looked long enough to land my Cessna 175 single-engine airplane. I circled back and slowed down to get a better look at the gravel bar. I decided it was worth a try. I began my approach about one mile north of the touch-down point I had selected, a spot marked by a drift log on the bank of the river.

With my heart beat increasing rapidly and adrenalin gushing, I began to throttle back and pulled full flaps to slow my speed. At about 10 feet above the rushing Post River, I gradually pulled back on the throttle, raising the nose of the plane slightly until I was literally hanging on the propeller and was on the ragged edge of a stall. God help me if the engine should miss a beat! With the stall warning screaming and my heart sounding like a tom-tom drum in my ears, it occurred to me what a position I was in: 100 miles from the nearest human being—alone—and nobody knew where I was.

I concentrated on landing as slowly as possible and at the same time keeping sufficient speed to maintain enough lift on my wings to stay in the air until the wheels touched the gravel. To my horror, I began to see that some of the gravel was not actually gravel but river rocks six to eight inches wide. Too late! The wheels touched down amid the sound of rocks flying up and bouncing off the wings. The strip now looked about the length of my driveway at home in Austin and was disappearing rapidly. Ahead, I could see the drop off of the gravel bar rushing at me. For a brief second, a scene flashed before my mind of an old western movie showing a covered wagon headed for a cliff and sure death and destruction.

I was jerked back to my present situation as the plane's wheels bounced over the rocks that lined the riverbank and the drop off ahead came speeding toward me. The brakes could not dig in and kept skidding under the wheels. I cut the master switch and prepared for a crash into the Post River. . .

BREAKAWAY

Walter Yukon Yates

the memoirs of

WALTER "YUKON" YATES

COMMENTS —

YUKONYATES@AUSTIN.RR.COM

Inquiries should be addressed to:

Post River Productions
2900 Post River Road
Cedar Park, Texas 78613
yukonyates.com

First Edition
First Printing February 2011

Cataloging-in-Publication Data

Yates, Walter
Breakaway

p. cm.

1. Yates, Walter—memoir 2. Biography—Walter Yates
3. Adventure—United States—twentieth century 4. Adventure—Texas
5. Adventure—Alaska 6. Adventure—Survival 7. Adventure—Flying
8. Adventure—Wilderness 9. Alaska—Gold Mining

ISBN: 9780615438832

LD 5309 8 2011 818.54. LCCN: 2011921299

Book designed and edited by: Allison Devereux

Although information herein is based on the author's extensive experience and knowledge, it is not intended to substitute for the services of qualified professionals.

Printed in the United States of America
at Ginny's Printing in Austin, Texas

I dedicate this book to my wife Tracy who with untiring efforts kept the home fires burning day after day, and year after year, as I pursued my life long dreams of exploring lands beyond the arctic circle. She understood the passion that drove me on. Without her, this book may never have been written. She reached inside and touched me where I live.

Acknowledgements

My heart felt thanks go to Richard "Cactus" Pryor, who for years kept up with me by having me as a guest on his KLBJ radio show, KTBC TV. He urged me to write a book, convinced that the world would want to hear my stories—in some of which he was my co-pilot. Cactus was at my bedside many times as I spent six months recuperating from a helicopter crash in British Columbia.

My thanks to Allison Devereux and her editing skills as she transcribed my stories and edited my hand scribbled notes. I thank her for her faith in the story I had to tell and her encouragement for me to tell it.

CAUTION

FASTEN SEAT BELT BEFORE
PROCEEDING FURTHER

Part I
Impact!

The Crash

The sound was like someone had hit the tail end of my helicopter with a baseball bat. When the Bell Ranger shivered like a thing alive and started a slow spin, I knew I was in trouble.

It could not have happened at a worse time. I had tightened the friction on the collective control and had the cyclic control stick between my knees as I poured a cup of coffee from my thermos. I was returning to Texas after a three-month gold prospecting trip to Alaska and I wanted to relax for a moment and enjoy the wilderness fairyland that was unfolding 700 feet below me. A heavy spruce forest blanketed the soggy northwest British Columbia marshland as far as the eye could see.

It was as if I was sitting still and the earth below was spinning in a giant circle. I knew I was going to crash—I had lost control of my tail rotor. In a flash decision, I dove the aircraft in order to build up enough speed to weathervane into the wind, keeping the tail behind me to resume a straight course. But I was running out of sky. There remained only a few seconds to decide where to put down the helicopter. Instinct took over. I spotted a clear cut of land wide enough to accommodate a crash landing, a 30-foot wide survey line that had been cleared by the Canadian government for oil and mineral surveys some years earlier. However, there was nothing to break my fall and the aircraft was going down so fast that I was certain I would not survive the impact.

The opening was directly below me now, but I did not have sufficient RPMs to pull off a successful auto-rotation landing. At the last possible moment I made a split-second decision to go into a sweep of spindly spruce trees in order to break my fall and possibly avert instant death. I pulled the aircraft up sharply and flared, cutting the power and raising the nose in order to slow forward speed.

I was now in the treetops. Quickly, I pulled the collective control, which put additional pitch in the main rotor blades, causing them to take bigger bites of air and produce more lift. I was falling straight down through the trees, drilling a round hole into the forest.

There is an old saying that I am sure we have all heard about near-death situations: they say your whole life flashes before your eyes. Well, I just don't believe this is true. During an in-flight emergency situation, if you lose power or experience some other crisis that forces you to put the helicopter down, the first thing you do is go into auto-rotation. It is possible to make an auto-rotation landing without any power and get a helicopter down without harming it or its occupants. This maneuver is practiced extensively in flight school. In fact, auto-rotation is one technique that instructors really bare down on when teaching their students. What it boils down to is this: in order to execute a successful auto-rotation landing, you have got to get that collective down sooner than immediately. My instructor used to say, "One, two, down. If you haven't got the collective all the way down by then, it is too late." We are talking about split seconds.

While you lower the collective you must also chop the throttle. This prevents the tail from wagging the dog. With the thrust from the main rotor blades, you can reverse your lift by dropping the collective and free-wheeling your rotor blades; while you are falling like a rock, the air passing through those blades has the opposite effect, spinning them and giving you lift. The objective of an auto-rotation is to get those blades at the highest RPM possible before hitting the ground. Then, you pull the collective and put all your pitch back in the blades at just the right moment before you contact the ground. If done correctly, your helicopter will make a soft landing.

I may have been a little slow to get all of these things done. If I had been at a higher altitude when disaster struck, I would have had more time to perform these maneuvers, but I probably had less

Crash site as seen from the air.

than 10 seconds to keep the helicopter in the air. On top of this, I had to decide where I was going to put down the helicopter. I realized that I was not building up the RPMs in my rotor blades that I would need to slow my landing and I was really going down fast. That is why I made the decision to fly my helicopter into the trees.

I am here to tell you that in this situation, you don't have time for flashbacks of your life. You are simply too busy. It is your life you are trying to save and whether or not you do depends entirely on how quickly you react. What you have to do in an emergency like this is engage your brain. It feels as though the ground is coming up toward you much faster than you are falling toward it. Depending on your altitude at the time emergency strikes, you may only have seconds to perform all of these procedures—you just do not have time to play back your life. The only thing that flashed before my eyes in these short moments was the ground that was rapidly coming at me.

The only time ten seconds seems to last an eternity is in the fourth quarter of a football game when the losing team has just moments left on the clock to score and win the game. Otherwise, ten seconds goes by mighty fast. If Nolan Ryan stood 10 feet away from a brick wall and threw an egg at it, what flashes through your mind is what's going to happen to that egg. In this case, I was the egg.

It was a nightmare of cracking, chopping, jolting, and unbelievable confusion. The rotor blades were chopping spruce trees into two-feet chunks; one even came through the helicopter bubble, hitting me in my rib cage and glancing off the left side of my face.

Impact! The right door of the helicopter flew off as if it had been blown by a bomb. Instant fire covered the shattered bubble and the door opening was a solid mass of flames. Releasing my safety belt, I dove through the angry blanket of red. I felt the sickening warmth of the fire as I looked back to witness the horrible sight: in mere moments, my aircraft had become a burning inferno.

A helicopter is not designed to make long-range flights, but I had a ferry tank carrying 44 extra gallons of gasoline. Moreover, the main tanks were nearly full as I had flown only an hour since my last fill-up before the crash. Approximately 75 gallons of fuel were feeding the fire!

I was amazed that the auxiliary tank under the rear seat had not exploded upon impact, literally drenching me in fuel. This ferry tank was designed to rupture on the bottom and leak out its fuel in the event of a crash and, fortunately, that is what happened. Still, for fear that it might explode and burn me alive, I decided to put more distance between the roaring flames and myself. I was in a state of shock and did not realize that I was crawling on hands and knees through a mucky mixture of moss, water, and mud.

Thirty feet away from the aircraft I collapsed. That is when the popping started. I always carried a rifle with me on these trips. A rifle is a vital survival gear item in the Canadian bush country, and I had two boxes of cartridges in my helicopter. Exploding now, the brass hulls ricocheted off of nearby trees. This was a new danger, so I crawled a short distance farther from the wreckage. By this time, the pain from my wounds had become excruciating.

I pushed myself into a little depression in the ground full of brackish water. The muskeg-type moss was soft and easy to press into. I did not yet notice the cold, penetrating dampness of the

40° water. I lay there and watched the flames consume my beautiful bird and everything I needed for survival in this unrelenting wilderness.

A short while later, as the flames subsided, I watched the remains of my helicopter melt into the swamp. Things began to grow even fuzzier. I drifted off in a wave of unconsciousness.

By the time I came to the fire had burned itself out. Shivering from the cold, I started to get to my feet, but for the first time I realized that I could not stand—the pain in my back and chest was unbelievable. Later, I found out that I had a crushed vertebra in my back and had suffered seven broken ribs. I could feel the bone ends rubbing together as I moved. Cuts on my face and head were bleeding profusely and blood ran into my eyes, blurring my vision. I felt for my left eye to make sure it was still there. Nothing looked real: I was seeing a hostile environment through blood and pain.

I crawled close to the remains of my helicopter. Heat was still radiating from it. What had been a classy aircraft that had carried me across the Alaskan and Yukon wildernesses was now nothing but a pile of molten, twisted metal sizzling in the swamp.

I lay back against a tree stump. In retrospect, mine had been a good life. There had been adventures and close calls throughout my many years of flying in the North Country. I thought about my life in the Marine Corps during World War II in the South Pacific, action on Guadalcanal, and unbelievably close calls as I lost one buddy after another. I might have been closer to death now than at any other time during a highly adventurous life. I felt myself sinking into blackness again. I wondered: *is this it, Walter Yates?*

The Move to Burny Mountain

My life had been one of survival from the very beginning. I was born in 1924 to Andrew Jesse and Mae Elisabeth Yates. My father cut lumber and my mother stayed at home to take care of her seven

Yates family portrait, July 1940 (I am standing in the back).

children. The earliest years of my life were spent on a remote mountain in the middle of the wilderness, miles from the nearest town, and from an early age, I was taught how to live off the land.

When I was about four years old, and I do remember the story vividly, my family moved from Oklahoma up to Burny Mountain in Arkansas where my grandmother and the rest of the Yates clan had lived for years. Just outside of Kingston, Arkansas, on our way up to Burny Mountain, we had to cross Dry Creek. Dry Creek was a creek that was just that—dry—except when it rained, and when it rained, it flooded. That creek could really get on a tear.

It had been raining the day we were to cross Dry Creek. My dad had a trailer carrying all of our belongings behind the car and when he pulled up to the river, he stopped and studied it for a while. It was flowing pretty hard—even faster than my dad realized—but he made the decision to go ahead and cross it.

We were a little more than halfway across the creek when water got into the engine. The car died and we were stuck in the middle of the river. In the car were my mother, father, and sisters; the three older boys—Chester, Harris, and I—were out back in the trailer. We were all stranded and the water was getting higher.

Fortunately, my dad was familiar with the area and knew that the Holt family lived about half a mile up the road from that crossing. I do not know how he did it, but my dad managed to get out of the truck, make it across the water, and run to the Holt family to get some help—hopefully with a team of mules to pull us out of the creek.

In the meantime, my mother, sisters, brothers and I were still stranded in the creek. The water was coming up into the car and the trailer, and I know my mother was horrified. She was especially worried about us boys out back in the trailer. It was not long, though, before my dad came back with Mr. Holt and a team of mules. They backed the mules up into the water and were able to get a line on the truck, but when the mules pulled, the truck and trailer would not move. We really had a problem and matters were getting worse as the water kept rising higher.

My dad crawled over the back of the car and unhitched the trailer from the truck. He and Mr. Holt made another run with the mules and this time they were able to pull the car out of the creek. In the meantime, the trailer began shifting as it was no longer attached to the car, and it looked like it was about ready to go. Quickly, my dad got back in the water and managed to hook the line onto the trailer. That trailer was just like a wagon and the team of mules pulled it right on out of the creek.

We were out of the water and out of danger. My mother was terrified. We were *all* terrified. The Holt's realized our situation and invited us up to their house to dry out and put on dry clothes. They fixed us supper and insisted we spend the night at their home.

The Holt's house was crowded with all the guests—they had a pretty good-sized family themselves. My oldest brother Harris had been to Burny Mountain before and knew the route up to my

Grandma Sarah Yates, late 1800s.

grandmother's house, so it was decided that Harris, Chester, and I would continue up the trail to grandma's. Of course, I did not know where we were going or how serious the situation had been.

We had to cross a couple of smaller creeks to get up the mountain, but we came to one that we could not wade across. Harris must have been only nine or ten, but he was old enough to know better than to try to wade out into that deep water, particularly with me being just a little kid. So the three of us sat down under a tree, huddled up together, and spent a miserable night waiting for daylight.

During the night the creek ran down a little bit and at daylight we were able to wade across. We proceeded up the mountain to Grandma's, wild-eyed and exhausted, trying to explain to our grandmother what was going on. Although we were tired, we felt all sorts of excitement.

My Uncle Jimmy, who lived with my grandmother and my Uncle Loli, saddled up one of his mules and headed down the mountain to meet the rest of the family and to see if there was anything he could do to help. My dad was down by the creek working on the car with Mr. Holt, trying to repair the engine that had flooded. Eventually, they managed to dry out the electrical

Left to right: Uncle Loli, Uncle Marion, Aunt Madge, me, Uncle Jimmy.

system and the distributor and get the car started again. Dad hooked the trailer to the car and headed up the mountain with the aid of a saddle horse lent to us by Mr. Holt. The mountain was so steep that Dad had a little bit of trouble dragging that trailer, but it had all of our family possessions on it and he did not want to lose them. Dad got the trailer to within half a mile of grandma's house before the car failed and he could not go any farther. Over the next few days, everything was stored in my Grandma's barn.

We all moved in with Grandma, Uncle Jimmy, and Uncle Loli while Dad started construction of a log home on 40 acres of land about a mile up the mountain from Grandma's house. Dad built that house in record time. Of course, I was having fun out on the farm with all the animals and Uncle Jimmy's coonhounds. The passage of time did not mean much to me at that age, but I know it was pressing for the rest of the family—particularly my mother—not to have our own home, so Dad really worked hard to get that house built.

When Dad completed the main part of the house, which had everything but a kitchen, we moved in. Dad and my older brothers later added a kitchen in a lean-to fashion that extended all the way across the back of the house and was nearly 12 feet wide. In total, our log house was about 30 feet wide. Dad also built a loft where my brothers, sisters, and I slept, while my mother and father slept in the main room downstairs—which was the entire cabin except for the kitchen. We had a ladder to the loft that we climbed to get to our bunks at night, and I know my mother used to worry about us falling off that thing.

My father built a split-rail fence that zigzagged around a small pasture to hold in our Jersey cow, which gave us delicious, creamy milk. Dad cut Water Oaks, which were not very good for firewood or lumber—or anything else for that matter—but they grew straight and with a nice grain. Dad cut the oaks into 10-foot logs and then split them into rails. These rails were the same kind that Abraham Lincoln used to talk about splitting. My father and older brothers then constructed the fence by stacking and overlapping the rails five or six tall, then angling them around the pasture. Many a time I used those rail fences to prop up my trusty rifle and pick off a rabbit, a bird, or some other critter.

Living out in the wilderness, we always had to consider our water supply. There was a spring about half a mile away from our house that ran year-round from which we obtained our water, and we relied on that spring for our water until my father dug a well. Dad selected a draw about a hundred yards from our house that water flowed down when it rained. It was his opinion that the head of this draw would be a good spot to dig a well. Living out in the sticks as we were, my father employed the help of his brothers, my Uncle Jimmy and my Uncle Loli, who occasionally assisted my father with his projects. The three of them dug at that well for quite some time, and it must have been 18–20 feet deep.

In order to build this well, my father and uncles dug the hole wide enough to swing a pick. They also had a ladder that they stuck down into the well to climb up and down while they were working.

Once they got the well dug deep enough to hit a little underground stream, they figured that it would supply all the water we needed and stopped digging. Next, they took field stone rock that we had gathered from around the area and lined the interior of the well. This lining was simply dry stacked rocks; my father did not use any kind of mortar. At that time, I did not even know what mortar was. Finally, to finish the well, my father built a rock housing that surrounded the mouth of the well and hung a bucket on a rope to draw water.

Throughout the season that my father built the well—one in which we were not suffering a drought—it always held at least 8–10 feet of water. It was good water and it adequately supplied our family's needs. One year, however, we had a heck of a drought. Everything dried up and the well was parched. My dad decided that while it was dry he would climb down and dig the well a little deeper to reach more water, but it didn't work. After he dug just a little bit farther down, he hit rock. My father knew there would not be any more water down below that rock so he stopped digging.

Without a new source of water, my father instead did some maintenance cleaning on the well and replaced many of the rocks. And he had a lot of free help for the task. It's funny how these old-timers could manipulate their neighbors and friends. Most all of our neighbors at that time drank a homebrew beer of some kind, so my dad let the story out that a bucket had broken carrying 10 bottles of his own homebrew. He said that the bucket had fallen down the well and was probably covered up with silt, but that whoever helped him clean out the well would get a share of that beer. Without further ado, Uncle Jimmy, Uncle Loli, and a couple of neighbors who lived as far as five miles away came over to our well. In Tom Sawyer style, Dad could almost sit back and lean against a stump as he watched the others do the work. They were really after that homebrew.

It is sad to say, but as it turned out, my father had only dropped two bottles of beer into that well, and one of them was broken.

Everyone got a taste out of the remaining bottle but that was it. Nevertheless, everybody took it good-naturedly.

Eventually, we all started complaining about having to hand-rope the water out of the well, so Dad made a big roller to draw up the line. He chopped a log that was about 10 inches in diameter and cut it down on each end until it looked like it had two round handles. He supported those handles on a wooden frame, setting the big log roller on top of it. He then attached an L-shaped board at the end of the roller enabling him to turn it like a crank. Finally, he tied the rope that carried the bucket to the log and turned the roller around, bringing the rope up or down. It made fetching a bucket of water from the well much simpler.

Helping my dad with the well was one experience that caused me to realize certain abilities that were developing in me. I was learning that I could build. I kept looking at the roller that my dad had built and was reminded of the kitchens of my Aunt Nora and my Grandmother. I had been in their kitchens and seen that all the women-folk had rolling pins to make pies, but my mom did not have one. Instead, she used a bottle for a rolling pin. It dawned on me that the roller my father had made for the well was exactly like Aunt Nora's rolling pin, and I decided that I would just make one for my mother.

Right away, I proceeded to start work on the rolling pin project. We had a lot of hickory wood out in the yard and I found a log my dad had drug up that was about three inches in diameter. A portion of this log had really straight grain and no knots, so I cut off a section about the length of a rolling pin. My dad had a handsaw in his tool bin; I took it and sawed down each side of the log to about an inch in diameter. Then, with a hammer and a chisel, I split off the ends until I had handles sticking out. My contraption did not swivel like modern rolling pins do, but you could use it in your hands to roll out dough.

There was a lot of sandstone around our home. Sandstone is like any rock except it breaks apart easily and is somewhat like compacted sand. Sandstone is good for smoothing down wood, so

I got a chunk of it and I rubbed and rubbed and rubbed on that little log, smoothing it out until I thought it was perfectly round (although it probably wasn't). I also rubbed on the handles of the roller until they were smooth so that my mother would not get splinters in her hands. I kept working until I believed I had made a perfect rolling pin.

I presented the rolling pin to my mother and she was overjoyed. I am sure she just wanted me to feel good about myself for making it, but she praised me to everybody for making her that rolling pin. And I, of course, probably got the big head over it. My mother kept that rolling pin for years and used it all the time. However, years later when we moved to Texas from Arkansas, the rolling pin got lost. My mother used to mention how sad she was about losing the rolling pin, but by that time we were in a position to easily buy one from the store. Nevertheless, that rolling pin was where it all began: where I learned to work wood with my hands.

My next project was more ambitious. I had helped my Uncle Jimmy with his wagon and team of mules that he used to haul lumber, hay, and other material to town, and I decided that I would build a wagon of my own. I made slower progress on the wagon than I did with the rolling pin because by that time I had to start doing work around the house. My dad always had some chore for my brothers and I to do, so I did not have as much time as I wanted to work on my project. However, when I did not have anything else to do, I was constructing that wagon. My dad was good enough to let me borrow some of his tools that I previously had not been allowed to use because he was afraid I would ruin or dull them. He had a drawing knife, a foot adz, and several different kinds of axes and woodworking tools, all of which came in handy while shaping the pieces to build the wagon.

The only things that I did not make original were the wheels. At that age, I could not figure out how to make a wagon wheel with spokes in it. As an alternative, I took rough-sawn boards and put them together running one way on one side and the other way on the other side, and I nailed the boards together making a round, solid wooden wheel. I cut a hole in each wheel with a wood auger and I put a tongue on the wagon so that I could adjust the frame that held the axel and pull the wagon by hand. The axel also had a piece of heavy timber on it that was rainbow-shaped on the bottom with a spindle going down through it, enabling the whole axle to turn. When the mules were pulling the wagon, the wheels would turn on that spindle. Of course, the wagon was too small for an animal to pull, and the front side of the wagon was difficult to make turn. The rear was built in the same way as the front except that it was solid and would not turn at all. I cut a square hole in the center of each one of those frames where the tongue could slide in and out, adjusting the length of load that I could put on the wagon.

I did not put a bed on the wagon, but I put upright boards on each side of those forms. Then, I would lay a log or some other object in the wagon and pretend that I was hauling big loads. I often hauled wood to add to our home's woodpile, and I got a lot of comments for my wagon. That's the way I have been all my life: I love to work with wood. Many years later, I built a complete western-style stagecoach. The skills I learned on Burny Mountain stayed with me all my life.

The Mushroom Hunt

Part of living off of the land meant hunting for food. One of the best prizes that you could earn living in the wilderness was to find wild morel mushrooms. I did not know at the time what the name of this mushrooms was, and I do not think my dad or mom or uncles ever used the name morel, but that's what they were called. To them, it was just mushroom hunting.

Morel mushrooms are prized the world over. I have heard stories of Europeans who have gone to their deathbeds before telling anyone the location of their patch of morel mushrooms. They are just that good. When they were properly prepared—and my mother sure knew how to do it—the best way I could describe them in those days was that they tasted just like beefsteak. They had a good flavor to them and there wasn't anybody who did not like those morel mushrooms. We had to be careful because there were also poisonous mushrooms in the area, but the good thing about the morel mushroom was its distinct appearance, entirely different than most other wild mushrooms. The best way to describe a morel mushroom to the uninitiated is that it looks like a brain with the different cells and lobes. The appearance is so distinctive that once you learn what they look like, you do not forget.

One day, Uncle Jimmy came by our house carrying a gallon bucket. I noticed it was empty.

"Youngin'," he said, "it's been rainin' for four or five days and the time is right to go mushroom hunting. Ma' has got her heart set on some mushrooms so I'm going out to see if I can find some. Why don't you come with me?"

Uncle Jimmy never failed to teach me something beneficial. I admired my uncle considerably because he had such a knowledge of how to live off the land. I told my mom where I was going and that I needed a bucket like Jimmy's. Mom had also had the pleasure of tasting these mushrooms and so she was anxious to help. She found me a bucket and away my uncle and I went.

Uncle Jimmy and I walked for miles. The morel mushrooms were not easy to track down because the ground where they grew was not necessarily consistent. I have found them on the sides of hills and I have found them in draws and I have found them on flat-level ground. But not always. That day, the woods were damp from the rains and the ground was covered in leaves. We were searching partially on my dad's land and partially on Uncle Jimmy and his mother's land, and Jimmy would point out what to look for. Often these mushrooms appeared around a dead tree, an old stump, or a rotted log, but sometimes they would pop up in places for no explicable reason.

Uncle Jimmy explained something to me that was very important, which I exercise to this day: when collecting a mushroom, you must take a pocket knife—in those days, any kid living on the mountain big enough to walk had a pocket knife—and cut the mushroom off at the base of the stalk.

"Don't ever pull one up," he said. "If you leave the roots in the ground it encourages their growth next year."

The other thing Uncle Jimmy taught me about morel mushroom hunting was that they only come once a year, so enjoy them while you can.

Pretty soon, we both had a half-dozen of these morel mushrooms in our buckets. Uncle Jimmy was fair: the first person to find a mushroom got it, but the next morel that was found belonged to the other guy, and so forth. Uncle Jimmy taught me much about fairness in life.

Uncle Jimmy and I stayed out in the woods all day long. By the end of the day, each of us had about two dozen mushrooms. Morels vary in size from two inches high to as much as six or seven inches high, and as thick as two inches in diameter. Of course, the large ones were really prized, but most morel mushrooms on Burny Mountain averaged about three inches in height.

That was one of my better days mushroom hunting. Uncle Jimmy and I returned to the house and my mother offered to cook a few of our mushrooms right there on the spot. To prepare the mushrooms, you must first slice one in half and check the hollow interior for certain insects and bugs that might have taken up housekeeping inside of it. After rinsing them off, you season them. I do not know what my mother used for seasoning in those days, but I know there was salt and pepper and a few other ingredients that she sprinkled on the mushrooms before frying them in bacon grease. Boy, were they ever good! My Uncle Jimmy sure loved those things. Anybody that tastes a morel mushroom is going to love it. I have hunted mushrooms all my life, and I even found them during the time I spent in Alaska years later, a place I did not even know existed at the time.

Early Life on Burny Mountain

My Uncle Jimmy was also instrumental in me learning how to swim. All mothers admonish their kids and tell them, "Stay away from the water until you learn how to swim." I used to wonder, *how am I going to learn how to swim if I have to stay away from the water?* We did not live too far—maybe three miles—from King's River, which had several great swimming holes that Tom Sawyer would have admired. King's River was about the only place where we could gather to meet our neighbors' kids because our homes were all several miles apart. We just did not have playmates everyday, so on Saturdays our dads and uncles would take us swimming at King's River.

One day at King's River, we picked a spot that had a somewhat level, grassy bank surrounding it and big trees hanging over the river. It was a beautiful site. I was about five years old and the bank seemed awful high to me, but it was probably only four feet above the water. All the other kids jumped in the river and started swimming, but I stayed down at the lower end of the swimming hole where the water was only knee-deep, just wading around because I could not swim yet. Nobody wore swimsuits in those days, everybody skinny-dipped, except when there were girls around. In that case, we would jump in fully-clothed, overalls and all.

On this day at King's River, Uncle Jimmy walked up to me and said, "It's time you learned to swim."

"Well, that's what I'm trying to do," I said.

"You can't swim in knee-deep water!"

"I'm not allowed to get in that deep water yet."

Uncle Jimmy looked at me coyly. "Walter, let's take a walk. A little higher upstream there is a shallow spot where you can learn to swim. I'll give you a hand and show you how to do it."

Well, I was pretty nervous. I didn't completely trust Uncle Jimmy when it came to things like this because he was somewhat of a prankster—and that's to put it mildly. It turned out I was rightly concerned. As we walked together along the bank of the river, Uncle Jimmy suddenly stopped, picked me up, and threw me into the water.

I came up slobbering, blubbering, and gasping for air, frantically waving my arms and kicking my feet. And, wouldn't you know, I suddenly noticed I was swimming. Dog-paddling, I guess you would call it. But I was staying afloat! Of course, Uncle Jimmy jumped in right behind me to be there in case this did not happen. Later that evening, when he was describing all of this to my mother, he told her that this was the way everyone in the Yates family learned to swim. Someone just threw you in the water and yelled "Sink or swim!" You really learned to swim in a hurry.

After that, I was allowed to go to the river with my older brothers without an adult along, and I really enjoyed that new freedom. I never did get much past the dog-paddle in style until years later when my family moved to Corpus Christi, Texas and I began swimming in school like everybody else. But for those first few years, I just dog-paddled around like Uncle Jimmy taught me.

Another lesson that my Uncle Jimmy taught me—very carefully—was how to grapple for catfish under rocks in the river. During the spring seasons, wild walnut trees blossomed throughout the countryside. When the walnuts grew to about half the size of a golf ball, you could take a few to a watering hole where the stream runs, crush the walnuts on the rocks, and let the juice run down through the water. The juice from the walnuts would temporarily addle the catfish, causing them to float to the surface of the water, turn over on their bellies, and flop around so that we could catch them by hand. If the juice stayed in the water for too long, though, it would probably kill them.

This practice was definitely illegal, so we always had someone on the lookout in case the local game warden came around. We never did get caught, and we brought home an awful lot of fish that way. Although it was against the law, I am sure that it is safe 80 years later for me to tell this story—I don't think anyone is going to come and arrest me—but it was a practice that all the kids up there on Burny Mountain knew about. Fishing was one of the more exciting things that young kids could do, and to be able to come home with a string of catfish was like a badge of honor. My brother Chester also took to grappling catfish. He and I would go down to the river frequently and return home with enough fish to feed the whole family, every time we went. I don't believe we ever did tell our mother how we were getting all these fish, she just thought we were good at fishing. But my dad knew what we were up to and warned us to be careful because the game warden would lock us up if we ever got caught. Still, he did not put his foot down and make us stop.

I never will forget the day the big catfish came up. Chester, Harris, and I were all at the river that day. Harris was the more conservative one of my siblings and he frowned upon grappling for fish like this. Harris was fussing at us while we were grappling when all of a sudden we heard a splash repeated downstream. I looked down and saw the biggest catfish I had ever seen, probably weighing over 15 pounds. We did not have any way of weighing it but it was big.

After we threw in the walnut juice the big catfish started gasping for air and struggling for oxygen. It was not quite turned over on its back but it was sticking its head out of the water and swimming on the surface of the river. Catfish have horns sticking out of them—spikes, really—on either side of their gills and one just above their shoulder. Those horns are sharp, and they must have some kind of poisonous fluid in them because if one sticks you, it doesn't just hurt right then, it keeps on hurting. We were scared of the horns on this catfish but the prize of getting the fish before it got itself together and went back underwater was too big to pass up. All three of us, even Harris, jumped into the water after that catfish. We missed it the first time and it went under water. We stood very still and waited because we thought the fish would come back up to the surface, and pretty soon it did. This time, we did not miss. Chester got his hand in the catfish's mouth and gripped its lower lip while I held the tail section. Then, the three of us dragged it up onto the bank.

That fish was coming alive now, really flopping, but pretty soon it was subdued. That was the biggest fish we ever brought home and I thought it must have been the biggest one in the river. We took the fish home whole, of course, taking turns carrying it because it was so heavy. That night, my mother filleted the catfish. We must have gotten two or three meals out of that fish and I never will forget it. Later, I told one of my uncles about the catfish.

"Just how big was that fish?" my uncle asked.

"Well, it was so big, you couldn't see it all at one time." They laughed about that, and it was almost the truth.

In those days, none of the kids had any money to speak of, and anything we could do to earn a little bit of pocket change we were right in there knee-deep doing. One of the things that we could do in the fall of each year was to pick peach tree pits. There was an abundance of peach trees on and in between the farms around Burny Mountain that grew what we called free-stone peaches. The trees had probably grown from somebody throwing a seed down on the ground after eating a peach years earlier. The peaches would fall off of those trees and leave seeds after they rotted.

There was an agricultural department out in Fayetteville, Arkansas that would buy those pits, sprout new trees, graft a good peach on them, and then sell the peach trees in various nurseries around the country. This agricultural department needed people to collect those seeds, and that is where we came in. I do not remember the price we got for the pits, but I remember if I collected 40–50 pounds of seeds in a toe sack and took it into town to this agricultural department, they would buy them from us. We could take them into Kingston—only five miles away from Burny Mountain—and get a fair price for the pits, but if we took them into Huntsville, about 15 miles away, we could get three or four cents more per pound. So we would wait until somebody in the area had to go to Huntsville for supplies with a wagon and send our peach pits with him. We did not make a lot of money, but until the peach pits were all gone or the department quit buying them, I could collect as much as $2 for a sack of pits. To a kid who never had a nickel in his pocket, that was a lot of money.

The first thing I did was spend that money on a Stevens Crackshot .22 Single Action Rifle, which I bought for $2.95 from a Montgomery Ward catalog. It would shoot the .22 ammunition that came in sizes for short, long, and extra-long rifles. The shorts did not shoot very far but they were a lot safer for a youngster to use. To get ammunition, I had to go down the mountain, cross King's River, and then walk a mile up the road to the country store in Loy, Arkansas which had a little bit of everything, including the shells. I never had enough money to buy a whole box of shells so I would buy them individually, two for a penny.

I improved my ability to squirrel hunt after that rifle purchase. I spent a lot of time trudging through the trees, sometimes several miles away from home, with that little .22 rifle, and I would always bring home three or four squirrels. Squirrels were part of our regular diet in those days. The best to eat were the young squirrels—they could be fried and we ate them just like fried chicken. The older squirrels we would stew and make into dumplings. That was just an average meal two or three times a week up there on Burny Mountain. If we did not have anything else to eat, we would go squirrel hunting. We did not shoot these squirrels for the fun of shooting, we shot them for food.

I learned a lot from my little .22 rifle. After every shot I had to open the bolt, eject the empty shell, and then put another one in. If you have a squirrel that is trying to get away from you and you aren't good at handling your rifle, that squirrel will be gone before you can get another shot at him. The best hunting for squirrels, when I could always count on bringing one home, was in the spring and early summer when they cut on hickory nuts. Like pecans, hickory nuts have a thick hull, and as soon as the nuts are about two-thirds grown the squirrels will start nibbling on them. My brothers and I would find a hickory tree with the droppings of the chewed hull underneath and just sit down quietly on a log under the tree and wait.

Pretty soon, we heard the *flip flip flip* of the hull droppings falling to the ground. Very carefully, without shifting my body, I would move my eye in the direction that the sound was coming from up in the tree. All that was left to do was to shoot the squirrel. I could shoot a lot better with an armrest than I could free-hand, so I often selected a spot where there was a bush or a branch in front of me that I could hold the rifle against. Then, I would zero in on that squirrel and shoot him. Sometimes there was more than one squirrel in a tree and when I took my shot they would all run and hide. But if I waited long enough in my spot, staying completely still, it was not long before the other squirrels came back out and started chewing their hickory nuts again. I guess they did not miss their buddy yet.

My brothers and I were taught early on to shoot a squirrel in the head so that we would not mess up the meat. Our shots had to be very accurate and it was a long time before I got good enough to always hit a squirrel in the head. Most of the time I went hunting by myself. Chester was a lot better shot than me and Harris was even better than Chester. When I went hunting with my brothers, they would always get a squirrel before I could even get my rifle ready; when I hunted by myself, I could take my time. And I was glad that I did when I was able to come home with a squirrel. To transport the squirrels home, I took a forked stick and cut a prong on one end. Then, I cut the stick about a foot long and cut a notch into the leg of the squirrel, ran the stick through it, and carried it home.

I learned to shoot a rifle at a much younger age than most kids who lived in towns and cities. The skills I learned squirrel hunting really helped me as the years went by, particularly later on when I joined the Marine Corps where I would earn a medal for my marksmanship. This skill stuck with me throughout my life and, as it turns out now, I am here today because I am a good shot.

Stranded

When awareness came again, I tried to make myself believe that my helicopter crash was all a horrible dream. But the pain, the cold, and the miserable swamp—evidence that I really had crashed my helicopter—would not go away. I took stock of my situation. This particular flight leg was from Fort Nelson, British Columbia, to Red Deer, Alberta, with planned refueling stops at Fort St. John, Grand Prairie, Whitecourt, and Dawson Creek. I had avoided some bad weather to the south and was out in the forested flat country, approximately 30 miles north of the Alcan Highway and the Canadian Rockies. Everything had looked so beautiful. Evidently, I had been lulled into a false sense of security.

For some reason, at this time I thought it important to recount the miracles that had kept me alive through one of the most traumatic moments of my life. First, if that chunk of wood that flew through the helicopter bubble had hit me in the head, I would have been knocked unconscious and burned with the aircraft. Second, although the helicopter had crashed hard, I had not been knocked out. Third, the right door of the helicopter flew off upon impact—if it hadn't, I surely would have been trapped in the flames and burned to death. Last, my auxiliary gas tank had not exploded and drenched me in fuel—this would have been certain death.

I wondered, *what is the next step?* Tomorrow, once the melted aluminum and weird, twisted steel that had been my aircraft had cooled sufficiently, I would go through the ashes and the part of the helicopter's tail section that had not burned completely to see if there was anything that could be used to keep me alive until help arrived.

Then, I saw my heavy boots and jacket. I remembered pushing them into the baggage compartment last. The compartment was so full that it had been difficult to close the door before I left on my flight. Upon impact, it had burst open with such force that these items landed far enough away from the aircraft to escape total destruction by the flames. The fact that this was yet another miracle which could contribute to preserving my life did not penetrate my intense shock and made little impression on me in that moment. The pain was so severe that I'd rather sit and shiver in the cold and wet than retrieve my boots and jacket. Every moment was pure torture.

After lying in the cold water that first night—half awake and half unconscious—I began to realize that I was in even worse condition than I thought. All movement had to be done on hands and knees. I made several attempts to stand by supporting myself on a tree, but it was simply impossible. I had lost approximately two quarts of blood, but I had to do something. I could not just sit there and hurt.

I crawled to the wreckage in hopes of finding anything that would help keep me alive. First, I inspected the tail section of my helicopter. I had been so right! The tail rotor pitch control drum assembly had come off. This effected complete loss of control of the aircraft.

Next, I began sifting through the ashes. The baggage compartment, although it had burned completely, did not get as hot as the cabin and engine area. Before I left Anchorage some friends had given me a five-pound box of prunes. I found the box, now a chunk of black charcoal lying underneath the baggage compartment. Those were the prunes, all right. A few were only half charcoal, their inner portions still moist. There would be a small amount of food value in these so I set them aside, went through the glob again, and found half a dozen more prune pits that were not burned completely, although they were well roasted. For the next two days I would suck on the charcoal prunes and eat the pits, which tasted like almonds. There could not have been more than a tablespoon of food value altogether in these burnt prunes, but at that time of desperation they were a big help.

Sifting through the ashes, I came upon my hunting knife. Deformed by the fire, it was now almost unrecognizable but it would still be useful. My camera equipment had also burned. Most of the lenses had melted out of shape but one had not been damaged. This was a real find! Later on, if the sun came out, I could use this camera lens like a magnifying glass to start fires. I had done this as a boy. I would dry some moss by holding it inside of my clothing next to my body; then, holding a magnifying glass to the sun, I would concentrate the heat on the dry moss until it ignited.

My metal detector was completely fused and melted together. I also found my ELT. This emergency locater transmitter activates upon impact and turns on a radio signal for the search and rescue team to zero in on, but it had probably worked only a couple of minutes before the heat rendered it useless. A tape recorder had also melted and fallen into the water.

The most valuable find was my toolbox. It was made of heavy metal but was burned so badly that most of the tools were ruined. However, a few tools, including my hacksaw, were still usable. Although the saw was twisted and warped from the heat it could still cut. Another valuable item in my toolbox was a roll of aircraft safety wire, damaged but also still usable.

On my trip through the North Country I had found an antique bucket at an old ghost mine in Alaska. Now, here it was, burned and blackened, but I could use it to catch rainwater. It was at this point that I began to realize the miracle that had sprung my boots and jacket to safety. The right elbow was burned out of my parka and the boots were scorched at the top, but they had been thrown far enough away from the fuselage to escape serious damage. Still, I did not yet realize what an important role these heavy boots and jacket would play in keeping me alive.

Then there were the items that were on my person when I went down. I had my pocket calculator that gave the date and time, one small package of M&Ms candy, and a tiny box with seven matches.

These items, added to what I had found in and around the wreckage, brightened my spirits and gave me new hope.

I was concerned about my broken ribs and afraid that my movement about might cause one of them to puncture a lung. Using the remains of my hunting knife, I carved some splints from spruce limbs and bound them together with the safety wire in the form of a rough corset. I wrapped this around me and twisted the wire to draw it tight. I thought, perhaps, this would keep the ribs in place.

As I became even more aware of my impossible situation, I realized that I must call upon my determination and will power to the utmost if I was to survive. I had always had great pride in the strength of my will power, which I had called upon many times over a lifetime of survival study. Now, I was facing the supreme test. I had to convince myself that I could withstand the intense pain, but more and more, I realized that if I were to experience the miracle of survival I must depend upon divine guidance. I prayed for relief from pain, for food, and for guidance to those who would be searching for me. Most of all, I prayed for strength.

When you are lying beside a crashed aircraft, injured to the extent that you are not sure if you are going to make it, one thing you've got plenty of is time to think. Lying there thinking about my situation, it was natural for my thoughts to go back to my childhood. My mind again wandered back to my early years living on Burny Mountain in the Arkansas Ozarks. *Will I ever see that place again?*

Living Off the Land

Growing up on Burny Mountain, I did a lot of exploring with my brothers and became very familiar with the lay of the land, 40 acres completely covered with timber and a large bluff. The land we lived on had belonged to our family since my father homesteaded when he came home from World War I. As a young boy, those 40 acres might as well have been the whole state of Arkansas! To me it seemed huge, and there were no fences or boundaries to tell me when I was leaving our land and wandering onto someone else's. I could roam for miles and never know whose land I was on until I returned back to our log home. That is how I spent many of my days: exploring, hunting squirrels, and chasing rabbits.

Eventually, I was allowed to wander the woods by myself, as long as I did not stray too far or stay out too late, and this is where my education in wilderness life really began. Uncle Jimmy would often go with me on these jaunts and he taught me about nature and the wildlife. He taught me how to recognize different types of wood and trees, and I learned which wood was best for building furniture and which was best for building fires. Uncle Jimmy also showed me the location of some wild plum trees. At the right time of year, we would always get into them.

Living out in the wilderness, we raised our own food as much as we could. We raised chickens for meat and eggs, and hogs to butcher. My dad also started a garden plot by our house, but this was part of wilderness life that I really did not like. There always seemed to be sprouts and weeds growing out of the ground that my brothers and I had to get rid of with grubbing hoes. I was probably five or six years old and had my fair share of work cutting out those sprouts.

We raised potatoes and corn and had apple trees near our home. Anything we could store away for the winter, we would. Although I did not like tending to it, the garden was an important resource for our family. I remember the times when the whole family sat around a large wash tub in the evenings shelling corn. We would take ears of corn and twist them in our hands to remove the kernels and let them fall into the tub. My hands were sore for days afterward, but we all shared in this chore, even our mom. The corn we produced was traded at the little country store in Loy for cornmeal and flour. A man we called Old Jucks ran the mill that ground our corn, and I still remember watching his machinery run. It had a one-lung engine that operated a big fly-wheel that went *whoosh whoosh whoosh whoosh pop!* I was fascinated by that big machine.

My dad started a tradition of always having homemade ice cream on the Fourth of July. You might think, how could we make ice cream in the middle of summer? Where would we get any ice? Well, my dad was pretty good at solving problems like this and I think that to a great extent I inherited some of those traits.

Dad dug a pit in our backyard about four feet wide, six feet long, and seven feet deep. When I was helping him dig the pit, Dad would stick a ladder into the hole and I had to climb down it to fill a bucket with dirt. A few miles away from us on the mountain there was a man who had a sawmill. He kept a huge pile of sawdust and it was available to anybody who wanted it. My dad would go over there with a team of mules and a wagon, load up a bunch of that sawdust, and then dump it in the bottom of the pit about two or three feet deep. When winter came—and we had some pretty cold winters—some parts of the river would freeze over with a layer of ice as much as five inches thick. We would break off the ice and bring several hundred pounds of it back to our house. Dad then put the ice down into the hole of sawdust and poured several more feet of sawdust on top of it. Finally, he would lay some boards over the pit to seal it shut and then throw on some dirt.

The following summer, when the Fourth of July came, Dad would open up the pit, dig down deep into the sawdust, and pull out huge chunks of ice that had remained frozen in the ground which we could use in our homemade ice cream freezer. We would make ice cream several times throughout the summer until the ice was gone. My mother also loved making ice-cold lemonade. That ice was a real treat for us living up on Burny Mountain.

Whenever my mother had to wash clothes, she would bundle up the dirty laundry, go down to the spring, and take all the kids with her. She built a fire under a big, iron pot that our grandmother supplied us and boiled water to wash our clothes. Then, on a piece of rope that Uncle Jimmy had rigged up for a clothes line, she hung the clothes out to dry. My mother insisted that her children have clean clothes. She always used to tell us to be sure to change our underwear because if something ever happened to us, we don't want to be caught with dirty underwear. We would spend the whole day at that spring on wash day and eat a lunch that Mom had packed. Mom did the wash about once a week—frontier life was rough on the women-folk.

My mother was from New Jersey and had been a real city girl for most of her life. I know she often wondered what she had gotten herself into when she married Andrew Yates, but Mom was a real trooper and I rarely ever heard her complain. She was always working. With that many kids to take care of, three meals to fix each day, and clothing to iron and mend, she did not get much time to herself. She had an old iron that was really just a piece of iron that she heated on top of the stove. Even though we lived in the sticks, she still liked to look nice when she could, particularly if we were going to church (which we did not do as often as we should have because it was so far away).

My mother never had it easy. In 1929 there was a serious outbreak of diphtheria, and it was mandatory for everyone to get diphtheria shots, including babies. My baby brother was nine months old at the time. The whole family marched down to where the health department was administering the shots. I suppose with thousands of people receiving the shots they got careless in the process, and there were a few cases of blood poisoning caused by unclean needles. My baby brother, Robert Eugene, got infected, and I still remember the huge, reddish-purple spot on his arm. It just kept getting worse, and after three days he died. This was my first experience with death and I just could not understand why an innocent child had to die. My mother bore eight children—"Bobby Gene" was number 8—and it was not until I joined the Marine Corps that I had any other vaccinations. I was afraid to get shots after that tragedy in our family. We all mourned the loss of Bobby Gene and for years after his death I could still see the grief my mother had to bear.

Over the next few years I became more familiar with the land and kept wandering farther away from the house. Little did I know that I was learning skills I would use much later in life. Neither did I realize how privileged I was to be able to learn the things I was about life at such an early age. I did not have any little buddies to play with but I amused myself in the forest. As all kids do, I built hideaway camps, one of which I made in a cave down by the bluff. This spot provided good shelter and I built myself a little clubhouse where I could build fires and roast potatoes.

There was not much I didn't learn about living out in the sticks. That's the way my mom used to refer to it when she wrote to her mother: "living in the sticks." But she was a good sport. I never heard her complain about the hard life that she led. I will say again, those frontier women—and that is what my mom was—had a rough row to hoe, and they hoed it. I am really proud of the folks I had who taught me the lessons that came in so handy throughout my entire life.

Bee Hunting

My Uncle Jimmy also taught me how to go bee hunting. Every family on the mountain knew how to hunt for wild bees in order to obtain their honey, and we always had plenty of honey year-round. At first, I did not think too much of the idea of robbing the honey and getting stung by all of those bees, but Uncle Jimmy had a technique of wrapping up his head in mosquito netting and wore gloves to protect his hands. It would not eliminate bee stings altogether, but it would keep them down to only a few. I always got at least one or two stings.

When roaming around the mountain, the men-folk kept their eyes peeled for bees flying around old hollow trees. If they saw one, they would stop for a minute and watch for bees flying in and out of the knothole. The men always carried an axe or a hatchet with them and if they found a bee tree they would carve an "X" into the trunk, indicating to any other mountain residents that this tree had been claimed.

The idea is to cut down a hollowed-out bee tree and let it fall to the ground. When the former bee home falls, the bees are extremely confused and hundreds, if not thousands, of bees swarm around wondering what happened to their home. During this time of confusion, we would drag the log a little ways off and notch it with the axe above or below the knothole. Once we located the honeycomb, we cut the tree about two feet beyond it, creating a sort of cylindrical tube containing all of the honeycomb. Then, we took our knives and cut out several racks of the honey-filled comb. The bees have sealed up each chamber and this will keep it fresh for years. The process involves a delicate balance of removing large chunks of honeycomb and several of the bees while leaving enough of the comb so that the bees do not abandon the hive altogether.

By this time, the bees realize what has happened to their hive and begin to swarm around furiously. Then came the tricky part. In order to trap the bees to take them back home to our bee boxes, we had to locate the queen. It isn't *too* difficult because she is always surrounded by a mass of other bees trying to protect her, and she is about half-an-inch longer than all of the other bees. As Uncle Jimmy taught me, you reach your hand under the mass of bees, pick them all up, and put them into some kind of container. This can be a bucket or a tub or even a piece of hollow tree whose ends can be closed up with cloth.

I do not know how they do it, but it doesn't take long for the other bees to figure out where the queen is and work themselves into the container. Then, we left the log on the ground for a few days before returning to close up the open end of the container and bring it home. We would then farm the bees and harvest honey right in our backyard!

One time, I wanted to surprise Uncle Jimmy. I knew he had marked a bee tree about a mile from our house and I went out there one day with an axe and a tub. Just like he taught me, I cut the log down, carved it open to the honeycomb, and filled up the tub with what must have been 30 pounds of honeycomb. I then found a hollow log nearby, and with some old feed-sack canvas I made a trap for the queen, caught her, and put her in the hollow log. After a little while, a whole mass of bees was swarming into the log to find and protect the queen. Before I left, I sealed up the other end of the log with another piece of canvas.

When I got back to the house I put the tub filled with honey on the kitchen table, awaiting Uncle Jimmy's return. I knew he was going to be so proud of me when he got back. But instead, as soon as he saw that tub of honeycomb, he knew I had chopped down his latest bee tree and grew very angry.

"You didn't cut down my bee tree, did you boy?" he asked.

"Yup, Uncle Jimmy, I sure did. I cut down the one over in Stillhouse Hollow."

"Well, I was planning on catching those bees, not just gettin' the honey!"

I told him that not only had I collected the honeycomb but that I had also trapped the bees in a hollow log, which was ready for us to carry on home. He looked at me, shook his head and said, "You did good boy!"

Uncle Jimmy had a way of looking at me like I had just done something wrong or that I was just about to. He kept me on my toes but we got along really well. He knew how to keep me in line and taught me almost everything I know about living in the wilderness. I do not mean to diminish my dad because he taught me a lot too, but with all those mouths to feed, he had to work every waking moment to make a living for our family. I am still not sure why Uncle Jimmy, who never married and lived with Grandma, never seemed to have anything to do, but I guess it worked out well for both him and my dad.

The Turkey Shoot

On another occasion, Uncle Jimmy took me on a turkey hunt. Between our land and the King's River there were two bluffs which we called the Upper Bluff and the Lower Bluff. On this particular day, Uncle Jimmy had seen a flock of wild turkeys at the Upper Bluff and asked me if I wanted to go turkey hunting with him. That sounded exciting, so I grabbed my trusty rifle. I loved to shoot my .22 Stevens Crashshot rifle, and I loved the way turkey smelled and tasted fresh out of the oven. Although my gun was only a single-shot, bolt-action rifle, I had gotten pretty good at shooting accurately. I'd had plenty of practice on squirrels in the miles of forest surrounding our log home. The rifle was nice and broken-in, and I could reload it quick-and-easy.

Uncle Jimmy told me that if I did not hit a turkey just right on the first shot it was liable to get away before I could fire off another round. He always encouraged me to "shoot for the head" or else I would lose the turkey. We set off into the wilderness toward the bluff and it was not long before we found feathers and tracks in the dirt: evidence that the turkeys had recently passed. Jimmy told me to be silent because these turkeys had highly sensitive hearing, and eyesight as good as an eagle's. He said they could see us coming way before we saw them. I was very careful not to step on a stick or make any other noises that would scare the turkeys away.

All of a sudden, Uncle Jimmy reached over and gave me the signal. He touched me on the shoulder, indicating that he had seen a turkey and that I should be still and silent. Almost inaudibly, he whispered that the turkeys were about a hundred yards in front of us. We crouched down, nearly on our stomachs, and began to inch our way closer to the flock. After what seemed like an eternity, I eventually saw a few birds. Sometimes they would travel in bands of as many as 30 at a time so I was eager to get a little closer to see just how many there were. Remembering what Uncle Jimmy had told me about losing the turkey if I did not hit it right, I carefully moved closer to the flock and got into position. I pointed my .22

Crackshot, rested my elbows on my knees, and spotted a big turkey that looked to be a gobbler. I concentrated to hold my sight on his head, but this was no easy feat because a turkey will move its head around in all different directions and with no apparent pattern. His head was a moving target and it was a challenge to zero in on him.

Eventually, I got into a rhythm and could follow the turkey's movements. I had been taught very early by Uncle Jimmy and my father that you do not pull the trigger, you squeeze it very gently. If you did not squeeze it just right you would pull your aim off the target and miss the shot, and with my bolt-action .22, I would not get another shot unless I was super quick on the reload.

I was finally ready to make my shot. I zeroed in on the turkey's head and with deep concentration squeezed the trigger. *BAM!* As soon as I fired the shot there was a turkey explosion! Total turkey chaos ensued. Feathers scattered everywhere, and turkeys flew in every which direction—except for one of them: the one I had targeted did not fly away. But neither did he drop to the ground! Instead, he started to run as fast as he could. I realized I must have missed the headshot, but I had to have hit him *somewhere*. It must have been the wing or else he would have flown away like the rest.

The turkey was bolting away as fast as his little turkey legs would take him. Uncle Jimmy shouted, "Get after him, boy! Run. *Run!*"

I took off running as fast as I could, trying to reload as I chased this turkey down. I never took my eyes off of him for fear that I would lose him in the woods, and I knew that if I did not catch up with him soon he would make it to the Lower Bluff and escape me. Fumbling with the shells in my pocket, I tried and tried to blindly reload the rifle. I dropped two or three bullets along the way, the whole time wondering if this bird would ever run out of energy.

Although I ran like heck after this turkey, I never could get any closer to it than 50 yards or so. Every time I got that close, I would stop and try to reload. Finally, the turkey must have gotten tired because it slowed down momentarily. I knew if I missed this next shot he was gone. I was huffing and puffing and panting like a dog but I held my breath and pointed my rifle. I pulled the hammer back and squeezed off a shot. *BAM!* This time I made the headshot and that turkey dropped like a box of rocks.

Whew, success! All of that running and chasing had paid off. The turkey flopped around for a bit, and I caught my breath as he breathed his last. I picked him up by the neck and flung my rifle over my shoulder, ready to make the proud walk back to show Uncle Jimmy. He was really happy for me and said, "Youngin', looks like you got a real biggun' there."

Uncle Jimmy always called me 'youngin' when he was proud of me so I knew that I had done well. He picked up my turkey by the legs and hoisted it up.

"Boy, this turkey weighs 15 or 20 pounds at least!"

We did not have a scale at home so we were never able to weigh it, but it sure was a heavy turkey.

We took the bird back home and Jimmy taught me the art of cleaning a turkey. Basically, it is a really big mess, but we got all the feathers off and cleaned it up before I presented it to my mother. She did not seem as excited as Jimmy and I were; I guess she saw the turkey as just another job she had to do in the kitchen. We did not have it for dinner that night because it was a little late in the evening to start cooking a 20-pound turkey. This was around 1930 and we did not have an icebox to keep our food fresh, but we did have a cold mountain spring that flowed about 200 yards from our front porch. We used this spring to keep our milk fresh. My dad excavated a hole just beneath the spring so that water would collect and pool; we placed rocks all around the hole and a board on top to keep the animals out. I wrapped up the cleaned turkey in a towel, put it in the cooling pond, and closed it up good and tight for the night.

The next day my mother prepared the turkey and my whole family, including Uncle Jimmy and my grandmother, had a delicious turkey dinner. I was very proud of myself having been the big provider of our sustenance at the ripe old age of six years old. To this day, that was the freshest, best-tasting turkey I have ever had.

Making Moonshine Whiskey

Back in those days, all the old-timers, including my dad and uncles, made moonshine whiskey. It was just a way of life. My mother did not like the idea at all, but there was not a whole lot that she could do about it. She protested, and my dad would listen to her for a while, but sooner or later he would make another batch.

We had no extra money. As a matter of fact, we did not know what extra money was in those days. What little money was available to anybody during the Depression years went to taking care of the family. Because money was so scarce, my dad found some friends to back him in his moonshine venture. They would put up the money for the sugar and cornmeal in exchange for a percentage of the whiskey when it was finished.

It was not long before my brothers and I got involved in this venture. The place where my dad had his distillery was about three miles away from our house in an area that was very remote. No one lived nearby. It was called Stillhouse Hollow, and I am sure it had a good reason for having that name. There was a small flowing creek that ran over the edge of a bluff in such a way that we were able to catch the water in a trough and use it for distilling the moonshine. It was the perfect location for my father's operation.

I was seven or eight years old when I first helped my dad make whiskey. Chester, Harris, and I carried the supplies back into Stillhouse Hollow and we got quite familiar with the whiskey-making process. One batch of whiskey required 100 pounds of sugar, and my job was to carry that sugar to the still. Dad rigged me up a homemade backpack to carry the sugar, and I could carry about 25 pounds at a time.

We did not always have sugar in the kitchen for my mother to bake with, but she loved to make sweets and pies and cakes. It was a real treat whenever she had enough sugar on hand to make us a batch of cake or fudge. One day, on one of my trips to the still, I got to thinking, *Mom sure could use some of this sugar.* There I was at that young age starting to scheme, and I hatched out a plan. We had accumulated quite a few small metal coffee cans that could hold a pound of coffee. With my plan in mind, I began hiding some of those cans away in a hollow fallen log just off the trail halfway to the still.

When I came down the trail with the sugar, I stopped at the hollow log, pulled out a coffee can, and filled it up with sugar. Then, I put the filled can back in the log and continued on toward the still. It took me four trips to carry the hundred pounds of sugar, and by the end of it, I had four cans of sugar hidden away.

I do not know what my dad would have done if he had caught me filching sugar. He probably would not have been too hard on me, but the way things went around there, I thought it best that he did not know what I was doing. But I *did* let my mother in on the secret. She scolded me at first for doing such a thing, but when it came right down to it, she really loved having that sugar. So, a little bit at a time, I brought the sugar into the house and Mom stored it away. All of a sudden, she was able to make the family desserts. I know my dad enjoyed them, and he never caught on to what was happening.

I managed to smuggle sugar this way every time my father produced a batch of whiskey, and I did it for at least two years before we moved off the mountain and the whiskey production stopped. No one ever got wise to me—not even my brothers. My mother was the only one who knew where the sugar came from, but the whole family sure enjoyed the goodies that she made with it.

My father made a batch of that moonshine whiskey every two or three months. He wasn't a drunkard, although he did drink it, and neither did he sell the whiskey—he and his partners all shared it. My uncles also periodically made whiskey and they all took turns supplying one another. I used to listen to them debate about who made the best whiskey. Of course, each man claimed that his was the best, but my dad would always win the argument.

"If mine isn't so good, how come y'all are always after it? You don't mind getting a jar of it every now and then," he said.

But my Uncle Jimmy was a character and he always had a retort for remarks like that. One time my dad gave him a quart of his moonshine and, a week or so later, he asked Uncle Jimmy how he liked the last batch.

"It was just right," he said.

"What do you mean 'just right'?" Dad asked.

"Well, if it had been any better, you wouldn't have given it to me, and if it had been any worse, I couldn't have drank it."

Mom used to always worry about Dad getting caught making moonshine whiskey. Everybody knew—because you could not help but know—that whiskey was being made all over that mountain, and every once in a while somebody got arrested. The revenuers, as my dad called them, would come to the mountain to look for the stills, so the men who made the whiskey were very secretive about where their stills were located.

To make a distillery operate properly you need a lot of cool water and a huge pot, ideally made of copper, to boil the mash. We had to be careful because some metals could make the product poisonous. My father's pot could hold about 50 gallons of mash and had a wooden dome that fit on top with a pipe coming out the side. This pipe, called the lead pipe, was made of copper tubing about three-quarters of an inch in diameter and it connected to another pipe that was coiled by wrapping it around a post about eight inches in diameter. Copper is very malleable and if it was coiled correctly, it could wrap around the pole without forming any kinks.

The coiled pipe sat in a wooden keg with the end of it sticking through a hole drilled in the bottom. This is where the cold water came in. My father built a trough on a slope that drained spring water over the edge of the bluff down toward the keg. The cold spring water cooled the copper tubing and whiskey was made by the condensation of the steam.

The alcohol in the mash has a lower boiling point than the water—I believe around 195° Fahrenheit—and thus evaporated first. When the mash began to boil in the pot, which was heated by a wood fire, the steam that it produced was the alcohol. This steam alcohol ran through the coil tubing and, cooled by the running water, would condense into a liquid and drip out the end of the tube. A small stream of whiskey flowed out.

If they kept the fire going strong, the liquid came out at a fairly steady rate. My father would periodically take a spoon and taste the whiskey; when it tasted right, he caught the liquid in quart-sized fruit jars until the product pouring from the tube became weak. When the liquid no longer had an alcohol content, the operation stopped and my father would clean everything up and store it away until he made his next batch.

However, this was only the first step of the process. The liquid produced, which was called the "singlins," had only been run through the still one time. In order to really refine that liquor, the "singlins" needed to run through the distillery at least one more time. If we ran it through a third round we produced highly concentrated, pure alcohol. I believe my dad claimed that his whiskey was better than my uncles' because he refined his product through the distillery at least twice.

A batch of 100 pounds of sugar usually produced seven or eight gallons of whiskey, although the yield and alcohol content changed slightly from batch to batch. The first three or four gallons were absolutely pure alcohol, so my father diluted them with water until it got down to the average proof for whiskey, which was around 80. I do not know what percentage of the total batch of whiskey was given to the partners who furnished the supplies, but whatever it was, I suppose they were happy because they kept coming back for more.

Raccoon Hunting

Uncle Jimmy loved to go raccoon hunting. He had two full-blooded coonhounds that really made him proud. One of his dogs had two different colored eyes—one blue and one brown—and he called him Old Blue. Uncle Jimmy trained the dogs to come to him at the sound of a cow horn.

Back in those days, the men went hunting with the hounds at night up on the mountain where the coons were thought to be roaming. The men, which included my uncles, brothers, and father, would stop and build a fire while the dogs ran around the mountain, yodeling, barking, and hunting for the raccoons. The men kept track of the dogs' location by their bark, and whenever the hounds struck a trail, they made a different sound that Uncle Jimmy recognized right away. Uncle Jimmy could identify which direction the dogs were moving and we would all head that way.

On one occasion, my Uncle Marion, who lived in Oklahoma and was the oldest of my uncles, came to visit Burny Mountain. He was not so much the hillbilly type that the rest of the Yates clan was in those days, but one night Uncle Jimmy invited him to go coon hunting with us. I went along and so did Uncle Loli.

Uncle Jimmy just loved to hear the way those dogs howled whenever they struck a trail. That night, we were sitting around the fire and the dogs had been running for a good while. They did not howl continuously, but two or three times a minute they let out a yelp and Uncle Jimmy kept track of their whereabouts. We were sitting there telling stories when all of a sudden the dogs started singing a different sort of tune.

"That's Old Blue, he's on the trail. Let's just listen to it for a minute," Uncle Jimmy said.

The dogs were about half a mile away from us in the brush. Uncle Jimmy said, "Oh, I just love those dogs. Isn't that beautiful music?" He turned to Uncle Marion. "What do you think about that music, Marion?"

"What music?" Uncle Marion asked. "I can't hear anything over those damn dogs!"

Uncle Marion was a character himself. I think one of the reasons he came to visit Burny Mountain as often as he did was to pick up a gallon of whiskey to take home with him. There is one story about Uncle Marion that I heard so many times that I believe it must be true. Uncle Marion had an ingrown toenail that was really giving him trouble, so he went to the doctor to see what he could do.

"It's just going to have to be cut out," said the doctor.

Uncle Marion was just like the rest of us in those days and did not have much money.

"How much is that going to cost me?" he asked.

"By the time you get through recuperating it will probably cost you about a hundred dollars."

Well, he did not have a hundred dollars to spend on his toe, so Marion went home without getting it fixed and the toe kept on hurting.

One night, Uncle Marion decided to take matters into his own hands.

"I'm just going to take that thing out myself."

He set out a quart of whiskey and started drinking. By this time, his toe was in really bad shape. It was swollen and purple and was really getting painful. After he had gotten pretty well loaded on that whiskey, he took a wood chisel and a hammer, laid his foot on a log, and with one whack just cut that toe off. I don't expect everybody to believe this ridiculous story, but I was told it so many times by my other uncles that I think it really did happen.

Shortly thereafter, somebody discovered that Uncle Marion was bleeding profusely and took him to the doctor. The doctor had to work for hours on the toe to stop the bleeding and Uncle Marion ended up spending two days in the hospital. The bill was a hundred dollars. Uncle Loli used to ride Marion about this.

"You'd have been better off if you just paid that money to start with. You wouldn't have had all that misery."

Years later, when Chester and I returned to Corpus Christi from the service after World War II, we decided to visit our Uncle Jimmy up on Burny mountain. He stayed on the mountain long after my family had moved, and I had not seen him in years. I bought a battery-operated portable radio to give to my Uncle Jimmy, and he really enjoyed listening to it. There was a county agent who had a radio program everyday at four o'clock discussing topics that interested Uncle Jimmy—farming, raising butchering hogs, and whatnot.

About six months later, Chester went back to the mountain to visit Uncle Jimmy and he asked him how he was enjoying the radio.

"It broke. It quit talking," Uncle Jimmy said.

"Well, it's battery-powered. The batteries are probably dead."

Uncle Jimmy looked at Chester skeptically. "No, it couldn't be that because there are a lot of stations on that radio that I haven't even used yet!"

This was the mentality of some of my kinfolks.

Oh, I'll tell you, the stories that go through your mind when you don't have anything to do but think! And so many of my memories involved Uncle Jimmy.

Fighting to Survive

How could anyone ever find me here, stranded in the wilderness of British Columbia? The very thing that had saved me from immediate death might prove to be my undoing in the long run. My helicopter blades had drilled a neat hole straight down through thick growth that was 50–60 feet tall. A search plane would have to fly directly over me if anyone was to see the wreckage.

The ground beneath me was wet and the muskeg-type moss was easy to press into. This soft footing had formed from millions of years of accumulated, decayed vegetation and the moss that grew upon it. The trees formed a spruce jungle, and at no point could I see more than 30 or 40 feet beyond me.

My pocket calculator indicated that I had crashed on Sunday, September 2nd, 1979. I guessed the time that my helicopter had gone down. It must have been roughly 10:30 a.m.

It started to rain then. This was the storm I had circumnavigated early in the day before the crash. It was fortunate that at this time I did not know it was to drizzle for seven days and seven nights! Still, I thought that I could not have been in worse circumstances. With the total wetness of the swamp beneath me and rain now falling from above, I would be wet all day and all night. *Would I catch pneumonia?* Even a bad cold and coughing might kill me due to my broken ribs. I had felt the broken rib ends rubbing on bone before fashioning the corset. The only good thing about the rain was that it supplied me with fresh water to drink.

Those first three days and nights I drifted in and out of reality. I had to call upon that strong will. I did not allow my thoughts to travel beyond one day. I thought of making it only through the day, even the next hour—then one more hour and one more day. I tried not to think about how many days I could last. This way, I was able to fight off the feeling of sheer hopelessness.

I heard voices every day that I was in this muskeg wilderness. There were literally thousands of Canadian geese and sandhill cranes in a small lake that I later found was only 100 yards from the crash site. The geese were constantly honking at each other, and this might have contributed to one of the weirdest experiences I had during the entire ordeal. One day, I was sure that I heard an old man and a boy talking to one another. Their voices floated right out of the trees surrounding me. Perhaps it was a man and his grandson preparing a trap-line for the winter. The man was singing an old Roger Miller song, "Dang me, dang me; they ought to take a rope and hang me; high from the highest tree, woman wouldja' weep for me?"

I was convinced that these were human voices—there was someone out there who could help. I started banging on the metal fuselage of the helicopter and shouted "Help! Help!"

Silence.

"Can you hear me? I am close to you and I need assistance! I am right over here, this way!" I yelled until I was weak and hoarse.

Then I listened. The voices carried on. I stuck my fingers in my ears so tight that it blotted out all sound. If the voices actually were coming through the trees, I would not be able to hear them. But I could still hear the voices as plain as ever. It dawned on me that I was imagining voices because I wanted so desperately for somebody to be near me—that my mind was becoming utterly confused. These voices were really getting to me. I thought how pathetic it must have been if somebody could have heard me yelling and banging on that metal! But the voices continued from day to day. Even though I knew what my mind was doing to me, I still listened and was almost convinced at times that they were real.

The geese were evidently preparing for their winter migratory flight. Large flocks would fly high above the trees and form their V's like they were ready to travel, but instead they would circle and honk furiously. Undoubtedly, this was for the benefit of the young geese that remained on the water. The old heads were trying to tell them that winter was coming and that they had to go South. They knew bad weather was nearing and they were goading their young to get up and out of there.

The geese flew around and honked furiously for four days in a row. On the fourth day they were finally able to get all of the young geese into the air and the sky was black with birds. I never heard so much goose noise in my life! They were really leaving this time. Their honking got dimmer and finally they disappeared into the distance. It was then that I realized just how much these geese and their chattering had meant to me. They had become the only friends I had out there and the deathly quiet that followed their departure made me realize that I was now completely alone. They were going south where I wanted to be—where my family and friends and my very life were centered. It was another in a series of growing disappointments to come.

The Move to Alabam

It was in the year 1932 that my young life changed. As a matter of fact, life changed for the whole family. My dad had fought in the army during World War I and with the country in such bad shape during the Depression years, the government made a decision to award a bonus to all the veterans of the war. At that time, we still lived up on Burny Mountain in isolation, and my friends were those that I dug up out in the woods while I was trampling around exploring. I do not recall how much these veterans were paid for a bonus, but it was enough to where my dad decided we could move off the mountain. He found some property with a two bedroom home for sale in Alabam, which was just a little wide place in the road near Huntsville, Arkansas. So we moved to Alabam.

I went to the Alabam school up to the fifth grade and for the first time I had neighbors and kids to play with. There were the Hatfields who lived just a little ways from our home. Albert Hatfield owned the general store one block from our house. I spent many hours over at the general store and when I was able to save a few pennies I would splurge on some two-cent candies.

There was also the Owens family who had a boy about my age, James Lee Owens (we called him J.L.), and his sister Jean. There were several other families within a couple miles of our home—next-door neighbors for the way I had been used to living. J.L. and I became really good buddies. I was just so anxious to have a friend. The thing that amazed me was how little J.L. knew about things I thought *all* kids knew—he could not identify the names of birds and trees—and I realized that I had learned a lot about life and nature living up on the mountain. The Owens family was pretty straight-laced; they went to church every Sunday, and now I started going to church too. Before, there had been no church within 10 miles of where we lived on the mountain. I know my mom used to be concerned about not attending service, but now we had a church nearby. It was not long before I found out I had to drop my hammer and tools on Sunday because you just don't bang around and make noise on the Lord's day. The few times that I violated that rule, the neighbors let me know in no uncertain terms that you do not do that on Sunday.

The thing that I missed most—and I did not realize I missed it until we moved off the mountain—was our Burny Mountain reunions. There were a few other people on the mountain who had young kids but we did not see them very often—only at our annual reunions when the community came together. Boy, did I look forward to those reunions. There were always lots of pies, cakes, sweets, fried chicken, and barbecued you-name-it. There was so much to eat at those reunions, and we had one every year. It started out as a family reunion, but in time, just about anyone within walking distance—and that might have been 8 or 10 miles from our house—would come to our reunions. We did not always have it at our house; the location changed from year to year, and sometimes we would make a weekend of it. We would all camp out, usually in somebody's barn because we didn't have tents in those days. I grew up with that kind of life and it stayed with me, many years later.

I also became good friends with a boy named Fay Smith. We ran around a lot together and we built a tree house down by the creek behind Fay's house. We also went possum hunting at night, walking for miles out in the woods with a coal-oil lantern. The best time to go possum hunting was when the persimmons were getting ripe. We normally just used them for baiting when we set up a trap for a possum, but occasionally we ate the persimmons ourselves. They were about the size of a large grape.

The possums loved those persimmons. When we went hunting at night, we found possums up in the trees eating the persimmons and we shook the trees vigorously (persimmon trees weren't very big, maybe 12–15 feet high and 3–4 inches in diameter at the bottom of the trunk). With a good hold on the tree, we shook like heck until the possum fell out. When it hit the ground, we would run over and lightly boot the possum so that it would sull up. You may have heard the expression "playing possum"; well, a possum really does play possum! That was their protection, they would just sull up in a ball and that was the way we got them.

Fay and I would stay out hunting late into the night and sometimes came home with three or four possums. For a normal-sized possum, we could get on average 30 cents for the fur. We weren't just hunting possums for fun, although we did enjoy it; we were doing it to make a little extra money.

Unfortunately, every once in a while we would catch a skunk, and that really created a problem. Usually a skunk will run away from you at night to try to escape, but they don't run very fast and we could easily catch them. And everyone knows what a skunk has got for protection. But we could get $1.25 for a skunk fur if it did not have too many white stripes on it. The blacker it was, the more valuable the fur. We would chase a skunk with clubs trying to knock it out, but sometimes it would get off a charge on us before we could get it. We would come home and you could smell us a mile away. Even if we bathed in coal oil, we could not get rid of the smell of that skunk.

One day, Chester and I went to school the day after we had gone on such a skunk hunt. With that skunk odor all over us, the teacher sent us home from school. Mom scrubbed and scrubbed us with homemade lye soap in a tub of hot water, but we just could not get rid of that skunk odor. It took about a week for that odor to wear off, but it wasn't so bad after two or three days. The teacher and the other kids in the class would complain when we came in, but after a while they got used to it and we were allowed to stay in school. After that, my dad told us there was no more skunk hunting during school days.

Trapping was popular in the winter season when the animal furs were thicker and worth more money. My dad trapped, my brothers trapped, and I trapped. We all trapped. We used little spring-loaded steel traps that would catch an animal by its leg, but the biggest problem for me was getting my hands on one of those traps in the first place. The traps that I used were No. 3's, and they could hold a possum. We had to have No. 4's for fox trapping because they could get out of the No. 3's. A No. 4 had a stronger spring on it, and a No. 4 double-spring was the best, but those double-spring traps cost about a dollar a piece and I could not afford them. I could only buy the little traps for 25 cents, and with them I made my own little trap line. I had four or five traps that I had accumulated and I would get up every morning before school and run my trap line.

I did not catch something every night, but throughout the week I would catch one or two possums. Occasionally I would catch a raccoon, and a coon skin was worth $3. For some of the fox skins we could get as much as $5. Harris and Chester were slightly better trappers than I was, but one time I did catch a fox. I caught mostly possums because they are not very trap-wary and I was able to outwit them, but a fox is pretty smart. It was not until I was older that I learned how to set a trap for a fox. Those were the lessons I learned as a youngster running around in the hills of Arkansas.

The Alabam school was a mile away from our house. A lot of kids complained about having to go so far to school—some of them had to walk two or three miles—but I thought, *my gosh, how much easier it is to walk a mile down a road instead of trekking up and down a mountain so steep you had to hang onto the bushes to climb.* There again, I was introduced to something I had not been used to. I had never complained about walking to school.

The Alabam School was just like all rural schools in those days—just a big box, two-stories high. The 1st through 4th grades were on the ground floor of the schoolhouse and upstairs were the 5th through the 8th grades. I did not know exactly what grade I was in when we left the mountain; although I had attended school before, I had to walk five miles to get there, so I did not attend it regularly. I was ten years old now and I assumed I must be in the 2nd grade, so that was where they put me, but all of those kids were a lot younger than me. I thought, *this is probably not right.* After finishing the 2nd grade and moving into the 3rd, I became a good student and was anxious to learn. Now that they were available, I loved to read books and I read just about every book that I could get my hands on. About halfway through the 4th grade, my teacher decided that I was ahead of everybody else and advanced me to the 5th grade, moving me upstairs. By then, I think I was probably at the level I should have been because my studies started getting pretty hard and I had to really push myself. I was making B's and occasionally C's on my report cards, but I was doing all right.

The Watermelon Patch

I spent a lot of time exploring around the countryside. Now I had a partner to go with me in J. L., and the good thing about him was that he did not resent the fact that I knew a lot more about nature and the wilderness than him. At the same time, J.L. knew other things that I did not know. We made a good combination, but I probably taught him a few bad habits, like stealing watermelons. I thought it was a god-given right for every kid to get into somebody's watermelon patch, but I found out that people in Alabam frowned on it considerably. I remember one particular incident that occurred before I left the mountain involving the Fanchers, a big ranching family in the area. They lived off the mountain but they had a lot of bottom land and Mr. Fancher would always plant several acres of watermelons down near the river. My brother Chester and I raided that watermelon patch pretty regularly whenever they began to get up in size, and you probably could have heard us half a mile away thumping on those watermelons. To those who may not know, it is very easy to tell when a watermelon is ripe by thumping it with your thumb. It is hard to describe the sound exactly, but I was taught by Chester who was taught by our oldest brother, Harris. We all knew the sound of a ripe watermelon.

One day I wandered off to the patch by myself. I must have been really mischievous that day. I thumped around and found a nice big watermelon that would have served eight people. I half-carried and half-rolled it over to the riverbank under the shade of some big oak trees, picked the watermelon up, and smashed it on the ground to break it open. I then start breaking off chunks to eat. This was a particularly sweet melon, but I did not eat enough of it to even make a dent. When I was full I thought, *I better get rid of these rinds and pieces so that nobody knows what I did*, so I threw them in the river.

Well, Mr. Fancher found these pieces of watermelon floating in the river. He got in touch with my dad and asked if his boys had gotten into his watermelon patch. My dad said he did not know for sure but that he didn't think we would do a thing like that. That evening, when Dad came home from work, he called me out onto the porch where he was chopping logs.

"Walter, what's this story about the watermelons?" he asked.

I put on my really blank look. "Watermelons? I don't know, what is it?"

Dad proceeded to tell me that Jim Fancher thought the Yates boys were getting into his watermelon patch and that he was getting tired of it.

"Did you get into that watermelon patch?" Dad asked.

I don't know why I did it—my dad was pretty strict with me and I had felt the result of his belt many times—but I just lied something awful.

"No sir, Dad!" I said. "I didn't get in that watermelon patch."

"I'll tell you what I want you to do. I want you to walk over there to Jim Fancher's home and you, Walt, look him in the eye and tell him you didn't do it." I did not want to do that, and he knew it.

"You know what's coming to you if you don't!" he said.

"All right, Dad, I'll do it," I said.

It was a five or six mile walk over to the Fancher's home. Mr. Fancher was out in the yard near the barn doing something with a piece of harness and I walked up to him, a six or seven year old kid, rubbing my toe in the dust and looking down at the ground. I was afraid to look him in the eye.

"What can I help you with?" Mr. Fancher asked.

I stumbled around a little bit and finally said, "Mr. Fancher, I didn't get into your watermelon patch."

"Well, it kind of looked like you may have," he said. "On your side of the river we found a lot of remains of watermelons that were broken open, and there are no other boys who live around here."

"No, sir, my dad told me I had to tell you that I didn't do it."

"Okay, son, but I don't really believe you."

I went back home with my tail between my legs and it slowly began to dawn on me what I was doing. I had this horrible lie that I'd gotten myself into and it was really bothering me.

Chester was just two years older than me and he did not like the way I was behaving. While I was gone, he told my dad that I had been the one who got into the watermelon patch. When I got home, my dad called me up again.

"You want to tell me again whether or not you got into Mr. Fancher's watermelon patch?" he asked.

I knew the jig was up. And I knew what was coming, too. At least I *thought* I knew. But it turned out later that I hadn't the least idea what was coming.

"Yes, I did," I told him.

"You lied to me," he said. "Now son, I have never caught you in a lie before. And we sure don't want to get started telling lies. You were taught to tell the truth in everything you do, regardless of the consequences."

He really read me the Riot Act. Dad took off his belt and had me lower my pants. Boy, you talk about a whopping. He really let me have it, and the worst part about it was that he would give me eight or ten licks then stop and stand there to talk to me about it some more, and then he'd do me again. By now my butt was really sore. To this day, I can still feel the sting of that belt on my behind and I vowed to never tell a lie again because the consequences just weren't worth it. And I did the best I could for the rest of my life not to tell a lie. It was a real lesson in life.

After that incident, it seemed like out of nowhere there were so many extra chores that I had to do—I do not know where they all came from. I took my punishment like I was supposed to and I carried wood, cut weeds, and cleaned out the barn. There wasn't anything I missed that Dad decided was something I could do around the house. To this day, I have not been in anybody's watermelon patch again.

Life in Alabam

My dad must have had a little bit of money left after we bought the house in Alabam because he suddenly showed up one day with a car. I could not believe it. This was a Chevrolet four-door with front seats and back seats—it even had a radio! This was really a prize and several times both Chester and I got a good lecture from Dad for running down the battery because we would slip outside and listen to the radio. We were not aware how batteries worked and that turning on the radio used up the juice. Another lesson learned.

We really enjoyed having a car, particularly my mother. We would all pile up in that thing—my older brothers Harris and Chester, my sisters Dorothy, Catherine, and Georgia Ann, the baby Donnie, and me—and Mom and Dad would take us on picnics.

It was six miles from our house to Huntsville, Arkansas. One Saturday, Dad loaded us up and we went into town and had hamburgers. This was the first time I had ever had a hamburger and I thought it was the most heavenly thing I had ever eaten. After dinner we went to the picture show at the theater. Huntsville is in Madison County and the name of this theater was The Madison. I had never been to the theater before and I was overwhelmed. Of course, it was a western; they mostly showed old western movies in those days and I believe the one we saw was about Hoot Gibson. This was before Roy Rogers came along. I was absolutely enthralled by the movie and, naturally, I assumed that everything on the screen had really happened and that it wasn't just play. The movie also set me off on a new tangent of wanting to have a horse. We had an old grey mare up on the mountain but Dad sold it when we moved to Alabam. Finally, of all things, Dad got a mule which he used to plow, but I also rode around on it, pretending to be a cowboy.

I was now nine or ten years old and I noticed that the people who seemed to have the most were those who were in business, whether it be a store, a blacksmith shop, a woodworking shop, or something else they owned themselves. That was about the time I discovered a newspaper called *Grit: The World's Greatest Family Newspaper*. I wrote *Grit* a letter telling them that I would like to sell their paper and right away I got a package from the post office with ten copies of the *Grit* newspaper and instructions on how to sell it. I was to sell the paper at five cents a copy and send them back three cents for each copy I sold. I could keep the remaining two cents. It did not take me long to figure: 10 newspapers, 2 cents—20 cents! That would be enough for the picture show and a bag of popcorn in Huntsville (at that time, theater admission was 10 cents). I started walking around the neighborhood and in the first couple of days I was able to sell all ten papers. I had been instructed to send *Grit* their share of the profits in stamps, so I took 30 cents worth of stamps, put them in an envelope, and mailed them in. I kept this up for two or three weeks and then I wrote *Grit* a little note that said "I believe I can handle more, send me 15 copies!" So they did. Now, it got a little bit harder to sell all my copies. Our neighbors all lived at least a mile apart and it was a long trek to reach my potential customers, so I began riding our mule to sell the newspapers and I was able to cover a larger distance. It was a challenge to sell all 15 newspapers but I did it. In fact, I continued my paper route until I had worked myself up to 35 copies a week with the help of that mule.

When I look back on it, 35 newspapers seems like such a small amount, but selling *Grit* further convinced me that a person had to be in business for himself. I felt really proud of myself and along the way I met new people and made new friends. I am sure a lot of my customers only bought the paper from me because I was a young kid—in those days, to spare a nickel for a paper instead of buying some food was a big decision.

At the peak of my sales I really had a downer. My dad sold the mule! I had a route scattered across a 10-mile radius that I now had to walk, and so began the slow decline of my paper route.

There were several people in Alabam who influenced my life in different ways. It was Kyle Fields who first got me interested in reading books. Mr. Fields had two young boys and he loved to tell a good story. J.L. and I used to go over to Mr. Fields' house and visit with him just to listen to him tell us stories.

Mr. Fields was really concerned about how his two young boys were growing up and he encouraged them to read as much as they could. He started them reading at a very early age. One day he came home with a big load of books. I do not know where he obtained them, but he had hundreds of books stacked in boxes. I happened to be at his house when he brought the boxes of books home and I curiously looked through them. Mr. Fields told me he got them for his boys to read but invited me to use them too. Any time I wanted a book I could take one home to read; when I brought the book back, I could pick out a new one. Those books began my adventure in reading and, to this day, I am an avid reader.

Vinnie Hines, another neighbor, wasn't any slouch either when it came to telling stories, but she was somewhat more reserved. Vinnie had a two-seat touring Model-T Ford. She drove the car into Huntsville two or three times a month then returned home and parked it in her garage. I used to admire that old car, and a time or two I rode along with her on those short trips just to catch a ride in the Model-T.

The Presleys were a prominent family in the area that lived about half a mile up the road from our house. Arty Presley and his wife had two boys. The younger son, Gile, was about the same age as my brother Chester and they got to running around together. The older Presley son, Glen, was three or four years older than Gile and did not run around with us younger kids.

Chester and Gile became active in fur trapping. The season did not open for trapping until the weather got cold and the animals grew thicker, heavier fur that was more valuable at market. However, sometimes Chester and Gile would jump the gun and go possum hunting before the trapping season began. They went into the forest at night and shook possums out of the persimmon trees, catching them alive. My dad had a cage in a shed behind our house that he used as an incubator to hatch chickens, and Chester and Gile used this cage to hold the possums they caught. Their idea was to keep the possums alive until the trapping season opened and then they could sell the fur.

The boys never got to cash in on their plan. Somehow or another, word got out that Chester—and, for some reason, only

Chester—was trapping for animals before the season opened. One day the sheriff showed up at our house with a search warrant. My dad knew that Chester and Gile were fiddling around out back, but he did not know that they were keeping possums in his cage. The sheriff searched our barn and eventually made his way to the shack. He spotted the incubator, opened the door, and found three or four live possums.

I never will forget that day. Chester was a minor so the sheriff instead arrested my dad and took him to the jail in Huntsville. Boy, I'll tell you, my family was all stirred up. We had ideas about who may have tipped off the sheriff, but there really was not much we could do about it.

One of my more embarrassing moments as a child occurred during this ordeal. As a veteran of World War I, my dad received disability checks from the government. In order to cash the check, of course, he had to sign it, but one of the checks came while he was still in jail. My mother handed me the check.

"You are going to have to take this into town where your daddy is and get him to endorse this check so we can cash it. We need the money, and we don't know when your daddy is going to get out."

I went into Huntsville by myself because I did not want anyone to know what I was doing. The sheriff at the jailhouse was named Jones, and there was a little diddy that people used to sing about him when someone got thrown in jail. "I wanna go home but it ain't no use, Old Jones just won't turn me loose." When I got to the jail I spoke to Sheriff Jones and told him what I was there for. He took me back to my father's jail cell and there he was, just sitting there. God, I felt horrible. Seeing his dad in jail is one of the worst things that can happen to a young boy. Dad had not committed any crime, but he had allowed his son to. He had not stopped him.

Dad signed the check and told me to tell the family he loved us and that he would be coming home soon. He tried to make as little of the situation as he could. I went back home, Mom cashed the check over at Albert Hatfield's store, and we were able to use the money while we waited for Dad.

They kept my dad in jail for ten days before turning him loose. Things got back to normal as much as they could, but we all felt branded that our dad had been put in jail. When I went to school kids teased me about my father, and it was a really rough time in my young life. I still think back to how mortified I was on the playground at school when children brought it up. Of course, in a town that small, everybody knew what had happened. Something like that really makes an impression on a young kid like I was.

Another thing happened at that time that really devastated me. All kids, when they reach a certain age, start falling in love—or so they *think* they are in love. And it happened to me. There was a young girl in my class named Dorma. She was a member of the Presley family and I was as smitten with her as a boy that young could be smitten. Dorma sat four desks in front of me in class. Each day our teacher would call a student up to the front of the class to sit at a bench and recite a spelling. After his turn the student would return to his seat. One day when I was called to the front I handed Dorma a note that I had written on a scrap of paper. It said "I love you!" I had the note in my hand and when I walked by Dorma, I paused just long enough to lay that note on her desk. My heart was beating like a drum, but she hardly looked at me.

After spelling my word I went back to my seat and sat down. I kept my eye on Dorma to see if she was going to read my note, but I could not tell whether or not she had even picked it up because she sat in front of me. I waited for several days for any response. Finally, a week later, Dorma approached me on the playground during recess.

"Walter Yates, I'm going to give you this note back. I don't even want to read it," she said.

"Well, *did* you read it?" I asked.

"No, I'm not going to read it," she said. "Okay, yeah, yeah, I read it."

And this is where she really got me.

"If you think I'm going to have for a boyfriend somebody whose daddy has been in jail, you've got another 'think' coming!" Then she turned and walked away. Boy, I was destroyed. It was a long time before I made my feelings known to a girl again.

Things began to pick up for my dad and he got a contract with a company that supplied railroad ties to railroad companies. Railroad ties were made out of oak or some other durable, hard wood and were laid on the ground under railroad tracks. The ties were usually eight or nine square inches and six or seven feet long, and they were sawed in sawmills by squaring off a 12-inch log with a saw blade.

My dad was skilled with a broad axe, one of the tools used to make railroad ties. The difference between a broad axe and a standard woodsman axe is its wider blade, nearly a foot wide rather than four or five inches. My dad kept his broad axe as sharp as a razor. Hewing out the logs by hand, Dad would square off one side of the log, turn it over, square off another side, and repeat this process until he had hewed all four sides down to a square railroad tie. On a good day, Dad could make as many as four ties. He got $1.25 for each, so he could make about $5 a day cutting railroad ties.

Dad cut logs from our own land, which had some pretty good timber on it, but once he used up all the trees that he could take off of our land he had to find a new source. Our property adjoined several hundred acres of government land that also had a vast supply of timber. I do not know whether or not my father had permission, but he just moved over onto that land and began cutting new logs. In a day he could cut a dozen or more logs and drag them back to our property with a mule. Then, with those logs, he would continue to hew railroad ties.

This project lasted for about a year. Can you imagine, with a family as large as ours, that we could support ourselves on $5 a day? You would not last an hour with that today. In those days, a dollar was worth a dollar.

The Bluff

When I was about ten years old I started getting the urge for bigger adventures—maybe because of the books I was reading, or maybe because my imagination was just running rampant. Our house was about three miles from the War Eagle River. Approaching it from our property, we had to traverse a huge bluff that stood at least 100 feet high in order to get down to the river. We walked as much as a mile along that bluff before finding an area where the ground dropped off and we could climb down to the water.

My first adventure to the river was with my brother Chester. He went to the river all the time by himself, but sometimes he just could not get away from me and I would tag along with him. Tired of the long walk around the bluff, Chester started exploring for a quicker path to the water and found a crack in the bluff that appeared to go all the way down to the river. However, you could not see the riverbed from the opening in the bluff. Chester was pretty adventurous himself—more so than I was at the time—and on one of his trips by himself he decided to see if he could get directly down to the river through that crack. And he did. He went all the way down through the crack, spent a few hours on the river, and when he was ready to return home, climbed right back up through it.

On this trip that I tagged along with him, Chester decided to let me in on his secret and told me he had found a faster way to get down to the river. He showed me the crack in the bluff, but I had no desire to climb down into that small, dark opening with no end in sight.

"What about snakes?" I asked.

Chester assured me he had been through the opening three times before and had not seen any snakes.

"Come on, follow me," he said.

I was really hesitant to do it, but I was not going to stand up there on the bluff by myself. Chester crawled down into the crack and quickly disappeared. I wanted to keep up with him so I jumped in behind him.

Although it was not completely dark, there was very little light, and after we descended about 50 feet, things got really dingy. We had to squeeze through openings just barely big enough to pass through. I was halfway afraid to squeeze through the tight spots for fear that I would get stuck, but I slowly managed to get through them. Chester moved quickly and I hollered at him to wait for me but he just kept going.

Portions of the route through the crack had a sandy bottom that was easy to walk on, but most of it was rocky and rough with craggy rocks to climb over. Finally, I made it to the opening at the bottom of the bluff. I had reached the river.

Chester kept a couple of fishing poles at the river. When I say fishing poles, I do not mean the standard rod and reel. My rod was just a cane pole with a string and a hook. We fished for a few hours before I started to complain to Chester that Mom was going to worry about me and that we better go back. We had caught a few perch and one or two catfish, and Chester agreed that we had fished enough.

Climbing back up through the crack was significantly harder than coming down it. The tight spots were particularly difficult to squeeze through and I had to fight off panic a time or two. To my relief, Chester took pity on me this time and stayed with me. He knew I was going to have a little trouble getting up through the tight spots and reached down to grab my hand and pull me up. It was not long before I could go up and down through the crack in the bluff by myself, but that first time was not easy.

We started back for home, but before we reached the house Chester swore me to secrecy.

"Do not tell our mother what we've been doing because she is just going to worry! And don't tell J.L. or anyone else about this crack. Let's keep it our secret."

So I kept the secret. It was not until years later when we had moved to Texas and were sitting around rehashing old stories that we told our mother about our trips to the river through the crack in the bluff, which shortened our travel time by nearly an hour. Mom said she was sure glad we had not told her then because she would have been scared to death.

Traversing the crack in the bluff gave me a lot of courage, which came in handy years later when I took on much more hazardous adventures than crawling through a crack. This early experience gave me the courage I needed to take the adventures that eventually earned me the reputation in Alaska as "That guy who is living on the edge." Some of the adventures I would take throughout my life were considerably risky, but the stories I am able to tell today are the result of learning from an early age that it is okay to take a risk.

As I have grown older, I realize that a lot of the things I did as a young boy were due to the low-esteem I had of my family and myself. Because of events like my father going to jail, I believed our family had a poor reputation in the neighborhood. Although the neighbors probably did not look down on our family as much as I convinced myself they did, you can imagine a young boy's feelings about insulting and embarrassing remarks made by other children on the school ground. Thus, I believe I started taking adventures like the one through the crack in the bluff to prove to myself that I was better than they thought I was and that I could do things that they were too afraid to do.

I built up an awful lot of self-confidence. I was trying to prove myself *to* myself. I needed self-respect, and I acquired it by doing things that other kids would not do. In the long run, the events that tormented me as a young kid and made me think that the neighbors had little respect for our family all helped to shape my life. In fact, my risk-taking has gotten me out of a lot of tough scrapes because I was willing to take a chance. Lying beside the wreckage of a helicopter, severely injured and without food, I was able to keep myself alive, and I credit all the experiences that started in my childhood which taught me to take chances. Amidst the wreckage of the plane, I had no choice. I had to survive, and I did.

Don't Go Away, I'm Alive!

There was no way that I could keep dry. Even without the rain it would have been impossible. Any weight put upon the marshy tundra would sink into water. When I crawled, I was in water. When I lay down, I was in water. The water appeared to be at ground level, but when I took a step I sunk down four to six inches.

Some sort of shelter to keep out of the rain and chilling wind was imperative. But could I build anything in my severely handicapped condition? I had to build something—or die. *The door that fell off my helicopter would make a good roof*, I thought. On hands and knees I pulled it, one inch at a time, to a spot where there were four small tree stumps cut off by the rotor blades of the helicopter. The stumps were about three feet high. Getting the door on top of those stumps was my hardest task yet, but I did it.

Fortunately, the terrain here was slightly higher and slanted upward, allowing me to stay a little drier, but I needed something to lie on. There was plenty of tall grass growing out of the marshy wetness and I collected enough of this growth to make a sort of mattress, but when I lay down, the lower part of my body was still in water an inch deep. The upward slant at least kept my chest and head clear.

I lay back and surveyed my handiwork. *How had I been able to do this when every movement of my body caused searing pain?* I began to wonder about man's pain tolerance. I reasoned that the pain had reached such a point that my body was beginning to accept it. At times, I was completely oblivious to it.

With renewed hope for shelter, I used the burned roll of safety wire to secure the helicopter door. Around this "roof" I placed

The shelter I built out of the helicopter door.

parts of the wreckage and then banked it with spruce boughs that had been cut by the rotor blades. This crude shelter got me out of the rain and my spirits began to rise for the first time. I caught rainwater as it dripped from the door into my antique pot from the ghost mine.

The wind seemed to blow colder and harder. The chill factor was plunging and at night the water began to freeze. Wet boots and icy water were taking their toll. Now, I was suffering from frostbite and trench foot. My feet were lifeless stubs with no feeling.

As it grew colder, I realized that I needed to seal my tiny shelter to keep out the icy winds. I used a piece of metal from the tail section of the aircraft for a door. When I crawled into the shelter, I could pull the door shut behind me and wire it secure. Most of my time now was spent resting in the shelter. Each day I stuffed cracks and openings with moss, but it was impossible to completely escape the vicious wind. It seemed like a thing alive, relentless and cutting at my very insides. I spent the nights rubbing and massaging my body, legs, and feet. Still, my feet began to swell.

The headaches and cramps in my stomach that resulted from not eating stopped after the third day, but I noticed a rapidly increasing weakness. I rationed out sugarcoated candy for two days, but I had to forage for food. That is when I found a low bush of cranberries. There were plenty of cranberry bushes, but birds and other animals had eaten most of the berries. I had to reach down underneath the bushes to find berries that the wildlife had missed. Perhaps here was another link to survival—if I could only find enough berries to sustain me.

Realizing that my body needed fiber, I remembered from my survival studies that the leaves and stems of most plants and trees producing edible fruits are not poisonous. For roughage, I ate cranberry leaves and their tender stems. They were bitter but the additional bulk and roughage proved a big help in controlling my digestive system.

During these forays for food I started gathering dry wood for signal fire purposes. I found wood in the form of limbs hanging from dead spruce trees, and I called the pile of dry wood my mound of hope. When it stopped raining and the search planes came, this would be my signal fire. Then there were the small spindling spruce trees that had died years earlier and were nearly ready to fall. These were on average two inches in diameter at the bottom and 15–20 feet tall. It took me over an hour to drag one of these trees to my survival mound, but it did so much for my pride and hope that it was worth the effort. Small accomplishments such as this help to sustain a person during periods of utter hopelessness. I had to feel rewarded for anything I did in this impossible situation.

On the fourth day I decided to try to move the tail section of the helicopter into the open cut of land roughly 40 feet away. There, it could be seen when the search and rescue team showed up. I struggled with the tail section for over an hour trying every possible way to move it, but it would not budge. I gave up and crawled back to my little shelter. I had thought about this task for several days but had put it off for two reasons: first, there was no hope for search planes to show up until the rain stopped; second, I knew it would add to my growing despondency if I could not move the tail section, and I did not know just how low a person could sink before giving up completely. Now I knew. I was at the bottom of the pit—but I was not giving up! Along with my almost unbelievable will for survival was my equally strong will power. It had never been tested to this extent and I was pleased with my display of mental strength thus far. I lay down in my little shelter and slept.

I awoke feeling refreshed and alert and crawled outside to hunt for cranberries, but a rustle of wings stopped me cold. A large, black bird landed in a nearby tree. We regarded each other quizzically.

Then, quite plainly, the bird said, "Talk!"

I stared at the raven, or crow, or whatever type of bird it was, in unbelieving silence. *I must be hallucinating*, I thought.

The bird tilted his head and repeated, "Talk, talk!"

This was in perfect diction. I could not believe it. *The pain must really be getting to me now. If I am really hearing and seeing this, let's see what happens if I talk back to him.*

"Well, you talk," I said.

Immediately the bird answered, "Pete Pickle." It repeated the name. Then the bird flew away.

My mind raced. I thought: a man crashes into a spruce jungle, is severely injured, has no food, very little shelter, and is crawling around in a boggy marsh when a bird comes along and starts talking to him, calling out his Central Texas congressman's name. *No question about it, Yates, you are hallucinating!*

I worried about my encounter with the bird until he reappeared at approximately the same time the next day and repeated the very same performance. It was obvious to me now that the bird was somebody's pet. Either a person named Pete Pickle owned the bird or he had been named that by somebody else. At any rate, those two words were the extent of his vocabulary.

When he announced himself this time, I replied, "Is that your name? Glad to know you, Pete. My name is Walt!"

"Pete Pickle," the bird replied. Nothing else, but it helped. After those long hours of silence, just to hear two words was uplifting.

The bird repeated this performance for five days, each time coming a little closer to me. If I could only catch Pete and put a message on him—or would I succumb to the need in my shrinking stomach for food and roast the little talker? All I was thinking of was rescue, so I decided if I could catch the bird in any manner I would tie a message on him and hope someone found it.

The big, black bird was not afraid of me but was a bit aloof and skittish. I came to look for Pete each day, but after five days I could hear him only at a distance. He was still repeating "Pete Pickle." It was one of the most gratifying experiences throughout the ordeal, but it left me with a sad, empty feeling when the bird disappeared completely.

I was so cold and miserable at night that sleep was impossible. I would sit up, massage my body and legs, rub my feet together, and then stomp them in order to keep my blood circulating and bring about some feeling. When it warmed up the next day, my fatigue and pain had advanced to such a point that I could sleep only an hour or two at a time. Upon awakening, I would forage for berries. I was able to gather only about a quarter of a cup each trip, but this was sufficient to keep me going even though I felt myself growing weaker each day. I had to keep doing these things or I would have gone completely nuts worrying about my plight.

About an hour before dark on the fifth day, I heard something large moving through the brush. It was a black bear—the last animal I wanted to pay me a visit. The big bruin did not stop until he was within 30 feet of me. He rose up on his hind legs and began looking around and sniffing the air. I was just plain scared. The only weapon I had was a burnt hunting knife, and in my weakened condition, the last thing I wanted was an encounter with that bear. I had salvaged some aluminum metal from the wreckage and I began to holler and bang these pieces together. To my horror, this seemed not to disturb the bear at all—much less frighten him away.

Instead, the bear dropped down on all fours and came even closer! It was obvious that he was trying to identify what kind of animal I was that had strayed into his forest domain. What could I do? I could not run. I could not climb a tree. I could not defend myself. I was at the animal's mercy.

Slowly, the big bruin narrowed the distance between us. I continued to holler and beat the pieces of metal together. The bear stopped no more than eight feet from me and stood up again. He was enormous! Now he was showing his teeth and low growls were coming from deep within his throat. The guttural outbursts seemed to begin down in his body and rumble upward. It was a bloodcurdling sound and became even more so as I grew ever more convinced that an attack was imminent. I was quiet, petrified with fear, awaiting my fate. *What an ironic twist*, I thought. Hunger, cold, pain, and exposure—they all seemed minor now. This animal was going to kill me. I could feel it in the icy pit of my stomach.

The bear was so close now that all I could see was hair. It was like somebody was holding a huge hairy blanket in front of me. I began talking to the Lord and I continued to talk until the bear dropped down on all fours and made a circle around my shelter. He circled the burnt helicopter, seemingly walking away, and then circled again. The animal continued this way until he was out of eyesight, still circling.

My conviction that I would be mangled and destroyed by a mighty animal left me in a cold sweat. Since I was in such an isolated area, could it be that the bear had never seen a human before? Why hadn't he struck out at an intruder? Was the bear merely waiting for darkness to attack? After 45 minutes of circling and making the low, guttural sounds, everything was quiet. It was the longest and most miserable night I had spent yet. I stayed alert until full daylight and then slumped back into fitful slumber.

On the sixth day, I was crawling around the shelter, stuffing moss into the cracks, and still thinking about my harrowing experience with the bear when there appeared a little frog that I uncovered from the moss. This frog was about five inches long. I was so lost in thought that I just stared at the frog for several seconds before it dawned on me what I was seeing. *This was food!* I snatched the frog and skinned it immediately. Then, I built one of the few fires that I would allow myself to start with a match and roasted the frog legs. Although the small legs were hardly more than a couple of bites, I spent ten full minutes consuming the delicious morsels.

As it grew colder each night, I decided to build a little stove out of parts of the metal pieces I had collected after repeated visits to the wreckage. I cut up some of the steel metal that had not burned and fashioned a little box approximately a foot high, eight inches wide, and a foot long. I literally wired it together. One of the exhaust stacks from the engine was perfect for a chimney. It curved, letting the stack turn and go out through the side of the shelter. Only nights when it seemed I could not stand the penetrating cold any longer would I use one of my precious matches. For two hours, I would sit there absorbing the wonderful warmth. It helped my spirits and kept me from suffering more hypothermia.

It continued to rain. I was miserable. A typical day consisted of dragging myself out of the shelter, crawling around in the wet bushes to pick berries, and then returning to lie down awhile and rest. Then, I would crawl over to the wreckage and go through the ashes, looking for anything that could be of help. Back to rest again, and the next trip would be to gather wood—small branches for the little stove and dead saplings for a signal fire. Then I would start the process all over again. It was tedious but it kept my mind occupied as the days passed and black hopelessness tried to penetrate my soul. Throughout those long, miserable hours, I kept the sound of a plane in the back of my mind. *When would it come? How would it sound? Or would it come at all…*

I woke up on the eighth day to a strange quietness. And then I realized that the rain had stopped! My face was radiant when I lifted it toward the sky. I said aloud, "Lord, don't let the rain start again—it's my only hope now."

It did not rain that night. And it did not rain the morning of the ninth day. *The clouds should begin clearing soon and they might just start the search immediately.*

Late that afternoon I heard the drone of an aircraft. *It's a search and rescue airplane!* I shouted and rushed to start a fire. The plane missed me by a quarter of a mile, but I could see into the windows as it went by, about 500 feet above me.

"Don't go away, I'm alive!" I shouted, knowing they could not hear me.

The plane was a twin-engine Buffalo used by the military, and I knew it had been the Royal Canadian Air Force Search and Rescue Team. After a few minutes, the plane came back the same distance from me as before but on the other side, flying in the opposite direction. It had missed me again! This was a horrible blow. One of the absolute lowest feelings even a healthy person can experience is to see help disappearing in the sky after it has come so close.

When I had time to reason it out, I figured this must have been their last pass of the day because the sky was beginning to gloom over. The rescue team needed perfect visibility for their pinpoint work. They would probably resume their search the next morning—*they had to resume their search the next morning!* I would arise early and get my signal fire going so that it would throw a column of smoke into the clouds. And they would find me!

I began gathering more wood to add to the stack I had piled up throughout the long days behind me. I collected a large supply of dead twigs from spruce tree limbs and moss from the sides of trees, stuffed them inside my parka, and zipped it up. They needed to be dry when the time came, and the time was coming. I was excited now—*really* excited for the first time since I had crashed. The first plane caught me off guard and I had been more confused than anything else.

I did not sleep all night. *They would find me this time.* I could hardly wait. This was the longest night of my life and it was miserably cold, but I refused to use one of the three matches I had left.

I kept imagining that I was seeing streaks of dawn hours before daylight actually arrived. When the first hint of light finally pushed at the blanket of darkness, I crawled out of my shelter. I was shaking from extreme cold as well as excitement. I had to do everything right this time. There was no room for mistakes.

When it was light enough to see, I took off my corset and used it for kindling wood. *This would be my last signal fire.* If they did not find me today, it was all over. When the tiny flame bit at the surrounding gloom, I added the moss and twigs from inside my parka and kept building the fire until I had the biggest one going that I had built since the crash. I inspected the green moss and spruce boughs stacked beside me. Then, I began listening for an aircraft.

It was full daylight when I heard the drone of an engine. Feverishly, I piled more moss and green limbs on the fire to produce smoke. Almost immediately, a billowing column sifted through the trees. But the wind was playing a cruel trick on me now. As soon as the smoke reached treetop level the wind rolled it right back into the forest!

The pilot was starting another search grid about a quarter of a mile from the spot where he had last passed over me the day before. As the plane neared, I could see the aircraft. They flew very low and were certainly close enough to see a smoke column—if there had been one high enough to escape the trees. The plane went right on by. They had not seen anything! I could not believe it. I thought, *now he will turn around as he did yesterday and keep the grid going. He will be a little farther away but if he is looking in my direction, he has got to see the smoke!*

My fire was burning beautifully. I stacked more green boughs onto the flame. The smoke column was billowing up into the trees but the wind was still wreaking havoc with it. *It isn't going much above the trees but they should still be able to see it!*

I heard the engine growing louder, but this time I could barely see the aircraft as it crossed approximately three-quarters of a mile away from me. They did not see the smoke. I began to wonder if they would even try again. This was the tenth day. The search and rescue team had passed me by four times now. There wasn't one chance in a thousand that they would come again. As the drone of the engine grew dim, I slumped to the ground and wept. For the first time, I lost all hope. I was completely enveloped in the gloom of grim finality. I had to face it now: the next step was death.

I spent part of the day writing notes to my family and making changes in my will. The only thing I had to write on was part of a brown paper bag that had fallen out of the helicopter. I would try to get these instructions and goodbyes to a spot above snow line in the unlikely event that a search party, or perhaps a trapper, came upon the wreckage during the fall or winter months. *How many times can a man die inside?* I wondered.

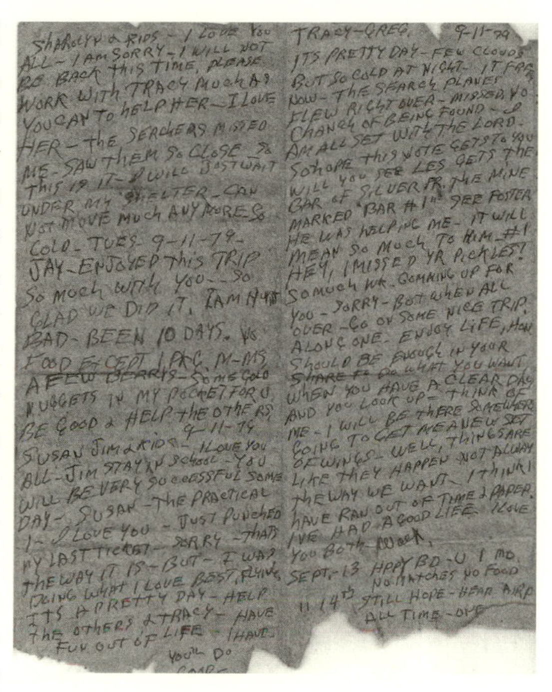

SHAROLYN & KIDS – I LOVE YOU
ALL – I AM SORRY – I WILL NOT
BE BACK THIS TIME, PLEASE
WORK WITH TRACY MUCH AS
YOU CAN TO HELP HER – I LOVE
HER – THE SEARCHERS MISSED
ME – SAW THEM SO CLOSE TO
THIS IS IT – I WILL JUST WAIT
UNDER MY SHELTER – CAN
NOT MOVE MUCH ANY MORE SO
COLD – TUES – 9-11-79 –
JAY – ENJOYED THIS TRIP
SO MUCH WITH YOU – SO
GLAD WE DID IT. I AM HURT
BAD – BEEN 10 DAYS. NO
FOOD EXCEPT 1 PKG. M-MS
A FEW BERRIES – SOME GOLD
NUGGETS IN MY POCKET FOR U.
BE GOOD & HELP THE OTHERS.
9-11-79
SUSAN JIM & KIDS – I LOVE YOU
ALL – JIM STAY IN SCHOOL – YOU
WILL BE VERY SUCCESSFUL SOME
DAY – SUSAN – THE PRACTICAL
1 – I LOVE YOU – JUST PUNCHED
MY LAST TICKET – SORRY – THATS
THE WAY IT IS – BUT – I WAS
DOING WHAT I LOVE BEST, FLYING.
ITS A PRETTY DAY – HELP
THE OTHERS & TRACY – HAVE
FUN OUT OF LIFE – I HAVE
YOU'LL DO
GOOD –

TRACY – GREG. 9-11-79
ITS PRETTY DAY – FEW CLOUDS
BUT SO COLD AT NIGHT – IT FREE[illegible]
NOW – THE SEARCH PLANES
FLEW RIGHT OVER – MISSED, NO
CHANCE OF BEING FOUND – I
AM ALL SET WITH THE LORD.
SO HOPE THIS NOTE GETS TO YOU
WILL YOU SEE LES GETS THE
BAR OF SILVER FR. THE MINE
MARKED "BAR #1" SEE FOSTER
HE WAS HELPING ME – IT WILL
MEAN SO MUCH TO HIM – #1
HEY, I MISSED YR PICKLES!
SO MUCH WK. COMMING UP FOR
YOU – SORRY – BUT WHEN ALL
OVER – GO ON SOME NICE TRIP,
ALONG ONE. ENJOY LIFE, HON
SHOULD BE ENOUGH IN YOUR
~~SHARE TO~~ DO WHAT YOU WANT
WHEN YOU HAVE A CLEAR DAY
AND YOU LOOK UP – THINK OF
ME – I WILL BE THERE SOMEWHERE
GOING TO GET ME A NEW SET
OF WINGS – WELL, THINGS ARE
LIKE THEY HAPPEN NOT ALWAY
THE WAY WE WANT – I THINK I
HAVE RAN OUT OF TIME & PAPER.
I'VE HAD A GOOD LIFE. I LOVE
YOU BOTH [illegible],
SEPT. 13 HPPY BD – U I MO.
NO MATCHES NO FOOD
" 14th STILL HOPE – HEAR AIRP
ALL TIME – [illegible]

Paper bag with last words.

I decided on a last prayer. Then, I would lie down and die peacefully. The pain, miserable exposure, weakness, anxiety, and gnawing worry would all be gone. I prayed aloud.

"Lord, I gave it my best shot. It isn't your fault, I just can't hold out any longer. I've always said I would never give up, so if it really isn't time for me to go and if there is something you want me to do to help someone find me, please give me the strength to do it."

A strange peace came over me. Then, something glowed inside. The horrible, empty feeling was leaving. The Lord had never talked to me but surely this was a sign. I began crawling toward the plane's detached tail section. *Why am I doing this? I have tried before*

Burned guns and hacksaw recovered from crash.

and failed. I am weaker than I was then. It was a strange feeling, like a magnet pulling me toward the wreckage. Something was happening inside of me.

I talked aloud while I crawled. *If they do come back, or even if a private plane flies over, there must be something for them to see in that open strip of land.* I did not know why they had not seen the smoke. Maybe it had blended in with the clouds. This time, they must have something to see on the ground.

When I reached the tail section, I disconnected the loose cables and crawled around behind it. Lying on my back, I took hold of the 200-pound mass of metal and began dragging the unwieldy piece of the aircraft. I was working without my corset now and each exertion brought blinding pain. My ribs had begun to mend, but now I could feel them breaking loose again. *What difference does it make? If they don't find me, the condition of my body won't matter. I'm grasping at straws anyhow—I don't possibly have but one more chance, and maybe not even that.*

But how could I have negative thoughts when I was now moving a possible lifesaver that I had not been able budge before? This had to be another in a series of miracles brought about by a belief in God that seemed to grow stronger even as my chances for survival grew dimmer. There was a mysterious new strength inside me now. My adrenalin had begun to flow. Instead of getting weaker, I was accomplishing something that I thought was impossible.

Part of the tail section got stuck on a tree, so I went after the hacksaw. In all, five trees blocked my path. They were each four to five inches in diameter at the bottom and it took time to cut them down, but I sawed away and then continued to drag the tail section.

When darkness came I crawled back into the shelter, rested, and talked to the Lord. Then, I got up the next morning and resumed the task. It took two days to move the tail section 40 feet, and when I got it into the opening, I shouted out my thanks to the Lord. I was in excellent spirits now, even though I had not heard a plane pass in 48 hours. Still, I was weak and tired as I crawled around in water and mud, attempting to prop up the tail section with sticks so that it would be more visible.

It was now the twelfth day. I had not picked cranberries in the past two days and I realized that I was badly in need of nourishment. I hunted for berries until I was so tired that I feared I might pass out and lay immersed in the water all night. In my weakened condition, I knew that I could not survive the exposure so I crawled back to the shelter and for the first time since the crash slept all night.

When I awoke the next morning I was horrified! It was drizzling rain and the fog had moved back in. With near superhuman strength coming from a weakened body, I had moved that piece of equipment out to the clearing where it could be seen, and now it was hidden by fog and rain. This was another almost unbearable letdown, but I could not allow that. *This is only temporary. The sun will come back out.*

That afternoon the clouds began to break and for an hour the sun shined beautifully. I imagined that I heard an aircraft. *I must get a fire going.* Quickly, I pulled some dry moss and twigs from my jacket pockets. There were only two matches left. I struck one. It flared and went out. *Only one match left now*—panic ate at my insides. I could not use this match until I was sure. *Maybe the camera lens would work*, I thought. Painstakingly, I concentrated the little dot of heat from the sun that came through the glass onto the moss. My hands trembled, but that pinpoint of light had to be held in an exact spot so that enough heat would build up and ignite the moss.

It took a long time, but finally, a tiny curl of smoke rose out of the moss. My heart jumped. The smoke grew and then there was a small glow. I gently blew on it. When the blaze at last appeared, I dropped the lens and built up the fire carefully. I was able to keep it going for an hour. The benefit I received from the heat was tremendous, but an aircraft did not show up.

This was now the thirteenth day and I had to fight hard to keep even faint hope alive. I picked more cranberries then crawled into the shelter and collapsed. I was weaker and more exhausted now than I had ever been. This alarmed me, but I still had faith. My mind was made up. I would not reach the low point of total despair again—even if I knew I was dying.

The fourteenth day of my ordeal dawned partially cloudy but with no rain. By now I was so tired, weak, and stiff that I moved with great difficulty. Common sense told me that I should lie in the shelter, conserve as much energy as possible, and go out only if the sun emerged. I could not keep the thought out of my mind: *was this the beginning of the end? Was I actually dying slowly, even now?*

It was ten o'clock in the morning when I heard the faint sound of an engine. The sound diminished, then it came again. Each second was pure agony. *Is my imagination going wild?* Now the droning hum grew louder. I covered my ears to blot out any outside sound. If this was merely my imagination, I would continue hearing it. The sound stopped. Quickly, I withdrew my hands. I could definitely hear the sound of an engine! My heart pounded. I scrambled outside, barely in time to see the aircraft passing low and directly over me.

I reached the clearing in record time. With renewed strength, I pulled my weakened body upright against a tree. I heard the aircraft circling. It was coming back! They had seen something at last!

Now I was shouting at the top of my lungs, "I'm saved! Thank you, God. I'm saved!"

I kept repeating it over and over. I picked up a piece of shiny metal that I had saved for signaling purposes and waved it wildly as the plane swooped directly over me again.

"I'm alive. I am alive!" I shouted. "Don't go away. Please don't go away!"

I had to make sure they saw me. Many times in similar situations, SAR crews would find wreckage but see no one alive, returning the next day by helicopter to examine the crash site. I wanted the search crew to know that I was alive and ready to go. I kept waving that metal and shouting. This time, they circled, came down low, and dipped their wings. This was a signal that they had seen me.

It was too much. Tears of relief streamed down my face as I kept shouting, "I'm saved! I'm saved!" I continued to wave the piece of metal. I had been disappointed too many times already. This was too good to be true. *Have I gone completely out of my mind?* The plane climbed higher, but then the pilot circled again, came down very low this time, and dipped his wings. This was positive proof that they had seen me! And that is when I allowed myself to relax completely for the first time in 14 days. I leaned against the tree. My knees felt like rubber, and I slid down to a sitting position. Now, I was losing strength fast. I felt completely used up. I could hardly raise an arm.

The aircraft continued to circle. They were probably radioing for a helicopter. But how could it land in this dense forest? It was up to them now, so I lay back and rested. Forty-five minutes later I heard another engine. It was a Voyager, the tandem-rotor Boeing Vertol helicopter that they used for search and rescue.

The giant yellow bird gradually worked its way over to where I was. Now, it was hovering over me. The down wash from those blades was literally slinging small logs and brush in every direction.

They inched directly over me, and then the bottom of the big bird opened up and two paramedics came down on a cable. They asked if I was Walter Yates.

My voice sounded strange when I answered, "Yes! Oh, my God, yes!"

I wanted to hug and kiss them. The paramedics went to work immediately, wrapping me in blankets and strapping me securely in a basket to airlift me out. It felt like I was being pulled up to Heaven as I was lifted into the helicopter. The two paramedics followed, and then I was on my way to Fort Nelson Hospital.

I wondered now if this rescue was real. Perhaps it was another dream that would end in a nightmare. I tried to focus on the friendly faces as they moved about in the helicopter. The rescue crew checked on my comfort; they were so kind, gentle, and efficient. I asked them if they had anything hot to drink. They did not, but one of the airmen produced a small can of orange juice.

"I'll let you have a few sips of this," he said, "but we really must be careful about what you consume until we get you to the hospital."

I began to feel more relaxed now. I wanted to go to sleep but the man who gave me the orange juice just kept shaking me. He told me that I had to stay awake, that I must not fall asleep. I motioned for him to lean down close. My voice was hardly audible and it was hoarse from so much shouting. The man smiled and said, "You're okay now." It was so very, very moving. I pulled him closer and whispered hoarsely, "You saved my life." Then I burst into tears.

The thought kept running through my mind: *maybe I am dreaming this.* I wanted to hear a voice confirm what I hoped was really happening, so even as they were wheeling me on the litter through the hospital halls I repeated over and over, "I'm saved! I'm saved!"

After a thorough checkup by a kind and efficient doctor I was given solid food. Later, I was x-rayed and the doctor explained my injuries in detail. My twelfth vertebra was crushed. I had seven broken ribs and most of them were compound breaks. The doctor thought it amazing that my lungs had not been punctured. He was further amazed that I had not caught pneumonia or even a simple cold! I had been in tremendous physical shape before the accident from climbing mountains and prospecting for gold all over Alaska. What was to bother me most was the trench foot. My feet had been cold and wet for 14 days, but they were to recover 90% efficiency in a five-month period. I was determined that my injured feet would not prevent me from enjoying life and adventure as I always had.

The search and rescue team told me that the flight on which I was discovered was to be their last. They had searched for me over 62,000 square miles. Later, an SAR special report referenced that fortuitous last day:

"Weather poor in Fort St. John area but mysteriously cleared to the north."

I underlined the word "mysteriously" three times. . .

One of the most satisfying reports I received came from the Canadian Department of Transport that confirmed the cause of my crash to be failure of the tail rotor system. The crash was not my fault as a pilot, and this I point out with understandable pride. I also want to declare that I owe my life and will be forever grateful to the Royal Canadian Air Force 442nd Search and Rescue Squadron. They always have their hands full with rescue missions along a strip through British Columbia that has been dubbed "Suicide Alley." In fact, there were three other crashes while the SAR team searched for me. In each case there were no survivors. One man was found sitting on a stump, chin in hand, dead.

The Canadian Air Force expressed to me their deep concern about the increasing number of inexperienced pilots flying through their country. Most of these pilots do not realize that there is a compass deviation of approximately 30° as you fly north. Also, in the heavily forested North Country, everything looks the same. The only real landmark is the Alcan Highway which is crooked and curves around bad terrain, and many pilots who decide to cut across will pick up a false highway that goes up into the mountains or stops in a box canyon. All of a sudden, their road is gone and they are confused. If the weather is bad and visibility poor, they are almost certain to crash. I desperately wish to convey a message to all pilots who fly through British Columbia and the Yukon country: for God's sake, take the advice that the Canadians so freely give!

Shortly after my crash I bought another helicopter. Quit flying? "Good Lord, man, that's my very life..."

Part II
The War Years

The Cactus Pryor Show

Before my crash, I had been a regular guest on Cactus Pryor's popular KLBJ radio show in Austin, Texas. He described my stories as "a drama in real life." Needless to say, my helicopter crash survival story only added to the drama. As soon as I was able, Cactus came to interview me from my bedside at Olen Teague Veteran's Hospital in Temple, Texas.

"Let's begin with the good news you just received from the doctor as I walked in here," Cactus began. "Give us a rundown of your physical condition."

"I think my physical condition is excellent considering what I've been through. In reference to the doctor who just left, I could not have received any better news. He says the crushed vertebra will heal by itself within three months and he sees no need for any future operations."

"You have, what, seven broken ribs? I just saw the pictures of them and, yep, they are broken! Did you doubt it?" Cactus asked.

"I didn't doubt it, but that was the first time I saw them on an x-ray myself. I wondered why something was hurtin' in there! Seven of them are broken on the left side."

"One report says that they were broken by the cyclic stick of the helicopter."

"That was my first appraisal, but after analyzing the situation I realized what really broke them: a tree. After an accident like this a man's mind gets a little fuzzy so I've had to stop and piece things together. I came down through the spruce trees, chopping them off with the rotor blades, but there was no way that the control stick could have done this damage to my ribs. A four-inch diameter spruce tree came through the bottom of the helicopter bubble, wiped out seven ribs, and cut three gashes across the left side of my face and ear. Had it been just a few inches to the right, it probably would have impaled me."

"I giant suppository! And we wouldn't be talking now, would we?" Cactus joked.

"To say the least!"

As I lay propped up on my elbows in the hospital bed, Cactus asked what the doctors thought about the makeshift splint I had whittled while I was stranded.

"The doctor didn't comment on it," I told him.

"Professional jealousy!" Cactus joked.

"He probably did not want to admit that I had fixed them! But he did say that the splint may have prevented me from puncturing something in there."

"Your feet, though, have caused you the most trouble."

"My feet sustained the most serious injuries. My back and ribs are *painfully* serious, but not so serious that they won't heal. My feet, however, soaked in 40° water for 14 days, and with the other injuries I sustained there was no way to get off of the wet muskeg ground. I suffered a combination of frostbite and trench foot, a condition that was common among our military personnel in World War I. It is an agonizing condition that does damage to the nerves, and it is a very slow process for these nerves to grow back. During the time that it does heal, it's just painful."

"To the extent that the doctors had to do a spinal block on you, I understand?" Cactus asked.

"Yes, they have done two now."

At the time, a spinal block was a new procedure that doctors performed for pain management. The spinal block took away all feeling from my hips on down and stopped the pain. It was just like heaven for what I was going through.

Cactus asked me to describe my helicopter flight leading up to the crash. I explained that on Saturday, September 1st, 1979, the day before the accident, I had flown into Fort Nelson, British

Columbia—the halfway point on my course across Canada. I refueled my airplane, got a good night's rest, and prepared for an early start the next morning.

When I woke up the next day—Sunday, September 2nd—the weather was not good. I talked to the weatherman for a briefing and filed my flight plan for the trip to Red Deer, a small town south of Edmonton. I had planned stops at Fort Saint John, Dawson Creek, Grand Prairie, and Whitecourt—all places I needed to stop for fuel. Fort Saint John being my first stop, the weatherman informed me that I might not be able to follow the Alcan Highway due to the poor weather. Nevertheless, I decided to follow the highway south to start out my flight. After about 50 minutes, I realized I should have listened to the weatherman. I ran into a solid wall of bad weather and was forced to land my helicopter beside the highway.

At least two dozen vehicles passed me in either direction while I waited in the helicopter on the side of the road. The weather ahead of me was not improving but behind me the skies were clear, so I decided to go back north to Fort Nelson. After about 20 minutes of backtracking, I noticed that the weather to the south was finally starting to improve, so I made the fateful decision to turn around again and just go around the storm.

The farther I flew the better the weather got. I could see my southeastern route to Fort Saint John and believed the weather was no longer a problem. Thinking that I was in the clear now, I poured myself a cup of coffee from my thermos and munched on a cinnamon roll that I had bought at a restaurant the night before. I was flying the helicopter with the stick between my knees and enjoying my snack when, out of nowhere, I lost the tail rotor.

I plummeted into the trees and hit hard. As I look back on it, landing in the nearby clearing would have certainly killed me—if not by the impact then by the fire.

I was approximately 30–35 miles north of the Alcan Highway but it never entered my mind to leave the crash site in order to look for help. Even if I had been much closer to the highway I would not have tried. You should never leave the scene of a crash because that is what rescue crews will be searching for. If I had been in completely good shape with no injuries, and three weeks had gone by without rescue, I *may* have made the decision to leave had I known which direction the highway was located. However, in the condition I was in, I could not have walked a mile. That alone would have been a miracle. The only thing for me to do was to remain at the crash site and wait.

Cactus asked me if I felt fear.

I told him that I felt fear just like anybody else. The constant fear was that I would not be found, but I never did give up.

"Walter, I knew we were good friends before, but I didn't realize the extent of it," Cactus said. "I guess it takes something like this to appreciate the value of friendships, of relationships, and of life itself."

"I guess it does, Cactus, and I certainly have the same feeling as you do about our friendship. I am just overcome by the number of friends who have helped me through this."

In fact, people I had never even met were praying for my recovery, and the outpouring of support that I received amazed me. One of my neighbors had a younger brother named A.G. Akin who lived in Louisiana and when he heard about my story he wrote a poem. He called it "Fifteen Days with God and Wild Cranberries."

Returning home from the Yukon back to Texas,
At last I have found the gold,
When suddenly, my engine fails,
Lord, are you ready for my soul?

As I crawl out of the burning wreck
I watch my gear go up in smoke,
Now wild cranberries are my only food
And God's my only hope.

Fifteen days alone with God and wild cranberries,
Without them both I would not be alive,

Fifteen days alone with God and wild cranberries,
Somehow I know that I will survive.

The nights are getting colder
And the weather's looking foul,
I must keep my campfire going,
There's a black bear on the prowl.

My heart pounds with hope,
I see a search plane in the air,
But it fades on the horizon
So I say another prayer.

Fifteen days alone with God and wild cranberries,
Without them both I would not be alive,
Fifteen days alone with God and wild cranberries,
Somehow I know that I will survive.

I must not give in to despair,
My will to live is strong,
My loved ones wait in Texas
And for them I will hold on.

At last the helicopter is above me
And I know it's not a dream,
God and wild cranberries have meant more to me
Than all the gold in those Alaska streams.

Fifteen days alone with God and wild cranberries,
Without them both I would not be alive,
Fifteen days alone with God and wild cranberries,
Somehow I knew that I would survive.

A.G. Akin 1979

"I want to make a testimony," Cactus said. "I want to testify to your wife Tracy right now. She, like you, never lost faith. She, like you, exhibited nothing but courage. She dealt with this emergency, I think, just every bit as effectively as you did."

I was sure glad to hear him say that. I knew my wife was a strong woman, and throughout the whole ordeal I just hoped that she would not break down. I felt that the experience had probably been much harder on her than it was on me not knowing *anything*. At least I knew I was alive.

My children, brothers, sisters, and mother also demonstrated this strength. Mom was 87 years old at the time of my crash but she came through with flying colors, displaying the same courage that she had taught me herself.

The accident was especially difficult on my son Jay. He had been up in Alaska with me on this trip but drove back with the supplies instead of riding home with me in the helicopter. Jay left just a few days ahead of me and it was rough on him thinking that if he had been there with me he might have been able to help.

While we were in Alaska, a friend told Jay and I a story about a psychic back in Texas who had predicted a creek where gold was later struck. This story stuck with Jay and while I was missing he related the story of the psychic to the rest of the family. Not to let any stone go unturned, Jay and my good friend Glenn Kirby went to see this man who lived in Brownsville, Texas. At that time, the man was about 80 years old and had a good reputation in the area for making accurate predictions. Jay told him about my situation and produced a map of the area where I was thought to be lost. The man took the map, spread it out on the table, and studied it for what Jay thought was a very long time. Jay later said the man seemed totally "out of it." The psychic then took a pencil, marked a spot on the map, and said that I would be found with some gold near a trail. At the end of the session, Jay offered the man money but he refused.

"I will lose my power if I accept any money!" he explained.

Jay and Glenn were both impressed with this man. When they

returned home they called the search and rescue team in Canada and suggested they search in this particular area marked on the map by the psychic. The rescue team had an inkling as to what Jay had done and asked him if he had consulted a psychic. Hesitantly, Jay replied that he had, but they told him not to be embarrassed because they used psychics all the time. The SAR team agreed to follow the lead, even though they had already searched that area.

When I was eventually found, I was only a few miles from where the psychic had marked on the map—and I had about 10 ounces of gold with me! Moreover, I was near a trail cut during an oil search years earlier. Jay's memory of the story of the psychic resulted in my rescue. The SAR team returned to the area one more time, and because of this I survived.

"What do you feel about the affect of prayer on your recovery?" Cactus asked.

"Oh, there is no question about it, Cactus—it saved me. And not just my prayers; I have since learned that my friends and family, and even people who do not know me, made special prayers in church, at home, and anywhere else they happened to pray. I got out of an impossible situation. What other proof could you want?"

Although at times I felt doubt, I always believed I would make it out of the wilderness alive. At the same time, being a rational person, I thought I should make certain preparations that everybody has to make when faced with the possibility of death. I wrote down instructions, notes, and letters to my grandkids, my children, my wife, and other members of the family. I did not have much to write on, but I found a large paper bag which I used to write all my messages on. I still have that paper bag today. Other than making those preparations, I really never felt that I would not be rescued. I had to believe.

Cactus explained to me that he and everyone back home got day-by-day telephone updates from the Canadian Rescue Mission. They were kind enough to give my family and friends reports on their daily activities. Cactus asked me for my perspective on

Air Force DC-9 bringing me home.

the Canadian Rescue Mission, and I told him that these rescue workers were without a doubt the finest, most dedicated people in the world. They made these types of rescue missions all the time—and I was just another to add to the list—but they treated each mission like the life or death situation that it was. They never wanted to give up searching for somebody who had gone down.

After my rescue the search team flew me to the hospital in Fort Nelson, but the resources there were limited. The doctors were concerned about my feet and other injuries getting worse, and I needed to be airlifted out of Fort Nelson on a stretcher case because I could not sit up. However, no commercial airliners would fly to Fort Nelson. We even tried to get a charter plane, but nothing was available. Finally, we contacted the U.S. Air Force and it was less than a day and a half before they arrived with a DC-9 airplane to fly me home. They airlifted me out of Fort Nelson and flew me to Olen Teague Veteran's Hospital in Temple, Texas.

The whole experience made me realize how precious life is, but I knew I was not going to stop flying. I *couldn't* stop flying. However, I did decide that I would exercise extreme caution in just about everything I did from there on out.

"All your friends want you to recuperate as fast as possible so that we can kick you in the rear-end for scaring the hell out of us!" Cactus joked.

"Well, I deserve that and I'll sure bend over and take it."

Bed-ridden and recuperating in my hospital bed, I had plenty of time to think back on my life. Just as I had done while stranded at my crash site in the wilderness of British Columbia, I recalled some of my earliest experiences as a young boy growing up in the southwest, slowly becoming a young man.

Young in Corpus Christi

Around 1934 my Dad got word of the need for construction workers down in Texas, and many nights I heard Dad talking with my mother about moving the family to Corpus Christi. Mom did not want to move, but Dad was determined to load up and relocate to Texas where he could get more work and we could live a better life. Part of Dad's argument was that the move would be better for the kids.

"They'll be able to attend better schools," he insisted.

My mother never could win a battle with my Dad. He was strong willed and never wavered in his opinions.

By this time, Dad had run up quite a bill at the Hatfield's grocery store, and Albert Hatfield was giving our family groceries on credit. After selling some logs that he had cut, Dad went to the grocery store but was only able to pay off about half of what he owed. This was another experience that taught me a lifelong lesson: don't allow debt to pile up beyond your means. Still owing Albert the other half, we loaded up the car that night. My mother had been quietly packing our belongings for about a week and when the time finally came to move, Dad pulled the car around to the back of the house where we would not be noticed by the neighbors.

Our four-door Chevrolet—what they used to call a touring car—had a big trunk in back. Once the trunk was filled we attached another trunk onto the rear and a couple more on top, and we stuffed the rest of our belongings in every conceivable space that there was room inside the vehicle. Besides his big family, Dad had several round packages wrapped with blankets rolled up like logs attached to either side of the car between the fender and the hood. These packages contained two rugs my mother had owned since marrying my father as well as some of Dad's tools. Also in the car with us was our dog Snowball, a little white Eskimo Spitz that I dearly loved. We looked like characters from *The Grapes of Wrath*, and we were certainly in the same category because at that point in life—during the time of the Great Depression—we did not have much. Everything we owned we could fit in that car.

The next morning, just before daylight, we pulled out of our driveway and departed for Texas. I knew this would be a whole new experience for me. When I look back on it, I cannot fathom how my mother endured that car trip. Here we were, seven kids crammed in a car, and we were no different than kids are today.

"He's touching me!"

"Move over!"

"You're in my seat!"

My mother probably looked ahead with panic—unless she was too afraid to—at the next two or three days it would take us to get to Texas in that car.

Sitting in the back seat listening to Mom and Dad's conversations, I realized why we were moving. A large naval air station was being built in Corpus Christi that had all kinds of jobs available, and we were moving there so that my dad could find work. I began to realize just a little bit more what life was all about—but not *too* much. I was still just a 10 year old kid, after all.

We must have been some kind of sight on the road. We had a few flats along the way and the engine overheated due to all of the stuff stacked around the radiator that prevented it from cooling, but we did not have too much trouble getting to Texas and, soon enough, we arrived in Corpus Christi. My dad must have had *some* money left over because we stayed the night at a motel near North Beach, a part of Corpus that turned out to be very popular. The next morning my dad went out to the job site where the naval base was under construction and he immediately found a position working in concrete. This eventually started my Dad on a new career path; several years later, he went into business for himself as a concrete contractor. He also did some construction work. And so we started a new kind of life, once again. My dad bought a home, and it was not long before my brother Harris got a job in construction as well.

Still too young to work, Chester and I spent most of the time that we could get away from the house fishing at the beach. Texas was a whole new world for us because here was all this water, the Corpus Christi Bay, just full of fish! We caught something nearly every time we cast our rods. When we fished the whole day on King's River back in Arkansas, we'd be lucky if we caught one or two catfish.

I started school at Menger Elementary and began cultivating new friendships. Then, I went to Winn Seal Junior High School. The only graduation that I ever had was from that school. Although Dad had work, my family still wasn't too well off and there weren't many extra dollars available for new clothing. I had worn the same overalls and denim shirt for quite some time and they were getting pretty ragged. With my clothes full of holes, I was too embarrassed to go to the Winn Seal graduation ceremony. I did *not* want to walk across that stage. Although my mom had given me a fresh haircut, at the last minute I decided not to go.

My new running buddy's name was Carol Wilder. He also came from a large family and had several older brothers and sisters, so we had a lot in common. Carol and I hit it off right away and we began hunting and fishing together. I started riding Carol's brother's bicycle and we went all over the countryside. Carol and I would pack some potatoes and, if we were lucky, a weenie and some marshmallows, and we'd ride our bicycles all the way up to the Nueces River about 10 miles from our neighborhood. We camped and fished and roasted our snacks. Carol and I were quite alike, but I was used to having more freedom to roam around than he and most other kids had in those days—although all of them had more freedom than kids have nowadays. Still, I seemed to have more. There were hardly any restrictions on where I could roam—except for the watermelon patches.

After a few years living in Corpus Christi, my family was forced to move to another neighborhood because my dad lost the house. Although he was making fairly good money, and Harris was helping a little bit too, the payments on our house were more than Dad could manage working out on the base, so we moved into a rental home on the other side of town. Although I was far away now, I still kept up with Carol. By that time, there were three or four of us that would get together and hang out, and one of the things we experimented with was drinking beer. With a father who had made moonshine whiskey up in the mountains, I was familiar with alcohol. Although my mother told me never to touch the stuff, the other kids egged me on and I would take a drink. None of us boys ever got into any trouble, but we probably did things that we should not have.

Work at Western Union

Around age thirteen I decided to sell newspapers again, so I wrote a letter to *Grit* Publishing Co. requesting to start a new paper route. I mostly worked on foot, but sometimes I was able to use Carol's brother's bicycle to make my deliveries.

I was in a larger city now, so the *Grit* publishers sent me 20 papers to start out. At first I had trouble selling them all, but I continued with 20 papers as I built up my route. The price of the paper had increased to 10 cents per copy, and I got to keep 4 cents. This was really a success for me because I could make up to $2 a week, and that was pretty good money in those days. I was living in a big city with many new prospects and felt like I was making out like a bandit! Selling *Grit* further cemented my belief that to do-it-yourself and have your own business was the route to go. I always kept my sights on that, and the dream of becoming a business owner stayed with me all my life.

At 15 years old I got what you might call my first "real" job. I went to the Western Union office to ask if they could use another delivery boy and I spoke with a man named Mr. Wilson who later turned out to be my boss.

"Son, I don't think you are old enough," he said. "You've got to ride a bike all over town."

"Oh, I can do that," I insisted.

"Well, what kind of bike have you got?" he asked.

"Sir, to be honest with you, I don't have a bike yet. But as soon as you give me a job I am going to get one."

I guess I impressed him enough to where he thought I ought to have the job.

"You can start next week," he said.

I had to get busy and locate a bicycle, so without further ado I went down to Western Auto Store. When I got to the shop, I asked one of the employees if I could speak to the manager. The young man looked at me kind of funny but then called for his boss.

"There's a young man here to see you," he told him.

The manager came out of his office. "What can I do for you, son?" he asked. "Are you looking for work? Because we don't have any."

"No, sir," I replied. "I need a bicycle."

"Well, you came to the right place! We've got plenty of bicycles for sale. The men on the floor can help you."

"There's only one thing," I said. "I just got a job at Western Union delivering telegrams and I can't go to work until I get a bicycle. . . and I don't have any money."

I just flat out told him.

The manager looked at me and I could see he was ready to run me off—or so I thought.

"Come on into my office, son."

I followed him into his office and sat down.

"What does your dad do?" he asked.

"He's a subcontractor. He does concrete work and builds houses."

"How much money can you get from your dad for a down payment?"

"I've already talked to him and he can't give me anything," I answered. "He doesn't make very much money and we've got a big family. He just doesn't have any money to spare. The only way I can get it is to earn it myself, and I can do that. There's no question that I can do it. All you need to do is just sell me this bicycle and I'll make you a payment every week until I get it paid off."

The bicycle I wanted was $19.95. Twenty bucks. The manager looked at me for a minute before responding.

"Son, I'm going to take a chance on you," he said. "You've got an honest face. But if you miss a payment, I'm going to take the bicycle away."

"Sir, I guarantee you, I will not miss a payment if you let me have that bicycle."

Well, the good Lord was willing that day. The manager agreed, and I rode out of that store on my brand new bicycle.

I went home and told my mom and dad what I had done. They looked at me kind of funny before walking outside to see the bicycle.

"You mean to tell me that the manager sold you this on credit?" my dad asked.

"Yes, sir. He said I've got an honest face."

"Well, you better have!" he laughed.

My parents were really proud of me for getting that bike. I stuck my chest out because I was proud of myself, too.

The next Saturday I pedaled down to the Western Union office, parked my bike on the rack in front of the office, and went inside to start my new job.

"Mr. Wilson, I have a nice new bicycle out there and I'm ready to go to work."

Mr. Wilson ran the Western Union office and he said I could begin that morning, but before I got started he asked me for my address and social security number. I did not have a social security number yet, so I asked him where I could get one. I went to the social security office, signed up, and got a social security card. I still carry the original card in my wallet today. It is pressed between plastic, but it is the first and only one I ever got.

I went back to the Western Union office and Mr. Wilson introduced me to a boy only a few years older than me.

"This is Joe," Mr. Wilson said. "Joe is the foreman for all the deliveries coming in. He will give you your orders and tell you what to do."

Mr. Wilson left the room and Joe sat me down. He told me what the job involved and how important it was that I be careful with the telegrams I pick up and deliver.

"Sometimes we deliver telegrams, sometimes we pick up telegrams, and sometimes we deliver packages. We go all over town."

Joe gave me a leather satchel to carry the telegrams and asked me how well I knew the town.

"I've lived here a long time," I said.

I really did know the town well, and with the help of the map of Corpus Christi hanging in the office, I knew I could find any street. To test me, Joe took me over to the map and asked me to locate a certain address. I pointed out half a dozen locations scattered all over town before he determined that I knew my way around the city.

"Sit on the bench with the other boys," he said. "We work on a next-man-up order. Sit in a row and when you get to the front, the next delivery is yours."

Pretty soon I was headed out the door with a telegram. I jumped on my bike and delivered it without any problem, came back to the office, and sat on the bench at the end of the line. I worked every evening after school and all day each Saturday, and it was not long before I knew every street and hamlet in the Corpus Christi area.

I did not make a lot of money. When things were slow I made about $1.25–$1.50 in a week. On a good week, however, I could make as much as $3.00 if I earned some tips. That was a lot of money in those days. I agreed to pay the manager at Western Auto Store $1 per week until I got the bicycle paid; the rest of the money went into a Prince Albert Tobacco can.

The thing that scared me the most while working at Western Union was singing telegrams. If you worked for Western Union, sooner or later you would get caught delivering one. I couldn't carry a tune in a bucket—I still can't—but one day, it happened to me.

Mr. Wilson had a boy with a good voice that regularly delivered the singing telegrams, but on this particular day the boy was not working. Mr. Wilson approached me with the news I had dreaded.

"Walter, you are going to have to deliver this singing telegram," he said.

"Sir, you know I can hardly whistle, let alone sing."

"You've got to start sometime," he said. "Just do your best."

"I can't do that, sir, I just can't sing a song, especially not to a stranger."

"Well, if you can't do it, we're going to have to let you go. You have to take whatever job comes up."

I was not about to lose my job, so I finally gave in.

"Okay, sir, let me have it."

I stuck the telegram in my satchel and jumped on my bicycle. The delivery was to a home out on Ocean Drive, the well-to-do section of Corpus Christi at the time. I arrived at a huge, two-story home set way back on the lot with a long sidewalk leading to the front door. It felt like a slow mile walking up to the house.

I knocked on the door and a man answered. Without even blinking an eye to tell him what I was there for—or even to ask if he was the right man—I started singing "Happy Birthday."

"Hold it! Hold it!" he said. "Wait a minute, son. That's for somebody else!"

He went and fetched the man that the telegram was addressed to. When they came to the door they were both halfway laughing, which did not help my composure.

"You have a delivery for me, son?" the other man asked.

"Yes, sir. You must be having a birthday because I've got a 'Happy Birthday' wish for you here."

"Well, let's have it!" he said.

The man was really encouraging and that improved my morale. Then, I belted out "Happy Birthday" so far off key that I doubt the man even recognized the song. When I finished singing I turned on my heel and nearly ran back to my bicycle to get away from there, but the man came hollering after me.

"Hey! Wait a minute! Come back, son!"

I thought, *my gosh, I'm going to have to sing it again?* I reluctantly made my way back up the sidewalk, but then the man reached into his pocket and handed me 50 cents. That was the biggest tip I ever received.

With the help of that tip, it was not long before I had the bike paid off. My debt was down to $4.00 and it was really important to me to get that bicycle paid in full. That week I made about $3.75, so I went to Western Auto to talk to the manager again.

"Sir, I sure would like to get this bike paid for. I owe you $4.00 and I've got $3.75 right here. If you will accept that in total payment, I'll pay this bike off right now."

He looked at me for a minute.

"Son, you've done real good, so we'll do that. Let me have that money and I'll give you a receipt and the bicycle is yours."

I was just as happy as a clam.

Buying that bicycle was another experience that showed me if I was going to get anything in this world, I had to work for it. It also taught me that there are good people all over the place. The manager of Western Auto Store really helped me. As I got older, I used to stop in and see him from time to tome. He would give me a Coca-Cola and I drank it while we talked. He was just a really nice guy and I think he was as happy as I was that he had helped me out.

With school and a job, I did not have much free time. Whenever I did get some time to run around with my buddies, one of the things I loved to do most was go floundering. We would go out to the beach at night with a lantern and a gig and wade around in the water just off shore, usually in the shallow water of the bay. It was best if the water was no more than a foot deep so that we could see the flounder as they fluffed themselves up and down and then buried themselves in the sand with just their eyes sticking out. If we looked closely, we could see the eyes and the shape of the flounder under the sand, but we had to be very careful or else we would pass them by.

I first went floundering with my friend Carol who had an extra gig. We lived close to the causeway, a bridge on the north side of town that crossed the bay into Corpus Christi and had nearby areas of shallow water. We were just wading around when all of a sudden Carol jerked and soused his gig into the water. I had not seen anything in the sand, but Carol came up with a big flounder. Once I realized what we were looking for, it was not long before I was catching flounder myself.

To this day, I get more pleasure out of floundering than almost anything in the world. Of course, now I can't walk around with a lantern all night like I could in those days. It was always a thrill to come home with those big flounder, which I consider the best eating fish on the market, other than catfish. I went floundering every chance I got, and there is nothing I would like better than to jump in the car right now and drive down to the coast to go floundering. But, the way things are, I can't do that now.

The Marine Corps

I became acquainted with a boy named Robert Adams, and we got to be good buddies and ran around a lot together. We were talking one day when Robert brought up the idea of joining the service.

"Walter, let's join the Navy," he said.

"I'm not old enough yet to join the Navy," I said. I was only fifteen.

"Well, I'm not either, but as soon as we are, let's do it."

"I'll think about it," I said.

For the next few months I looked things over and researched the different branches of the service. I was pretty sure that joining the military was what I wanted to do.

By the time I turned seventeen, I was still in high school and working for Western Union. One day, Robert and I got together and decided it was time.

"There's just one thing, Robert," I said.

"What's that?" he asked.

"I don't want to join the Navy. I want to join the Marine Corps."

"Well, why?"

"Because they've got a better uniform!" I told him. "Did you ever see them? Look how nice that blue uniform is with the gold stripe down the side."

Finally, Robert said "Okay!" and we decided to join the Marine Corps.

The sergeant I spoke to at the recruiting office questioned me considerably. My buddy, only a year older than me, looked a lot older than I did—although he looked older than he was.

"I can't let you in unless your parents sign the papers," the sergeant told me.

I went home with the papers and talked to my parents.

"Dad, I'm going to join the Marine Corps, but I need you to sign the papers because I'm only seventeen."

"Son," he said, "this is not a good time for you to be joining any military service. A lot is going on in the world around us and you won't like it. It won't be the adventure you think it is."

Despite my Dad's warnings, I talked him into signing the papers and I joined the Marine Corps.

That week, the recruiting sergeant drove me, Robert, and one other boy to a larger recruiting base in Houston. As we were being processed I ran into another snag: I only weighed 113 pounds.

"We can't take you if you weigh under 115," the sergeant told me. I was a pretty small guy.

"If I come in later today and weigh that, will you take me?" I asked.

"If you can do that, we'll take you."

I left the station, went straight to a nearby corner store, and bought half a dozen bananas and a pound of cheese. I sat down on a curb and I ate it all. Then, I went and got two cold RC Colas and drank them. Man, did I ever have a bellyache!

I beat it back down to the recruiting base and said, "I want to weigh in."

I just barely tipped the scale over 115 pounds. I did not mention the lead washers I had in my pockets. The sergeant processing me said, "Young man, you are now going to be a Marine. You won't thank me for this later."

At the time, I did not know exactly what he meant by that.

Finally, I was an official member of the Marine Corps, and Robert and I were sent on a train to Camp Pendleton in San Diego, California for basic training. Neither one of us had ever left town by ourselves. We followed directions, did as we were told, and reported to Camp Pendleton as new recruits—and then the processing began all over again. We were issued clothing, new boots,

Portrait with marksman and pistol medals.

and a hat. I looked at Robert after he put on his new clothes and was really proud of him.

"I hope I look as good as you do," I said.

"That's not possible," he replied. That was Robert.

We began a regular routine of boot camp, waking up every morning at reveille. Reveille came early, and when you heard that bugle you had better be out of the sack. We learned the order of the arms and how to manipulate the rifle around. You had to be sure you started off on the right foot.

We did an awful lot of marching. A sergeant or a corporal would walk alongside his platoon and call out the cadence. *One, two, three, four!* We did that all day long. March. March. March. And then we did calisthenics. I was always glad to get back to my bunk in the barracks at night.

We never finished basic training at Camp Pendleton. On Sunday morning, December 7th, 1941, we were all lying around the barracks and I was reading the funny papers. An announcement was made over the P.A. system telling us of the attack on Pearl Harbor. I had joined the service on November 29th, 1941—one week before Pearl Harbor, which thrust the United States into World War II. The United States went to war, and I realized that what my dad had warned me of had been true. Nevertheless, I was still young and adventurous and I did not feel any regrets.

Our lieutenant told our platoon that our boot camp training would be expedited—we were going to be moved to another location to finish our training. It turned out that we would be the first expeditionary force to leave the States after the start of the war. In early January, after only three weeks of boot camp—which normally lasts two to three months—we were shipped to the South Seas. It was decided that we would finish our boot camp training in the jungles of the South Pacific islands.

The Battles at Guadalcanal

Less than 30 days after joining the Marine Corps I was loading a ship with supplies in preparation to depart for war. We put hundreds of sacks of cement down into the hold of the USS *Lurline*, a converted luxury liner. I did not know whether this cement was something that would actually be used later or if it was just ballast. The sacks were lifted to the ship in a big net and then dropped on deck for us to distribute.

Nobody could tell us, or were willing to tell us, exactly where we were going. We only knew that we were headed for the South Pacific. It was not long before the up and down motion of this ocean liner began to make me seasick. It took us two weeks to get to our destination and I was sick nearly all of that time.

Our first destination was Pago Pago on the island of Samoa. There, we continued our training in jungle fighting. Samoa is a mountainous country and for training we ran up and down those mountains with 84-pound packs on our backs. The climate on those islands easily reached temperatures over 120°, particularly in the heavily forested jungles where it would rain every day around 2:00 p.m. The storm clouds would build up on the mountains and you could almost set your watch by them. After the sun came back out, the island became a steamy jungle. Our sergeant kept telling us to get acclimatized to the conditions because he did not know where we were going next, only that it would be a similar climate and that we needed all the conditioning we could get. The extreme heat is a tough climate to fight in, as I am sure our troops fighting in the hot deserts of the Middle East are finding out today.

I was in A-Company, First Battalion, Eighth Marines (we called it A-1-8). After completing our boot camp training, A-Company was transferred to the other side of the island to a small native village called Alawala. Most of the natives moved out of their big, open-air, thatched-roof grass huts and turned them over to the Marines to live in. The huts were called follies, and the Marines took them over as the Samoans willfully vacated them and went on to build new ones.

There were probably only 180 Samoans living in the village of Alawala, and these guys were big. They looked like linebackers to me. The guy in charge of the native contingent was named Pai Tee and I made it a point to make friends with him. Pretty soon, Pai Tee and I were good buddies. Pai Tee began teaching me the Polynesian language and I picked it up quite well, but I had to be careful because some of my Samoan friends were jokesters and I never knew what they were going to teach me. The first phrase Pai Tee taught me was, phonetically, "*Saw oy mia tah owa ai avatu lua safula tah lah*," which meant, "Let's go have push-push in the bush and I'll give you two dollars." It never failed to make those guys laugh.

We continued our fitness training and I was gaining weight like you wouldn't believe. I was feeling pretty tough by now and had no trouble getting around, even with my heavy marching order pack. I had filled out, now weighing a little over 125 pounds. The regimen of boot camp training and regular meals—which I had not been used to back home—really took a hold of me and I put some meat on my bones. The clothes I had been issued in California were all too big at first, but now I realized why—they knew I was going to grow into them. I began to feel that I was going to make a Marine after all.

There was all sorts of scuttlebutt as to what we were going to do after we left Samoa, but nobody really knew. The major in our battalion wanted more experience in the jungle, and I happened to be one of the men appointed to accompany him on his exploratory trips. This major was terribly hefty, and it would not have hurt him to lose a little weight. There were four of us who went on these little jaunts, and we each carried loaded rifles into the jungle. Being young and fairly wiry, we had no trouble running up and down those mountains, so we got our heads together and decided to make things a little harder on the major. We ran up and down those mountains without stopping until he called for a break, and then he'd just sit there panting and blowing as the four of us looked at him innocently. We knew what we were doing to him, and I suspect he probably knew what we were doing too.

Rumors started circulating that we would soon be leaving Samoa. Sure enough, within a few days we departed Samoa to make practice landings on the islands of New Caledonia and New Hebrides. A practice landing meant that we would hit the beach as if we were attacking. For our first practice run at New Caledonia, we climbed down rope nets hanging over the side of the ship and boarded a landing craft. We carried our rifles, ammunition belts, and extra bandolier ammunition. The seas were fairly rough and the landing craft bobbed four to five feet up and down with the tide. If you did not time your release from the rope net just right, you might fall the rest of the way down, or the landing craft might rise up and hit you. It was a tricky procedure, but we learned to do it well.

Our next practice landing was a few days later on the island of New Hebrides. This time, we did it with our heavy packs on our backs. Throughout my jungle training and all the regimenting we endured on the island, I had increased my strength significantly and now weighed 130 pounds. Still, it was all I could do to handle that pack, my rifle, and ammunition on that second practice landing.

After New Hebrides, we cruised the seas for what seemed to me like two or three days. Again, nobody told us where we were going, but we knew these practice skirmishes meant we were going *somewhere*. Eventually, word got around that we were going to make a landing at Guadalcanal in the Solomon Islands to fight the Japanese.

We woke up at daylight one morning and realized that the ship had stopped. I looked outside and saw a huge, coconut tree-covered beach about a mile from where we had anchored the ship. The landing craft was circling and the deboarding net was hanging over the side of the ship.

This time, it was no practice landing. U.S. naval ships surrounded us, firing heavy guns at the island. Shells were landing on the beach and we could see them exploding and trees disappearing. We were bombarding the island prior to landing. This bombardment lasted for about 30 minutes as we all loaded onto the landing craft. We went out squad, platoon, and company at a time, trying to keep our formations together as much as we could as we exited the ship. I never did know how many troops it could hold, but that landing craft was nearly 50 feet long and it was full of us. As we loaded onto the landing craft, we circled the ship until the last platoon had boarded. When everybody was ready, we headed for the beach of Guadalcanal, guns still firing at the island. I thought, *with the barrage of shells they are laying down on that beach, we shouldn't have anything to worry about when we get there.*

I was mistaken on that count.

We did not need to wait for orders to debark. As soon as we hit the beach and that front gate dropped, out the ship we went. Those of us going out the front of the landing craft were met with machine gun fire. Watching this happen, I jumped over the side of the boat instead of running out the front as soon as I felt the landing craft hit the sand.

It was another big mistake.

The nose of the landing craft had touched the beach, but there was a shelf where the sea floor dropped off to 12 or 15 feet deep. I sank to the bottom like a rock. If it had not been for my sergeant, I would have drowned right there on the spot. He was not loaded down with gear like the rest of us were, and when he saw me go over the side he jumped in behind me and managed to pull me onto the beach. He gave me hell for that exit.

"We are still alive," was all I could think to say. He had saved my life at only the beginning of the battle.

It was there that the war started for us. Anybody who goes to war and has fought in any battle or firefight and says he is not scared is lying. We were *all* scared. And we were all green troops, thrust into a battle as soon as we hit land. I saw quite a few of our troops fall as we ran up that beach. I will never forget that day.

We moved up and down the beach and pushed as far inland as we could before our advancement came to a halt. We were bottled up on the beach and were kept hunkered down all through the night and the next day by small-arms fire. Out of 192 men in our company, that day we lost 30, a large majority of which had been killed outright. The others were severely injured and were waiting to be evacuated off the island.

After we hit the beach on Guadalcanal, we spread out and dug foxholes for protection. The Japanese had us pinned down on the beach and were getting some pretty good hits on us. To protect ourselves from their shellfire, we dug foxholes every time we were stopped for more than a few minutes. As we moved out and then stopped again, we dug more foxholes.

We had a battleship, a cruiser, and several destroyers supporting us from the water. Some of the ships had 16-inch guns that were laying shells on the Japanese and it felt like the whole island was shaking. The Japanese would periodically shell back at us from the higher ground they were positioned on. A shell makes a whistling sound as it passes overhead, but I was taught that you never hear the shell that hits you. We soon learned not to sweat the ones you hear.

The aircraft carrier the *Wasp* was supplying air support, but a few days later we were to lose her. In the last minutes of life on the *Wasp*, the SBD Dive Bombers and Grumman F4s were forced to land on what was later to become Henderson Airfield, but which we were still battling for at the time. We were in the process of securing the airstrip, but part of it was still under the control of the Japanese. As these guys landed the plane and taxied up the strip, the Japanese were firing their guns from the ground.

One thing that is very important in life, particularly in the midst of a war, is a sense of humor. You just cannot afford to lose it. My squad of nine men took the right flank and secured about 100 yards of the beach. That is when I looked up and saw a sign stuck in the sand facing the water. I thought, *what the hell is that?* I walked over to see what it was. The sign read: THE FIRST MARINE RAIDER BATTALION WELCOMES YOU TO GUADALCANAL.

The First Marine Raider Battalion was in fact attached to us, and one of their jobs was to recon areas where troops would be sent. The men of this battalion were on a smaller landing ship that had rubber boats attached. Two of these guys had lowered one of the rubber boats at night, gone on shore while the Japanese still had the island occupied, and planted this sign without making any contact with the enemy. What these guys did to plant this sign and give their fellow troops a laugh made us feel a little better about being there ourselves.

Our platoon eventually reached an embankment and we waited behind it for over an hour while some adjacent troops managed to get behind the enemy machine gun nests and take them out. We then moved farther inland, secured a position on the island, and got ready for what looked to be a pretty easy week. We were not being sent to the front immediately, so it looked as though we were just going to rest. But that was not the case. We continued practicing, training, and digging foxholes.

Constant guard duty was the order of the day. We changed shifts every four hours, and I began to wonder what had happened to the Japanese. Finally, word came that we would move out. We formed our standard marching order, headed west on the island,

and moved a few miles to the mouth of the Matanikau River. We stopped and set up camp, but by now we were again receiving shell fire from the Japanese Army stationed across the river. We still had not engaged the enemy, but they had us stopped. We dug in again and made our foxholes.

One fight we could not win was apparent right away: land crabs. These things would scoot along in a sideways fashion and drop into our foxholes at night, trying to claim our territory. Sharing a foxhole with one of these crabs was something else. They were about four inches wide and knew how to use their claws! Their pinches were painful, but if we jumped out of our foxholes, we stood the risk of exposing ourselves to enemy fire. These crabs were nuisances that could have led to greater danger.

I began to see what I was in for fighting in this war. We had to be careful moving about during the day, and most of the time we just stayed in our foxholes. We were all hot and sweaty and we had no fresh water to bathe in. When we got to the point where we could not stand the sweat and filth any longer, we took dips in the ocean. The sticky salt water felt refreshing while we were in it, but it did not make us feel clean once we got out, so I decided to do something about it.

Each of us carried an entrenching tool. One of us would have a shovel and a buddy would have a pick. I got out my entrenching tool and started digging a hole. While I was doing this, my sergeant came and found me.

"Yates, what the heck are you doing?" he asked.

"I'm digging a well."

He looked at me with an odd expression.

"How do you know there's any water down there?" he asked me.

"This close to the beach, and with all the rain we get down here, there is bound to be a water table close to the surface. I am going to get us some fresh water."

The sergeant left me alone and I kept digging.

After digging six feet down I hit water, and I kept digging until the hole was eight feet deep and five feet wide. It was easy digging in that sand, and the hole filled up with water about three feet deep. Everybody in our company came to take a bath in my well. When you are faced with a problem and don't know what to do next, you improvise. That is what I did, and I got us all fresh water.

One day our sergeant informed us that he would pick a nine-man team for a reconnoitering patrol. The job was to make contact with the enemy—more accurately, simply to locate it. I do not know whether I lucked out or not, but I was not sent out on the first skirmish. However, the *next* day, I was. Our team advanced, wading across the Matanikau river and slowly making our way through the thick, heavy jungle. I could not see anywhere in any direction and just picked my way through the heavy undergrowth and banana trees.

We had travelled maybe 400 yards when a sniper shot at us. We dug in and determined that we had caught up with the retreating Japanese troops. They had also dug in and were now firing at us. We used the field telephone to report our position and call for fire. Then, we adjusted fire for the mortar crew, telling them where they were hitting.

Eventually, we received orders to return to camp. We went back, opened our C rations—our daily subsistence which, if we were lucky, we supplemented with some coconut—and crawled into our foxholes for some very needed rest. We had not lost any men in this skirmish, and I began to feel just a little more comfortable about what we were doing.

Our next serious engagement was at the Tenaru River. That was one battle we almost lost. By this time, we had gotten acquainted with some of the natives and they were very helpful in spotting the Japanese and filling us in on their troop movements. I got the impression that the Japanese had really treated them badly because the locals were more than willing to help us.

The Japanese had found a cave up on high ground and installed a large artillery piece which they cleverly laid on tracks so that it could be rolled in and out of the cave. They really gave us a fit with that artillery piece. They would come out of the cave with this 160-millimeter gun, fire off half a dozen rounds, and then retreat back into the cave on those tracks. They would then cover the entrance to the cave with brush and were concealed in such a way that our observation aircraft just could not find them.

The natives came to us and gave us a big hand with this problem. I do not know how they were able to do it, but they circulated amongst the Japanese and acquired information to bring to us. Somehow they had located the position of the field piece and one of our SBD Dive Bombers was able to put a bomb right into the cave. We really praised those local guys, and we gave them tobacco and anything else we had to let them know how much we appreciated their help. With their support, we were able to gain control of Henderson Airstrip in the Tenaru Battle.

From that point on, all day everyday—and all night every night—there was some kind of battle taking place. We had to be very careful because the Japanese troops were slick. Somehow during the night they would slip through our lines and hide in the trees behind us. They would wait until daylight and then try to pick off our officers. Needless to say, officers stopped wearing their rank on their collars because it did not take long to figure out that they were the first targets.

One of the most annoying ploys was a Japanese bomber who flew over our camp every single night. We nicknamed him Washing Machine Charlie because he never had his engines in sync. It sounded like an old washing machine was running whenever he flew past us.

Washing Machine Charlie would come in every night and drop one bomb. In turn, we would fill the sky with anti-aircraft fire. The worst damage he caused was by the fallout of our own shrapnel, which came down like missiles. The little chunks of steel from the bursting anti-aircraft fire went *zip, thud, zip, thud* all around us. I found that the best defense against this was to stand up pressed tightly against a tree trunk. Had one of these pieces of shrapnel hit me, it would have been like a bullet.

There were some battles for which I was only an onlooker from the beach of Guadalcanal. One of these, the naval battle of Guadalcanal, took place about 12 miles off shore. It happened at night, and it lasted all night. From the shoreline we watched a constant barrage of tracer shells flying through the air and flashes of bombs going off on the decks of the ships. It just went on and on.

I do not know how many ships we lost in that battle, but it was a historic event. With all the bursting shells and tracer shots in the air, the battle was a sight to behold. It lit up the whole sea.

A-Company was on the front line for 45 days before we got any relief. We began getting replacements for the troops we had lost and were able to pull back a short distance for some R&R. A tent camp had been set up near the airstrip and my company was given two days rest, which we sure needed. Best of all, our chief cook Sergeant Mauhn had moved in with some field ranges and ovens and fixed us a few really good meals. We had two hot meals both days that we were with him.

One evening Mauhn made us a cake. At about 2:00 a.m. later that night, hunkered down in my foxhole, I woke up thinking about that cake and wondered if there was any left. I decided I would sneak over to the cook shack because my sweet tooth was really gnawing at me and I was sure some of that cake must still be left.

As I got close to the tent everything was quiet, but there was a Marine from another company on guard duty and the first thing I did was run in to him. He wanted to know what in the hell I was doing. So I told him.

"I think our cook had some of that cake leftover," I said.

He looked at me kind of funny and said, "You know, I didn't think of that."

The two of us slipped over to the tent and raised the flap. What greeted us was Chief Cook Mauhn lying on a cot and snoring like a fog horn. When our eyes got accustomed to the darkness in the tent we saw the cake pans on a table in the corner. They were large, flat pans, about 2-feet by 3-feet, that the military used to make bread.

One of the pans had half of a cake leftover, just sitting there on the table, and we crept over to it inch by inch. My partner in crime pulled out his bayonet and sliced the cake in half. We each took a piece and slowly backed out of the tent. Our cook never missed a beat with his snoring.

We walked about 100 yards away, sat down, and ate the cake.

"Sergeant, if we get caught," I said, "I don't know who is going to be in worse trouble, you or me!"

I slipped back to my foxhole and went to sleep with a full belly.

After a few short days of rest we were right back on the front line. It was on this second deployment to the front that we fought in what we called the Battle of Bloody Ridge. This battle was something else. We lost 30% of our company right there.

The Japanese Imperial Marines came at us in waves and seemed hell-bent to get killed. They just kept coming. One day, 300 of these Japanese troops came at us at once. We were ready for them, set up with .30 caliber machine guns and Browning BAR Rifles. I was shooting a Bolt Action 1903 Springfield.

We held the Japanese off, but they kept coming, and we kept shooting them, until the battle was over. We counted later and every one of those 300 Imperial Marines was killed in the assault. They had not gained a thing.

At the time I did not feel much for the fallen Japanese troops, but later I got to thinking about how many of them were shot down. They were right in the open rushing at us, and it was certainly one of our bloodiest battles. Many of our troops were killed too, and many more were injured.

About this time it dawned on me that it was now October and on October 19th I was going to have a birthday. I did not feel any different once I had actually turned eighteen, I just felt fortunate to have survived what I did. I did not feel good about shooting people, but I felt good about myself.

A couple of days before the Battle of Bloody Ridge, we had just finished clearing out Japanese soldiers who were embedded in foxholes and caves throughout the area. After the Battle of Bloody Ridge was over, we had to start mop up operations all over again. This entailed going into caves and foxholes where the Japanese soldiers might be hiding to make sure that they were not occupied for a sneak attack from behind. If they were inhabited, it was our job to remove them.

I was among a group of about 15 troops that was assigned to clean out these tunnels. Believe me, it was not easy to do. The caves that the Japanese dug into the sides of the hills went about eight feet deep. At the end of that tunnel, the caves turned to the right and went back about another six feet. This was a common technique, as we found later. Even if a bomb went off at the mouth of the cave, someone hiding deep inside could survive.

We found many dead Japanese soldiers in the foxholes, but we had to go into each and every one of these caves to make sure there were none hiding out. The Japanese were going to end up behind us if we missed them.

There was just enough light to see as a soldier began his crawl back into the cave, but as he moved deeper in, there was barely any light at all. When it came my turn, I crawled on my elbows and knees with my rifle cradled in my arms, letting my eyes adjust to the dimness. When I got to the turn in the cave, I peered around the corner and looked straight into the eyes of a Japanese soldier, sitting in a crouched position with a rifle across his knees. To this day, I do not know how I got out of that cave alive. In a situation like this, everything goes into slow motion. I can still see it now as his .25 caliber rifle came around, the end of that weapon looking like a storm sewer to my face. Today, I can still see his eyes bearing into me.

This is where my training paid off—I acted by instinct and I didn't have time to do anything else but shoot. I did not even think. I just swung my rifle at him and fired. I dropped down on my stomach, pulling my rifle in front of me as I went down, trying to make myself a smaller target. I do not recall aiming at all. I just swung and shot. One shot.

The only thing that saved me was that his rifle was lying across him, not aimed and ready, pointing straight out in front of him. The hiding Japanese troops could hear us coming, so we knew they were going to be ready for us, and why this guy did not shoot me sooner I will never know.

I got him before he got me. I hit this man in the upper chest, just below his chin, and I had completed my task. I did not see anyone else in the cave so I turned to head back. As I came out of the cave I was met by my lieutenant.

"Yates, couldn't you do it with one shot?" he asked.

"Sir, I did it with one shot."

"You shot twice."

"No sir," I said. "I only fired one shot and I got him."

"Well, we heard two shots."

We assumed that the Japanese soldier had gotten his shot off but had missed me. I had not even noticed. I quickly came to realize that the mopping up operations could be as bad as, if not worse than, an actual battle.

Later in life, I still think about that experience. I believe the only reason I was able to crawl into that cave was because I was so young. To this day I have visions of that cave encounter—I guess because I was face-to-face with someone who was going to kill me. This Japanese soldier was a human being, though his intentions were to shoot me. Because it was such a close encounter, the memory of the experience has been burned into my mind. I do have thoughts of the people who waited for him to return home, but he never did. Instead, I got to go home. Crawling into these caves was a different kind of warfare than a firefight battle, where at least you did not have to look into the eyes of the person you have killed.

In the aftermath of Bloody Ridge, we fought in another battle to attack the retreating Japanese troops. I was designated the forward observer, which is the spotter for the mortar crew. Somebody had to be up front to spot the barrage of mortar shells we fired on the enemy, so I was set up at a point where I could observe where the shells were falling. The mortar crew was back behind me firing .60-millimeter shells over my head.

The first couple of rounds generally land off target, so the forward observer tells the mortar crew firing the shells to either advance or back up. In those days we did not have radios, but we did have field telephones connected by wires strung behind us to communicate with each other. We also had a contour map with numbers that we referred to in order to indicate the location of the shell fire. We did not say "over there behind that big tree," or "to the left of that hill," but "the last one hit at 742." With the information I provided, the firing crew adjusted the elevation on the mortar and then fired again.

When a shell hit a target, the spotter called on the phone and ordered the mortar crew to "fire for effect." With this command, as many as 75 to 100 shells were shot into the air before the first one ever hit the ground. It was like a package of firecrackers going off.

We would wait a few minutes for it to quiet down and then check to see what the Japanese were doing. If we had been successful, we would advance and take the ground that we had just assaulted. This is the manner in which we advanced across Guadalcanal, taking a few hundred yards at a time.

There were enemy soldiers lying dead everywhere. Apparently, the surviving Japanese troops had not tried to recover those who had fallen in their haste to retreat. What few were still alive we captured and sent back for interrogation. Then, we continued our advance until we caught up to the enemy troops and could repeat the procedure all over again.

In this particular battle, when I called "fire for effect" and the shells were shot, there were a few seconds of stillness. Then, all of a sudden, everything around me exploded.

One of the shells had not been properly loaded. It was not a dud, but there had not been a full charge behind it. The shell fell short and hit the foxhole that I was in. I was badly injured. I had a concussion and shrapnel in my chest and back. My platoon quickly got a corpsman in there to give me first aid and some troops put me on a stretcher to carry me out. Then, to add insult to injury, a Japanese sniper shot me in the leg. A week later, I was carried back to the rear echelon, put on a ship, and sent to New Zealand to recover.

A few months later, what was left of my outfit also arrived in New Zealand. I got to reunite with all my buddies, but they filled me in on the horror stories of how many more men we had lost. Our battles at Guadalcanal for the large part were successful. We forced the Japanese troops to stop and turn back in their march through the South Pacific. However, they were not yet retreating home. It was well understood that their next goal was Australia and New Zealand.

When U.S. troops arrived in New Zealand, we were welcomed with open arms. The American troops were real heroes to those people because they knew what we had done at Guadalcanal. We knew, too, that our battles—as bloody and destructive as they were—had been a turning point in the Asiatic Pacific War. After World War II ended, our outfit received a presidential citation for being the first expeditionary force to the South Pacific.

Recovery

With the injuries I sustained at Guadalcanal, my fighting days in World War II were over. After my recuperation period in New Zealand I was shipped back to a hospital in San Diego, California. One day, I got in touch with my commanding officer and explained to him that I was from Corpus Christi where there was also a naval base. I told him that my home was not too far away from that base and that it sure would be nice if I could be transferred to the Corpus Christi Naval Hospital. I was subsequently shipped back to Texas.

I lay in that naval Hospital for four months while the doctors tried just about everything they could to correct my injuries. There was not much the doctors could do for my back, and my head injuries were causing constant, severe headaches.

One procedure the doctors tried on me I had never even heard of before, and I have not heard much about it since. The treatment was called an electro-insepligram, a procedure in which the doctors tapped my spine, drained out all the serum surrounding my brain, and then x-rayed the brain to try and determine the location causing the pain. Believe me, as horrible as the war was, undergoing that treatment was one of the worst experiences I have ever had. If I moved my head just the slightest bit, the pain was indescribable.

Every once in a while the nurses and their aides came by to turn me over in the bed.

"Mr. Yates, you've got to turn over," they said.

"No, no," I protested. "Don't move me. Don't move me!"

"You will get chest congestions and have all sorts of problems if we don't. We've got to flip you over."

With me screaming and yelling in pain and protest, every three hours two guys stood on either side of me, picked me up, and turned me over. Eventually, the brain serum regenerated and everything went back to normal, but the treatment was largely ineffective.

Shortly after these treatments I was discharged from the hospital—100% disabled—and I made the four-mile trip home. The doctors discharged me with the understanding that my injuries would eventually improve, which they did, but they were still problematic—particularly my headaches, which stayed with me for the rest of my life.

Early Career and the Start of a Family

After being honorably discharged from the Marine Corps I was in pretty bad shape, so I more or less just hung around the house. However, I was improving every day and I still had aspirations of starting my own business. As my health improved I got a job with a man named Joe Walker who was in the floor-covering business. I thought, *I'll just learn the floor-covering trade and see what I can do with it.* As it turned out, he had a daughter that caught my eye, so I always tried to be on my best behavior because of my interest in her. His daughter's name was Edith Jo.

I was doing really well at this company and I think I surprised Mr. Walker because he started turning me loose on jobs by myself within just a few months. Although I could not work more than half a day before I had to hang it up, I was learning the floor-covering business up and down. In the meantime, I began dating Edith and everything was going smoothly.

I still had the urge to get into something for myself, so on the side, while still working for Mr. Walker, I bought a big floor-buffing machine and went into the business of floor polishing. I ran an advertisement in the local paper and got many prospects. When I was not busy with my floor polishing business I worked for Joe and increased my knowledge of the floor-covering trade.

Finally, Edith and I decided that we really were meant for each other. Her dad did not think so and discouraged us as much as he could, but he could not stop us. We just eloped. This was an old-fashioned elopement: Edith handed me her clothes and belongings out of her bedroom window and we went off together. I thought at the time, *she sure has a lot of shoes.*

I had a close friend named Ralph McGee who had also been in the Marine Corps. I had become acquainted with his family and we had the wedding over at their house. My mother was present but Edith's parents were not—they did not know what was happening yet. It always bothered me that we were deceiving them that way, but that is how young people can be.

After Edith and I married we immediately moved to Austin, Texas where I got a job at Scales Electric and Plating. I was hired under a GI Bill in which the government paid part of my salary. The boss at Scales Electric was glad to find someone under those conditions, and so I began learning the plating business.

After a year working at the shop I was almost running the plating operation myself. There was another plating business in Austin across town that was operated by a man named Dan Taylor, but things were not going too well for him personally. He committed suicide and his business came up for sale. I saw this as the opportunity to finally own and run my own business, so I made a deal with the handlers of the estate and bought Mr. Taylor's plating shop.

I went in early one morning to Scales Electric and Plating and gave notice to my boss, Randolph Scales, that I would be leaving. Scales was a bit upset with me that I was quitting and, considering my health, advised me to be careful or else I would get hurt.

"You're not ready to run a shop by yourself," he told me.

"Well, I'm going to make a run at it, I've got to do it," I replied.

I had been a good employee for him and he had liked me, so he wished me well on my new business venture.

Soon enough, I was operating the Austin Electro-Plating company out on East 1st Street, and I ran that business for several years. Although business was successful, I realized that my health was no longer improving. In fact, it was getting *worse* and I did not know how or why. After visits to the doctor, I discovered that the fumes from the chemicals I was working with—mostly cyanides and acids—were getting to me and causing serious health problems. The doctor advised me to get out of that business, so I sold the plating company and moved on to my next venture.

I read in the paper that a local floor-covering company, Capitol Floors, had won a big contract with the government to lay the floors in the state government buildings. I applied to this company for a job, but I did not want to work on an employee basis. Instead, I requested to work as a sub-contractor rather than be on their payroll. They accepted my offer.

I laid asphalt tile for two cents a foot. There were dozens of buildings set to receive flooring under the contract, and each one was at least 4,000 square feet. I could lay about one and a half buildings a day; at two cents a foot—well, that was pretty good money for me! Equally important, I felt that I was self-employed, even though I was technically a sub-contractor.

I worked for Capitol Floors as a sub-contractor for about a year and I made really good money. Then, one day, the boss called me into his office and asked me if I would be interested in coming to work for him as the manager of his store. I accepted his offer and was the manager of Capitol Floors for the next three years.

Rocky Rundell, the owner of Capitol Floors, was expanding the business and he constructed a new building for a new store in north Austin. After about a year working at the north office, I started feeling really ambitious and sat down with Rocky in the office one day.

"I'm managing the business pretty well," I said, "and you know I am doing a good job. I want to make you a proposition."

"What's that?" he asked.

"Why don't you retire and spend some time at home. You won't have to work, and I'll run the business. We'll each draw $500 a month." In the early 1950s, that was pretty good money.

Rocky did not like my suggestion at all and, in the end, I decided to quit and open my own floor-covering business. Unfortunately for Rocky Rundell, about nine months after I left his company he went out of business. He just had not realized how much work I was doing for him.

I started my own floor-covering business and I called it Floor Craft, which I operated very successfully for over 20 years. I started out renting an old, deserted apartment building for my office. As I increased my number of customers and the company started seeing success, I bought a property on Lamar Boulevard in north Austin and opened a new store. After four or five years operating there, I enlarged again. I moved about a block west and built a huge, two-story building with a large warehouse out back and a floor-covering display area over 5,000 square feet. On the mezzanine of this building I established a home decorating business and hired an interior decorator. Business was really going well.

At home, Edith and I began having kids. We had two daughters, Sharolyn and Susan, and one son named Jay. As busy as I was running a business, I started to feel that I was not spending enough time with the kids. On top of operating Floor Craft, I dabbled in real estate, which kept me even more tied up. However, I started doing so well in real estate that it dawned on me this was the career I was cut out to follow. Plus, I enjoyed it much more than my floor-covering business. So, I made a career change: in 1972 I sold Floor Craft and its building for a nice profit, acquired a real estate license, and went to work buying, fixing up, and then selling old, dilapidated houses. Now, I had more time for the kids, and for the rest of my working days I worked in the real estate business. I spent a lot of time scanning the newspapers in various neighborhoods for houses for sale. Usually, they could be bought far below the market price because they needed many repairs, and I had discovered that I was capable of doing most of those repairs myself.

I continued this way for some time, but it eventually occurred to me that I enjoyed working with land—particularly ranch land—more than refurbishing old houses. It seemed I had a natural eye for picking out the right property (or maybe I was just lucky). I bought a 300-acre property in the city of Georgetown just north of Austin that almost adjoined the Georgetown airport, and to this day I am not sure how I ever managed to make that purchase. It was a big risk due to the huge debt it put me under. I started developing portions of the land and divided it up into lots anywhere from three to five acres. This was good land—tree-covered and close to Austin—and it turned out to be a very successful business venture.

I began reinvesting the profits I was making in real estate into more ranch land located within a reasonable commuting distance from town. Sometimes I kept the land for a year or two before selling it to a developer, and sometimes I just filed a subdivision plat and developed it myself.

I took to the real estate industry like a duck takes to water. It was a clean, healthy, outdoor business that suited me to a tee. I believe the reason I was more successful at what I was doing than others was because I bought my own equipment, including bulldozers and road graders, and when I started development of a subdivision, I did all the manual labor myself. I built the streets and plotted out the land, but here I needed the help of an engineer. Luckily, a good buddy of mine named Jim Watson was an engineer and his son was a surveyor. Everything fell into place and Jim did all of my engineering work to prepare the plats, which was quite an ordeal. I had to take the plats to city hall and get them approved—if not by the city, then by the county. I found that the Williamson County office was much easier to deal with than Austin City Hall, and so most of the properties I chose to develop were 10 to 15 miles outside of Austin city limits. All in all, I developed about seven suburban-type subdivisions in the central Texas area.

I was just going great guns so I started buying and selling fully developed ranches. I always tried to buy what I called a water property, a track of land with some kind of running creek or stream on it. Water properties always attracted me, and they attracted buyers as well.

Mine was a one-man business. I did everything myself. I had no employees, which was really a relief: at one point at Floor Craft I had worked up to 25 employees, including four salesmen and two people in the decorating department. I felt more free being in a business where I could do everything myself, and a sense of freedom was something I always valued. In fact, I thrived on it.

Part III
Flying Adventures

Itching to Fly

All my life I had been interested in airplanes and dreamed of becoming a pilot. One day, a good friend named Gene Dagel showed up at my office. Gene was a factory rep for a carpet mill that was one of the suppliers for my floor-covering business.

"Walter, I want you to come out to the airport with me," he said. "Let's take a ride."

"What do you mean 'take a ride'?'" I asked.

"I bought an airplane," he said. That got my attention.

We went out to the Georgetown Airport and Gene showed me the two-place air coupe he had just acquired. I walked around the plane and *oohed* and *ahhed* over it for a few minutes.

"Let's go!" he finally said.

I climbed into his airplane and prepared for what would be only my second trip in an airplane. My first time flying had been when I was about 15 years old in Corpus Christi and I took a ride in a Piper Cub. We took off and flew all around the Georgetown area, and Gene let me take the controls a few times. It was only a short ride, but I really began to think seriously about becoming a pilot myself.

Another experience really got me itching to learn to fly. I had a good friend named Steve Simmons whom I had hunted and fished with for years. Steve owned a Chrysler-Plymouth dealership in Austin and was always a big help to me whenever I wanted to buy a new vehicle. He was just an old country boy that had come off the farm and made good, and I felt we had a lot in common. One day, Steve called me up and told me about a friend of his in Abilene who was a pilot. His name was Norman Lawlor and he was also a car dealer. Steve told me that he and Norman were planning to fly up to South Dakota in his airplane to go pheasant hunting. There was room for one more man in the plane and Steve asked if I would like to join them. I was ready to go at the drop of a hat and I took him up on the offer.

Norman's plane was a 1955 Navion. It had retractable landing gear and reached speeds up to 160 MPH. We flew to Mitchell, South Dakota and went hunting every day for four days. By the end of our trip we had shot our limit of pheasants and we packed them into dry ice before heading home.

By now, Norman and I had gotten pretty well acquainted and he decided to let me fly the airplane from the right seat. One thing about Norman Lawlor was that he was a borderline alcoholic. Before we took off that day, Norman reached under his seat, pulled out a bottle of whiskey, and took a couple of good swigs. Once we got in the air and were on course, Norman said, "Walter, you go ahead and fly." Which I did. And he promptly fell asleep!

I was really getting the feel of holding that airplane on course, and Steve watched over my shoulder from the back seat to tell me when I needed to make a correction in my course. Steve had been a navigator in World War II and knew what he was doing. We were somewhere in northern Oklahoma when Norman Lawlor finally woke up. He looked around, snorted a few times, reached under his seat, and took another big swig of that whiskey. I assumed he really *was* an alcoholic at this point.

"Where are we?" Norman asked.

"We are now about 50 miles north of Oklahoma City," Steve answered.

Norman looked at us kind of funny and asked, "Was I asleep that long?"

"Well, obviously you were!" Steve said.

Norman took the controls and we landed in Oklahoma City. We got some sandwiches, fueled up the plane, then took off again and flew on home.

That experience was enough to where I could not stand it any longer. A few days later I went out to the flight school at Browning Aerial Service in Austin and signed up for flying lessons. They were always ready for a new student and told me everything that would be involved. I agreed to all of it and we got started.

Flight School

I was instructed in a J3 Piper Cub, a pretty easy airplane to fly once you learn how to land it. My instructor's name was Jack McAlpin and he and I got pretty well acquainted. After I had about four or five lessons under my belt, Jack was letting me follow through on landings. One day, I asked him how short of a landing you could make with this little airplane.

"Well, let me show you," he said.

We came in for the landing and that plane was just *hanging* in the air. I could almost see birds walking around on the ground, we were going so slow. Then, all of a sudden, about 50 feet above the runway, the airplane stalled. Jack had gotten it too slow.

Man, did we hit hard—so hard that the tip of the propeller got bent and one of the struts on the landing gear was broken. We had also snapped one of the bungee cords that control the amount of resistance to bounce. I learned then and there that an airplane could fall out of the sky if you flew too slowly.

For some reason or another, the flight school blamed Jack for the accident and put me with a different instructor, a young lady in her mid-twenties. She was really friendly and knowledgeable and she polished up a lot of my maneuvers.

Gene Dagel was very interested in what I was doing and we talked regularly about the progress I was making in my flight training. One day he called my shop and we discussed the possibility of buying an airplane together.

"Why don't we get us a four-place plane," I suggested. "That way, more of us can ride in it than we can in the little air coupe you have."

"I've been wanting to get rid of this little air coupe since the day I got it," Gene said.

We began looking around for airplanes and found a Piper Tri-Pacer, a small four-seat, single-engine plane that was a step up from the Cub because it had tricycle gear. We bought the plane and I started logging the hours I needed to earn my pilots rating. By flying my own airplane, I saved a little money because I did not have to pay to rent a plane from the flight school.

Finally, I prepared for my check ride, the thing that any student pilot both looks forward to and dreads when learning to fly an airplane. In those days, when a student was ready for his check ride, his instructors sent him to another flight school to take the test with a complete stranger—someone he had never flown with before. I was sent to a flight service in Waco, Texas about 100 miles north of Austin. Before I left Austin, Mrs. Browning, who ran Browning Aerial Service, told me, "These check pilots can be tricky sometimes. You better stay on your toes. We've never had a student fail a check ride so don't let us down!"

"I'm going to do my best," I promised.

On the morning of my check ride I got into the Tri-Pacer in Austin, did everything I was supposed to do for preflight—a little bit nervous, but not too much—and flew to Waco. When I arrived in Waco, I reported to the flight school and talked to the young lady at the desk.

"We've been waiting for you," she said. "Have a seat over there. I'll have a pilot ready for your check ride in just a few minutes."

I sat down in the pilots lounge and skimmed the flying magazines that were lying all around the room. A few minutes later my instructor appeared.

"Okay, son, I'm going to take you up," he said.

We went out to the tarmac and I went through my pre-flight exam. I did everything very carefully to make sure my instructor knew that *I* knew what I was talking about. Then we took off. At first my instructor just had me fly around the airport; then, he gave me a heading to the west and I flew 15 miles to an area without much flight activity where it was safe for the flight school to administer the examination. My instructor had me perform various maneuvers and sharp turns. I flew up and down a highway and, with a crosswind, made S-turns over the road.

"I want you to be the exact same distance out on the right side of the highway as you are on the left," he instructed me.

Depending on the wind, you are going to drift into the road in one direction and away from it in another. This can be a tricky maneuver, but apparently I did okay.

"Okay, let's head back to the airport," my instructor finally said. He did not indicate whether I was doing well or not.

"What's the heading back to the airport?" he asked me.

I had kept my eye on the Brazos River, which flows more or less west to east near Waco. A few miles south of me I could see the river running to the east.

"I'm going to set it at 93°," I said quickly.

"Okay, let's see what happens."

Visibility that day was 10–12 miles and we must have been 18–20 miles west of the airport. We were flying along and I was as happy as a clam because I thought I had passed my check ride. Then, all of a sudden, the instructor reached up and pulled the throttle closed. Immediately, the engine dropped to idle and the plane became a lead balloon.

"You just lost the engine. What are you going to do?" he asked me.

Glancing a couple of miles ahead of us, I saw what looked like an open field.

"I'm going to land right in that field over there."

"Okay!" he said.

My glide ratio was not very good and I was losing altitude quickly. We had been a little over 4,500 feet when he pulled the throttle closed. I kept thinking, *he'll hit that throttle any second now and I won't have to worry about this*, but before I knew it I was lined up for that field, preparing to make a landing. I was getting lower and lower and he still wasn't saying anything. And that sucker did not say anything all the way to the ground!

I had no problem landing. I bounced the plane a little because I did not have any power, but I got down all right. My instructor sat there for a minute without saying a word. Then, he reached out his hand.

"Congratulations, you are a private pilot," he said. I had passed my check ride.

That experience affected me for the rest of my flying career. It gave me confidence to know that I did not need an airport to land an airplane. I even began experimenting on my own with off-airport landings, and I gained a lot of confidence in the air. I believe this man started me on the path to becoming a bush pilot in Alaska, which I was for several years.

Flying Adventures

Gene and I got along just fine in our partnership with that Tri-Pacer. Now, we could even take our families out on trips. I learned something new every time I flew that airplane and I enjoyed every minute of it.

One day, Gene came into my office with his face hanging down to his knees. I could see that something was bothering him so I asked him what was the matter.

"I'm being transferred," he told me.

"Is that going to affect our partnership?" I asked him.

"Unless we cut the airplane in half, we are going to have to do something about it."

"Where are you being transferred? Maybe we can just switch back and forth," I suggested.

"No, I'm going all the way to Memphis."

"Well, that's too far for us to stretch a partnership, all right."

I decided I would just buy his half of the airplane. Once I owned the airplane in full, I did not feel nearly as guilty landing the plane in the middle of a field because I was not risking someone else's property and investment.

Around this time a buddy of mine told me about a place 40–50 miles south of Corpus Christi on the Intracoastal Canal where you could land an airplane right beside the water and go fishing. Being the type of guy that I am, I had to check this out for myself. I called Steve Simmons, told him my plans, and asked if he wanted to join me.

"I'm ready!" he said.

Steve and I flew down to Corpus Christi to look for this fishing spot. My buddy who had informed me of this place told me how I could identify it: in the same area there was a crashed PT-19 navy training plane. Around 1950, a couple of naval air cadets in training were flying through the area when one of them thought he had a problem with his engine. He landed his plane on the beach and the other guy came in and landed behind him. As it turned out, the first cadet was just landing for the hell of it. There was nothing wrong with the plane. But when he took off again, he crashed the airplane into the soft sand. He was not hurt, but his airplane was too damaged to fly. Since he had taken off first he just climbed into the other cadet's plane and they flew off.

I did indeed spot the crashed airplane. It had been lying there for several years and was very deteriorated, but you could certainly see that it had been one of those navy trainers. I circled over the spot a couple of times and looked for a safe place to land.

Boy, did Steve and I ever catch some fish! I had found a new pastime flying up and down the coast. I would fly along the shore at low tide and when I spotted a school of fish near the beach I would land on hard sand where the tide had just gone out. I spent many fishing days down on the coast. I usually had somebody with me, but I went down there by myself many times as well.

Steve Simmons decided that he also wanted to learn to fly. He was an avid fisher and our trips to the coast got him really excited about becoming a pilot himself. Steve had a little trouble earning his pilot's license. He was a good pilot when he took his lessons but he had trouble with the written exam. He just was not good at studying and had to take his written exam three times before he passed it. About that time, the Cessna factory came out with the Cessna 175, a departure from their standard airplanes. Steve and I decided to buy one of those 175s and start a partnership. I sold the Tri-Pacer and we ordered a brand new Cessna 175 from the factory.

Steve and I went on all sorts of trips in that Cessna 175. It had more power to get off the ground than the Tri-Pacer, and by using full flaps I could land the plane in pretty short distances.

Sometimes Steve and I would go dove hunting and land right in the pasture, but most of the time we flew up and down the coast to go fishing.

Steve realized that he could use an airplane for his business, particularly on his trips to west Texas where there was a test track to check automobile tires. Steve went out there pretty regularly by car, but he realized that he could just fly instead and land the plane right on the track. One thing led to another and we began looking for a new, high-performance type airplane. We decided to look for a Piper Comanche, but we were not ready to purchase anything right away—we were just in the market for it.

I was further motivated to buy a new plane when I had engine failure on one of my trips to Corpus Christi to visit family. The only engine failure I ever had in an airplane in all my flying days was in that Cessna 175. I landed right on the highway just south of Victoria and caught a ride into town. I then went to the airport and brought a mechanic back to check out the plane. He found a problem in my fuel pump; I had gone into fuel starvation, causing me to lose my engine.

The mechanic ordered a new fuel pump for me and we pulled the plane into a nearby farmer's yard. Of course, we asked the man first if we could park the plane there for a few days because we had to change a part and could not fly. He said, "No problem," so we pulled in beside his barn and parked.

About a week later the mechanic called. "Your part came in," he said. "If you want to come down now, we'll go replace the part and you can fly the plane home."

The mechanic changed the fuel pump and fired up the plane and it ran perfectly. I taxied back out onto the highway with the help of a few farmhands. With one man at either end of the road to watch for traffic, I took off and flew on home. That experience shook Steve and me up a little bit and it caused us to speed up our search for a better airplane. We wanted a faster one, too.

Steve was about 20 years older than me. He was no slouch by any means, but he had been getting on in age to start flying.

Nonetheless, we both really wanted a Piper Comanche and Steve located one with an automobile dealer in Denver who was in financial trouble. His Piper Comanche was a 1961 model in great shape and it had a lot of good time left on it, so we bought the airplane for $10,000. That would hardly buy a wing tip today.

These days, moving up to a higher-performance aircraft requires a considerable amount of training. Apparently, this was not the case in 1972—at least no one said anything to me about it. Practicing in the new Comanche, I had a little trouble at first with my landings and it took some time before I could make three-point, squeak-squeak landings on the runway.

In a plane with retractable landing gear, sooner or later, somebody is going to land gear-up. There is a saying among pilots about gear-up landings: "There are those who have and those who will." Everybody thinks, *it won't ever happen to me*, but it did happen to me one day and I did it at my own airport. I landed with the landing gear up! Fortunately, I was able to grease it in and did not damage the belly of the airplane at all—I just slid along the grass strip. I damaged the propeller slightly when I hit the ground, but that was the worst of it.

Steve started flying out to the test track in west Texas several times a month to bid on worn out test cars, and I started flying to destinations farther and farther away. I made many cross-country trips, and I picked up where Norman Lawlor left off going pheasant hunting in Mitchell, South Dakota. Steve and I went up there every year. We also flew to Colorado and Montana to go deer hunting. We were travelling all over the country.

Steve and I maintained a good partnership as co-owners of the Comanche. It is expensive to maintain an airplane, but if you've got someone to share the cost with you, it cuts down on the load considerably. We worked out a system: whoever asked for the plane first or reserved it on a special day got it, regardless of any last minute plans the other person might have made. That person just would not say anything about it. We charged ourselves $10 per hour to fly the plane and we put the money in a kitty for future repairs and our annual inspection. This way, we always had money for maintenance—we did not use the money for anything else.

Steve and I got along beautifully, but as time went by he started slowing down. He was developing some health problems and realized that something might happen to him while he was in the air. Eventually, he decided it was time for him to end his career as a pilot.

"I will go with you anytime you want to take me fishing, but I am just going to quit flying," he said. And he did.

We had to do something about our partnership. He was no longer using the airplane yet he still had half the money in it, so we decided to just sell the plane and that I would find something else for myself. We had put a lot of time on the airplane and had flown all over the country, but we were able to sell it for $15,000. We actually made a profit.

I put my part of the money aside and started looking for a new airplane. It was not long before I had another Comanche—I was just sold on that airplane. Some Comanche airplanes had long-range tanks, and I found one for sale that had two extra 15-gallon tanks in addition to the 60-gallon main tanks. With the 30 gallons in the two auxiliary tanks built into the wings, the plane had a maximum load of 90 gallons of fuel, and a 1,000-mile trip was no problem at all. I used the plane a little bit for my business, but for the most part I just flew for fun. I truly loved flying. Sometimes I made excuses to use the airplane for business because I just wanted to be in the air.

Fishing Trip to Mexico

I discovered a fishing camp in the Campeche area of the Yucatan Peninsula and, I tell you, it was probably the world's most satisfying fishing spot outside of Alaska. One day, I described this fishing camp to some of my buddies as we sat in the customer's lounge at North Austin State Bank drinking coffee. With me were Jack Ray, owner of a steakhouse called The Barn; R.W. Hoover, former dairy farm owner and real estate investor; and Eldin Bebe, president of the bank. Eldin was a regular on our hunting trips but he had never been with me on a fishing trip. The more I talked about Campeche the more excited they got, and the four of us decided to take a trip to Mexico.

I told them to count on being gone for five or six days, which included the flight time. After a few days, we all agreed on a date and I prepared my Comanche for the journey. I owned what I believe was one of the best Piper Comanche's manufactured. Apparently, some just turn out better than others. Mine was a 1968 Comanche B that flew about 7–8 MPH faster than any of the others I had flown. I really loved that airplane.

On the day we left for Mexico we all piled into the plane. Everyone was loaded with expectations—not only had I discussed these fishing trips in great detail, I had also shown them pictures of all the fish I had caught down there before. These guys just could not wait.

The route I took went south down the coast past Corpus Christi and Brownsville. I decided to land at Brownsville to top off my tanks. We did not stay for long, but I was reminded by the FBO (fixed base operator) to be sure and land when we entered Mexico to check in with customs. Apparently, the Mexicans were sticklers for their regulations on foreign aircraft flying into their country. I had obeyed these rules before, stopping at Matamoros, but I ran into all sorts of delays. Somebody always had his hand out for a *pelone*, a little under-the-table tip, but they did not do anything other than register the aircraft and the passenger names. I am prone to bend the rules a little bit from time to time, and my buddies with me were not aware of the requirements, so I chose not to discuss them. I did not land in Matamoros to check in, I just continued down the coast.

I also had another idea.

"You can see how the coast line runs down and hooks around to the left," I said as I showed them my chart. "We can save a whole lot of flying time by cutting across the water. If you guys don't have any objections, I will chart a new course to Campeche."

They all looked at each other.

"Will we be out of sight of the shore?"

"For a short time, we will," I answered. I suppose I was not being completely honest with them.

They said that if I thought it was safe then they would go along with me. With their permission, I set up a course starting just south of Brownsville that would take us straight across the Gulf of Mexico.

I was really enjoying myself on this flight and everyone was excited. But I made a serious error. I always watched my fuel pressure gauge very closely when trying to stretch a flight. I had plenty of fuel to make it to Campeche, but I did not want to stretch it *too* much so I kept an eye on the gauge. If the needle flickers just a little bit, it means that one tank is about to run out and that it is time to switch to another. This usually happens before the engine even coughs.

Well, we all got deeply involved in some conversation and for just a short time I was not keeping my eye on that gauge. All of a sudden, the engine sputtered and it almost quit before I got the tanks switched. In a situation like this, you flip the electric fuel pump on, switching the tanks immediately, and your propeller never stops spinning. It may slow down just a little bit during the transition, but then it picks up and you go on. Nevertheless, in that moment, I thought I was going to lose all three of those guys. They were shaken up and became adamant that I fly closer to the shoreline.

"We are over halfway there now," I told them. "That would be like turning backwards. We are okay. I am sorry I misjudged my tanks."

After that, each one of them was leaning over my shoulder watching that gauge. They would not take their eyes off of it.

We landed in a town called La Pesca at a semi-private airstrip. We told the man on duty we were going across the bay to a fishing camp for a few days and that we wanted to tie the airplane down and refuel. He could speak only broken English, and I could say only a word or two in Spanish, but he led me to understand that they were out of fuel and would have some within a few days. Since we were going to be fishing, he told us he would top off our tanks whenever we got back.

After tying down the plane, we crossed the bay in a boat to get to the fishing camp. Our feet had no more than hit the ground before these guys wanted to get out there in that water.

The most enjoyable fish to catch and release were the baby tarpon. These fish were on average 20 inches to 2 feet in length—and boy, did they ever give you a fight on the end of that line! I don't believe I have ever seen happier fishermen than these guys were down in Campeche. In addition to my own enjoyment fishing, I was enjoying watching *their* enjoyment.

The camp where we stayed had a small aluminum boat that could hold the four of us plus a fishing guide. Our guide was very helpful because he always knew where to find the fish. One day after lunch our guide took us into the back bay to go after the larger tarpon. There was a channel of deeper water running through the bay and quite frequently we caught large, full-grown tarpon. In that deeper channel we jigged for the fish off the bottom of the sea floor. We had several different kinds of jig baits and we just lowered them down until they touched the bottom of the ocean and then bounced them up and down to lure the fish. Those fish were masters at throwing the hook. We could hook a half-dozen tarpon before we ever got one into the boat. They came almost entirely out of the water, jumping around and shaking their heads, and you could hear their gills rattling a mile away. We stayed out on the water until four of five o'clock in the evening, and every one of those guys caught a tarpon that would make anybody proud, except for me. I caught several other fish but I did not get one of those large tarpon.

The guy who ran the fishing camp was named Hal Hassey. Hal originally came from Florida but when he discovered this place in Campeche he just knew that people would want to come so he set up the camp. Most of our meals were fish—some that we caught ourselves and some provided by the camp—but we did not eat the tarpon because catch and release of those fish was just for sport. Instead, we ate the grouper and sea bass that we were also catching left and right. The cook at the camp was a master at fixing up those fish, so in addition to enjoying the fishing, we had a week of great meals.

Time came for us to depart and Hal had one of his guides use one of the larger boats to take the four of us and all our gear back across the bay to the plane. When we arrived at the airstrip there was a different guy on duty. I do not know if he was the manager but he spoke fairly good English. I asked him if he had topped off our airplane with fuel.

"No, our fuel truck hasn't come yet," he said.

We were trying to get an early start so that I could get us back to Brownsville in one day, but this guy could not seem to convince us that he knew for sure when the fuel would be coming.

"We will just go on and refuel at Vera Cruz," I finally told him. We had enough fuel to get there and fill up.

That is when he hit me up for the *pelone*. He was trying to get as much as $100 out of me.

"What is that for?" I asked.

"Landing fee, landing fee."

"That is way out of line," I said. "I have been here before and you never charged us any landing fee."

I was sure he was extorting us so I fussed and argued with that guy for a good while. In the meantime, my buddies were waiting in the airplane thinking that I would come out at any moment and we would be ready to go. Finally I said, "Let me go talk to my *compadres* about this."

I hurried out to the plane and said, "Get in! Let's go! We're losing time!"

"What's the rush?" Eldin asked.

"We want to get back to the states before dark," I said. "We should get on and get moving, so jump in!"

They all got in and hooked up their seatbelts, and I started the engine. I looked back to the little shack that was the administration building and saw this guy speeding toward us in a Jeep. Knowing I did not have much time, I checked the magnetos as I taxied toward the end of the runway instead of stopping like you are supposed to do. By the time I got to the end of the runway, this guy was already mid-way down it. He stopped for a second and then I poured the coal to that thing. My buddies were absolutely mortified. They figured that we would be shot down before we even got in the air. They were yelling and hollering at me to stop, but I just floored it and went on. I was not about to have that guy extort any money out of me. When this man realized what I was doing he started speeding toward us in that Jeep, but it was a well-paved runway and I made a nice short-field take-off. We were 300–400 feet up in the air before we even intersected this guy and we just passed right over him. He shook his fist at us as we flew away.

I told my friends that this man was trying to extort $100 for a landing fee.

"I have been here so many times before and never had to pay any landing fee," I said. "I just wasn't going to pay!"

"Well, I would have paid it! I would have paid it!" Eldin shouted.

"I know you would have, but it just wasn't right."

I finally calmed everybody down, but then they began worrying about something else. I told them we were going to have to land at Vera Cruz to refuel because I did not have enough in the tanks to get all the way back to Brownsville.

"What if that guy radios ahead and arrests us?" they asked. "You really got us in a pickle here, Walter."

They were really giving me hell, and I was beginning to regret the decision a little bit myself. I respected all these guys and, in addition to being my good friends, they were also people I did business with.

"I don't think they even had a radio there," I explained. "When we first came in and landed I buzzed the field to let them know

I was coming. They didn't call in for a landing or provide a traffic report or anything."

"Well, he has a telephone!"

"Yes, he might have," I conceded. "But we don't have any choice. I don't have enough fuel to get us home. We've got to land at Vera Cruz."

We landed in Vera Cruz and I taxied up to the refueling station. The man working the airstrip waved his flags to guide us in and I told him to top off the tanks. He was a very accommodating young man and knew a few words in English. I made it clear what grade of gas I wanted and he topped us off.

"Do you guys want to go in?" I asked my friends. "They've got a restaurant in there, we could get some lunch."

"No! Let's just get out of here!" they said.

So we took off again. Nothing had been said by the authorities in Vera Cruz about our departure from La Pesca but I did not want to say "I told you so," so I just kept quiet. Those guys didn't say anything either, and it was not brought up again until we got home. When we had our next coffee meeting at the bank, they began telling everybody about that crazy Yates and what he did in Mexico. That story circulated around for a long time and it got to a lot of people that I wish it hadn't because they were good friends and business contacts; I had taken a lot of them on fishing trips before and hoped to again in the future. I finally convinced my buddies that they were exaggerating the story a little bit and it all passed. But for some reason or another, those guys never flew with me again.

The First Trip North

In the early 70s, a school buddy of mine who I had grown up with named Billy Gene Howard—we called him B.G.—got in touch with me. He was a petroleum engineer working for Marathon Oil Company and had just been transferred to Anchorage, Alaska. Bill began bombarding me with letters telling me how much I would love the North Country and that I ought to come up and visit to see what really was God's country. It did not take too much to convince me. I had to do a lot of planning because I had never flown that far before—the trip would be nearly 5,000 miles—but when I finally got my act together I set off for Alaska alone. I certainly invited my wife Edith to come with me but she chose not to go. She was not too sure that it was a good idea to fly that far in a single-engine airplane.

Bill was right. I fell in love with Alaska, so beautiful and so undisturbed. It was an absolutely splendid place with its scenery, mountains, glaciers, and *salmon*. Bill had a floatplane and we flew out to remote lakes to go fishing. You had to hide behind a tree to bait your hook, you would catch so many! I truly fell in love with Alaska and that love story would continue for the rest of my life.

After that vacation visiting Bill in Alaska I made many trips back, and it was on one of these trips that I first began to test my abilities as a pilot. On my first few visits to Alaska I flew up through Canada, most of the time following the Alcan Highway. However, it was not long before I learned about an alternate route between Seattle, Washington and Prince George, British Columbia. This was a route that few pilots took, but the ones who told me about it said that it could save me a couple hundred miles on my journey. They called this route the Trough.

The Trough was an enormous canyon several hundred miles long that came out at Watson Lake in Canada, but there was one major problem cutting through it: if you hit bad weather there were very few places you could set down your plane. In my younger days I probably would have tried to plow through any bad weather, but I knew better than to risk it in the Trough. There is a saying among pilots: "There are old pilots and there are bold pilots, but there are no old, bold pilots."

After flying through the Trough a couple times, I got familiar with the lay of the land. There was a large river that flowed down through the canyon with beautiful turquoise-colored water that meandered back and forth. The canyon was on average half a mile wide and there were mountains on either side that reached up into the clouds. There were various logging camps up and down the canyon and each of them had a small airstrip nearby. Most of these airstrips were not marked on the official charts used by pilots, so I marked them on my own chart as I went through the Trough. A few times that I ran into bad weather and poor visibility, I landed on one of those airstrips and just waited the weather out. Over time, I began to feel much more comfortable flying through the Trough.

Nevertheless, I had to be extremely careful. Unless I flew at a very high altitude I could barely get radio transmission. On one occasion that I hit bad weather, I was forced to fly very low through the canyon due to the low ceiling. Rugged mountainous country surrounded either side of the Trough so I did not want to stray out of the canyon, and I could not alter my flight plan because I had no radio transmission. I was beginning to wonder what I was going to do. Luckily, I passed over a logging camp that had its own radio system. They were kind enough to get a hold of flight control in Prince George and cancel my flight plan for me, saving me a lot of trouble. When you are flying in another country you sure do not want to violate their regulations, and I enjoyed flying up north so much that I did not want to jeopardize any future times I envisioned spending up there.

Flight to Watson Lake

It was on one of those trips through the Trough that I really had a problem. I ran into bad weather and the ceiling kept sinking lower and lower. It reached the point where I was almost flying in a tunnel because the ceiling was below the mountains on either side of me. I was flying only 500 feet above ground and had a visibility of only 4 or 5 miles. Despite the poor flying conditions, I was making it along fine; however, the weather quickly began to further deteriorate. It had been a long time since I had passed one of my marked landing strips, but I decided that I better make a 180° turn and go back.

Well, you can't always do that. The weather behind me was also rapidly growing worse. I felt like a baseball player caught between 1st and 2nd with both basemen trying to get me out. I really did not know what to do so I thought, *perhaps I might get a hold of another pilot flying up here on my radio.* Miraculously, some guy with a strong Canadian accent answered me. He called me Yank—I guess he recognized my accent too. I gave him my location, explained my problem, and told him I was getting low on gas. I had about 200 miles to go to get out of the canyon so I asked what he would recommend.

"I'm about 20 or 30 miles ahead of you," he said. "If you can get up here, there is a lake where we land Cessna 180s all the time with no problem, so you could probably land on it with your Comanche. Let's watch out for each other because the visibility isn't too good." I agreed. I did not have much choice.

It was not long before I caught up to him. He was flying a Cessna 180 on floats.

"You know I am on wheels," I said.

"That's all right," he answered. "There is a strip right beside the lake. We keep a cache of fuel there for just such emergencies. I can get you enough fuel to get you to Watson Lake."

Boy, this was welcomed news to me.

"Just follow me," he said.

I throttled back a bit because my airplane was faster than his. He took a left turn up a canyon, which I never would have even halfway considered doing myself, particularly in that kind of weather. However, after just a few minutes we came to a lake and right beside it was a long, flat, open area that looked to me like a safe place to land.

The other pilot prepared to land ahead of me on the lake.

"Where I beach my plane is where you touch down," he instructed me. "When you get even with my plane, plan on touching down on the runway and you will have plenty of room."

I turned around, flew back a ways, and watched him land on the lake. He came up to a bank and stopped.

This is where I really began to learn how to operate landings and take-offs on short fields. I lowered my flaps and landing gear and throttled back, halfway hanging on the prop. I could see where this pilot wanted me to touch down and I did it without a bit of a problem. I actually went a little faster than I should have for the length of that strip because I was concerned about stalling.

After I landed, the pilot, whose name was Trig, took me to a heavy brush area where there was a canvass tarp covering a small storage of square 5-gallon cans of fuel. There must have been 15 or 20 of those cans.

"To be safe, I would like to take at least 20 gallons," I said.

There was a metal box about a foot square also stored in the cache.

"We put money in that box for whatever amount of gas we use," he explained. "This is kind of a co-op. There's about half a dozen pilots involved in this and we work on an honor system."

I calculated what I owed for 20 gallons of fuel and was more than happy to make my contribution. I put my money in the metal box and Trig helped me carry the cans down to my plane. I poured the gas into my fuel tanks, carried the empty cans back to the cache, and hid them under the tarp.

The weather still had not cleared up so the man suggested we take a rest.

"Why don't we have some fish?" he asked.

I looked at him and asked, "You mean that?"

"Yeah, I have a rod and reel."

I also had my own fishing rod but it was packed away in the baggage compartment of my plane.

"Do you want me to get my equipment?" I asked.

"Naw, we will have a fish caught in just a few minutes."

Trig used some small artificial lures and, so help me, every time he cast his rod he caught a trout. I had my camping gear with me so I got out my stove and skillet. I had a bottle of cooking oil and we fried those trout right there on the spot. I thoroughly enjoyed the meal and visiting with Trig. In fact, I stayed in touch with him for years after and we got to be good friends.

I wanted to wait for the weather to improve before taking off again but Trig said he had to get going. The weather did seem to be getting better and the ceiling was gradually lifting, so we both decided that we would leave at the same time. That way, if I ran into any problems he would be able to hear me over the radio.

I loaded all my things and took off. Then, I circled around the lake while Trig got into the air and I let him lead the way. When we got back to the Trough, he turned southeast and I turned northwest. The weather was much better now and it steadily improved as I continued north, flying at an altitude of 2,000 feet with good visibility. When I was 20 miles outside of Watson Lake, I called air traffic control and reported that I was inbound for landing.

The airport sat right on the edge of the beautiful Watson Lake. In fact, you fly right over the lake as you land. I pulled into the airport, tied the plane down, and caught a ride into town with one of the guys who worked in the tower. He dropped me off at a motel in Watson Lake where I checked in and got some much needed rest.

Flying in conditions like those can really wear you down and put your nerves on edge.

Although my difficult flight through the Trough to Watson Lake was a new and highly unusual situation for me, it turned out that treacherous flights like this one were quite normal for pilots up north. They are always ready for an emergency and they always have an answer for it. Up north, the thrill of flying this terrain is a way of life. Passing through canyons and drainage ditches, I often saw bush pilots flying right down on the treetops. One beautiful, clear, sunny day, I was riding co-pilot with Bill Howard to Yakutat in southeastern Alaska and I asked him why he and other pilots flew so low.

"Bill, it is such a pretty day, why don't you go up to a little safer altitude?" I asked.

"Walter," he said, "I am not sure I can fly this plane above a hundred feet!" That was just their way of life.

A few days after my incident in the Trough, I left Watson Lake bright and early and flew to Whitehorse. The weather was excellent and I could fly at just about any legal altitude that I wanted. I passed mountain peaks exceeding 10,000 feet in elevation as the highway below me wound through the valleys.

About two-thirds of the way to Whitehorse I flew past a mountain peak and could not believe what I saw. I saw aluminum. I saw metal.

I had spotted an airplane that had crashed into the mountain peak and was now partially covered with snow. With one wing, the engine, and the nose cowling sticking out of the snow, I could identify the plane as a Douglas DC-3. I circled around, climbed a little bit higher, and then called Whitehorse over the radio.

"I want to report a crashed aircraft," I said.

"What is the position?" the man on the radio asked.

Using my chart, I told him the location. "Stand by, one," he said.

I did not hear from him for two or three minutes. I was beginning to wonder if I had lost the signal when he finally radioed back.

"You'd be interested to know that you are the seventh person in the last two years to report that aircraft."

"You mean, it has been there that long?" I asked.

"That's right. It's too difficult a terrain to try to salvage the plane so no one has even attempted it." There are many instances in the North Country where planes go down and rescue crews are never able to get to them.

I got to Whitehorse and visited a friend I had made named Bud who owned a fixed base operation in town. Bud had rooms for pilots in his building and I usually stayed in one for a night if the day was waning on me. I told Bud about the crash site I had seen and he told me that he was very familiar with it.

"That crash gets reported frequently. I guess somebody ought to go up there and try to remove the wreckage, but it's just not worth the effort."

"Well, I can understand why," I said. "That mountain juts straight up and down."

I sure liked the arrangement Bud had set up with these rooms for pilots. There were five rooms and you could take any one that was vacant. He kept the room keys in the doors so that pilots could come and go at any time; when you left, he just put the room charge on your bill for fuel. Bud only charged about $30 per night for a room but I would have paid more because it was right there on the airport and very convenient for pilots. He told me that he sometimes went two weeks without anyone showing up, and other times he had pilots asking to share a room.

"Traffic comes and goes," he said.

I will say again how accommodating, friendly, and nice the people were who lived up in Canada. The only time you might get the idea that they are a little hard-nosed is when you don't follow their regulations. I have inadvertently strayed off my flight plan a time or two, and they did not hesitate to let me know. With the number of aircraft flying through that desolate country it can be very difficult to find a plane that has gone down, so if you say you are going to be on a particular course, that is where you better be.

The next day I left Whitehorse and went up the highway past Haines Junction and Burwash. I re-entered U.S. territory at Northway, Alaska, another town with which I had become pretty well acquainted. I cleared customs and stayed the night in a rental cabin (which cost significantly more than Bud's lodgings in Whitehorse). The following morning I woke up to great weather and departed on the final leg of my trip to Anchorage. As I approached the city, I was pretty amused by the directive techniques used by the town's air traffic controller. When a pilot is about 20 miles outside of his destination, he radios the airport and they give him a route to fly. On this flight, those instructions really caught my attention.

"Fly over the Peanut Farm and turn right on a heading of 260°," he said.

"Would you repeat that?" I asked. "Peanut Farm?"

"Everybody knows where the Peanut Farm is," he said blankly.

"Everybody except me!" I said.

It turned out that the Peanut Farm was a bar that local pilots frequented. The main feature, to no surprise, was the many bowls of peanuts strewn about the bar.

I landed in Anchorage and parked my plane on Les Risley's lot. I met Les on an earlier trip to Alaska and we had gotten to be such good friends by now that he did not even charge me for tie down. Les had a nice home on the edge of the slope rising up into Anchorage's Chugach Mountains and he invited me to stay the night. As time went by, he actually gave me my own room. I left clothes in the closet and various other items that I would need in town, and that is where I was home when I visited Alaska. I used their telephone and felt like a member of the family.

Les and his wife Wanda had two children, a young boy—about eight years old at that time—and his sister who was twelve. Les and Wanda are both gone now. Les was later killed in a very serious motorcycle accident and his wife got cancer. It is a fragile life we lead.

Bill Howard and the Bear

In 1973, I told Bill Howard that I would like to return to Alaska the following summer to shoot a film on bears, salmon, and the natural landscapes of the North Country. I wanted to produce a documentary film on Alaskan wilderness to release by 1976, in time for the nation's bicentennial.

"No problem," Bill said. "Just figure out when you are going to come and I will arrange for us to take a float trip." We agreed that I would return in late May.

In keeping with the celebration of our bicentennial, I wanted to show Alaska as it was in the beginning. The wilderness was still thriving but I knew that, unfortunately, this would change someday. I wanted to bring my film through the civilizations that had come to Alaska and the change the land had made on the people—an entirely different breed of man than us down here in the Lower Forty-eight. Man seems more conscious of man in the North Country. In spite of the civilization and modernization of Alaska, they still have the frontier spirit to help their neighbor, and this is apparent everywhere you go. They are living life in God's most beautiful country and seem to have more concern for one another—but with one exception: every person who goes to Alaska and enjoys all its beauty wants to be the last. He does not want it to get crowded. You start thinking, *what can we do to keep people from crowding this beautiful land and destroying it?* I certainly had those thoughts myself. I decided I would devote about ten percent of the film to what was happening to Alaska in present day. I saw Alaska as our last frontier, and it was melting fast. This was the story I hoped to tell in my movie.

Down below Yakutat on the Alaskan coast lies the Setuk River which flows out of a large lake—large enough to land a float plane. Bill flew in there before I arrived that summer and reserved a government cabin that was available for people backpacking and camping in the area. He also went up and down the river searching for a good spot on the edge of the water to build a platform where we could watch the wildlife. He hauled in some lumber and built the platform in a big tree at a site bears frequented to feed upon salmon.

Bill had everything prepared by the time I returned to Alaska the following May. We got in his floatplane and he showed me where we were going on the map. From the air, I saw a tremendous amount of scenery in the way of glaciers, ice packs, and wildlife. I was happy to see that the landscape had not been affected too much by hunting pressure and civilization. Bill flew over the lake prior to landing and I was absolutely amazed: I had never seen so many salmon! We were flying at low altitude toward the lake's confluence with the Setuk river and it was absolutely loaded with fish. You could easily see the salmon from the air, and I immediately understood why Bill had picked this spot. The river water was so clear it was invisible and it looked like the salmon were lying on the ground. Some of my photographs captured this effect, and almost everybody who looked at them remarked on the illusion. One fellow looked at the pictures and asked, "What are the salmon doing up on these rocks?" I took several pictures of the salmon, which were so thick that it looked like you could walk across the river on their backs.

One of the most interesting sights, having never seen it before, was to watch the salmon swimming up the river to spawn. I have heard that once the salmon start up the river they do not eat until they spawn in order to conserve energy for the journey upstream; when the salmon finally do spawn, they die. Their whole lifestyle is built around this event—racing to get back to where they were spawned and then spawn themselves.

Swimming up the river, the salmon will come to a place you would think impassable and then try and try again until they finally make it through. It is true perseverance. They literally swim *up* the falls. Of course, they do not realize at first how strong the force of the water will be—when they first went down it they were just little fingerlings. After three or four tries, they realize they have got

Bill Howard and I prepare for the bear photography trip.

to give it all they've got, and they've got enough. That is the way our maker made these fish. Luckily, in the few truly impassable locations—the manmade dams—provisions have been made for the salmon to pass through in carriers.

Bill and I landed on the lake, set up camp in the cabin, and prepared ourselves for several days in the wilderness. I was really enjoying myself because this was the kind of lifestyle I loved. I had my movie camera and still camera with me and I was ready to start filming, so we fixed ourselves some sandwiches and went down to the river. We were able to wade across the river right where it flowed out of the lake and the salmon were actually swimming against our legs. It was a sight to see.

It was a little over half a mile down the river to where Bill had built the platform. When we reached it, we climbed up, set up my camera gear, and waited for the bears to show up. And we waited and waited. I had a telephoto lens on my camera that I used to take pictures of the salmon swimming through the river, but we saw no bears. Bill and I sat up there all day before we gave up and climbed back down the tree to head back to the cabin. The equipment was difficult to move back and forth so we decided to leave the movie camera on the platform until we returned early the next morning.

We waded back across the river, returned to the cabin, and fixed a delicious meal. We grilled fresh salmon, cooked a big batch of potatoes and onions, and made a salad with some lettuce and tomatoes. You can't beat a meal like that! Salmon tastes so much better when it is fresh-caught, and we had no problem catching them. We took a rod and reel with a lure on the end, tossed it out into the water, and the fish just could not avoid biting the hook.

We got up early the next morning, fixed breakfast, and went back to the platform, hoping that today would be the day. Along the banks of the river we could see bear tracks so we had great expectations that we would get to film some bears. Again, we waited and waited and waited. I really appreciated Bill going to all this trouble to help me; he had built this platform in the trees and taken off several days of work to accompany me. We were really enjoying the time we had together, but another day went by without seeing a single bear.

Again, Bill and I headed back to the cabin, ready to kick our feet back. We brought some beer with us to the cabin and had put them in the river to chill. We placed them right below the confluence of the river and the lake and bolstered them with some rocks so that they would not float away.

"One of those cold beers is going to really hit the spot," Bill said as we walked along.

"You bet," I agreed.

Well, when we got to the place where we had put the beer, there was no beer. There were, however, quite a few empty beer cans with teeth marks in them scattered along the edge of the riverbank. The bears had really beat us at our own game, and we got to wondering if there was a drunk bear somewhere roaming up and down the river.

Bill and I talked things over that night and decided we should look for bears at a different point on the river.

"I think the best thing for us to do is to float about six miles down the river," Bill said.

"How are we going to arrange that?" I asked.

"Let's fly back to my buddy Dale Hart in Yakutat. We will get a rubber raft and have him fly us back here. Then, we'll float down the river with your camera ready—we are sure to get some shots."

This sounded like more adventure to me, and it sure seemed like a good way to get shots of the bears, so we flew back into town, got ourselves a raft, and returned to the lake. Bill knew where we would come out at the end of our float trip—near a bridge passing over the Setuk River—and he made arrangements for a car to be waiting for us when we got there.

We loaded my camera equipment into the raft, as well as a few munchies, and I brought along a plastic bag to prevent my movie camera from getting wet whenever we hit rapids. Once we had everything in order we took off down the river.

At times we moved pretty fast, but at other times the raft barely seemed to move. When we hit slow water we paddled, and when we hit rough rapids we braced ourselves. The river did not run straight but turned and meandered through the countryside with an occasional sharp turn. Bill controlled the raft while I kept my camera ready. We believed that at any moment we would run into one of these elusive bears.

We could hear rushing water up ahead so we knew we were coming to some rapids. I slipped my camera into the plastic bag and grabbed one of the paddles so that I could help keep the boat straight as we went down the rapids. At the bottom of the rapids the water flowed swiftly into a sharp right turn. Very carefully, we maneuvered our raft through the rapids, slowed ourselves down as much as we could, and then rushed along the curve hanging on for dear life.

Then, the most unexpected thing happened. We rounded the corner and there stood a bear knee-deep in the water catching fish. We were headed straight for him.

With little control of our raft, we actually glanced off the bear! We startled him, but before the bear could even move we had bounced off of him. To our good fortune, the bear decided to move in the opposite direction.

Of course, my camera was still sealed up in the plastic bag. The opportunity of the trip had been right there in front of us and it passed without me shooting a single frame. And that was the extent of my photograph-the-bears trip. We floated the rest of the way down the river and eventually arrived at the bridge where the old truck was waiting. We then loaded up our gear and drove back to Yakutat.

Bill and I made it to town and spent the rest of the day with Dale Hart. Dale treated us to a nice steak dinner and we had a great time. The next day, Bill and I flew back to Anchorage in the floatplane. It was time for Bill to get back to work and for me to return home.

Fishing Trip with Jay

I began introducing my son Jay to faraway places in the wilderness when he was about 12 years old. One summer I suggested to him that we fly to Canada and go on a father-son fishing trip. Jay was really excited about this idea, which made me very happy because I wanted him to enjoy the same pastimes that I did. I arranged to take a week off from work and then Jay and I loaded up in my Piper Comanche, just he and I.

From Austin we flew to St. Louis, Missouri to refuel and rest for a little while. Then, we flew to upper Michigan, crossed the Canadian border, and landed at Sault Ste. Marie in Ontario, Canada. I had arranged to stay in a fishing community called Kirkland Lake but I needed instructions on where to land when I got there. Once I learned the location of the airstrip we got back in the Comanche and took off for Kirkland Lake, which was about 200 miles away. I thought how glad I was to have auxiliary fuel tanks, making cross-country flight much easier.

We landed at the small airstrip near Kirkland Lake and met our fishing guide. He helped me tie the plane down and drove us to the lake where he had a float plane ready. The arrangement was for him to fly us to the cabin where Jay and I would stay for three days and two nights, and then he would return to pick us up.

Jay and I hit that water as soon as we could. At the cabin we had an aluminum paddle boat and we had no problem catching fish. We brought food along with us, of course, but we also counted on supplementing our diet with the fish we caught. Most of the fish we caught were northern pike, a really tough fighting fish which made them all the more fun to catch and release, and another type of fish that looked like a rainbow trout without any color, which turned out to be really tasty.

The lake we were on was pretty large and Jay got bit by the exploring bug, so we went paddling all over that lake, stopping every once in a while to trudge through the trees and brush. Jay was on the lookout for arrowheads. We did not find any, but we both thoroughly enjoyed exploring the wilderness together. There was an abundance of maple trees and you could see scars on the bark where people had drawn sap over the years to make syrup.

Our exploring led us to another nearby lake. We had spotted this lake from the airplane when we came in to land, and it was only separated from our lake by about a quarter-mile. There was a trail connecting the two lakes so we pulled our little aluminum boat on shore, tied it down, and took off walking with our rods and reels. We reached the other lake and it looked very inviting so we began casting our lines. There were several nice fish to catch and it was just a fun place to be.

"What do you think about going back and dragging that boat over here so that we can explore this lake?" I asked Jay. He was ready to go at the drop of a hat. The 12-foot long aluminum boat wasn't all that heavy so we had no problem dragging it over the trail.

We got back to the new lake and spent the rest of the day exploring and catching and releasing fish. We were just having fun and I was really pleased with the way the trip had turned out. Jay and I had not been able to spend too much time together one-on-one; I had been working some awfully long hours for the past few years, not to mention my travelling. We really needed this trip together and it was well worth it just to see the happy grin on Jay's face. He was smiling from ear to ear the whole time we were there and he absolutely enjoyed every minute of it.

As the day drew on I told Jay we best drag the boat back over to the other lake and return to our camp before it got too late. When we got back, we had a great meal for dinner—for some reason, camp food always tastes better—and we decided to relax and take it easy because our guide was coming to pick us up in the morning.

When we got up the next morning I stepped outside and thought, *we may have a problem.* There were low clouds, a low ceiling, and misting rain. It was the kind of weather even I would not fly in. *Maybe we will have to wait out here a little longer than planned,* I thought. However, it was not too long before we heard the drum of an engine. Our guide came in about 100 feet above the lake and landed that float plane. Then Jay and I loaded up our gear while the pilot sat thinking.

"The way this wind is blowing, I think I will fly one of you over to the nearby lake first, then I'll fly back and pick up the other and all the gear. This is a pretty short lake and I don't like the way this wind is blowing." Being a pilot myself, I agreed. Our guide flew me over first, about a five minute flight to a small island on the other lake.

"I'll go get your boy and your gear and be right back," he said.

As I waited for the pilot to come back with Jay, I paid attention to the way it felt to be alone in the wilderness. Although it was only about 45 minutes, the aloneness made my head spin. Nevertheless, I felt tranquil. I wondered how long I could stay alone in nature, completely isolated. The thought attracted me. . .

The pilot returned with Jay and flew us back to the airstrip at Kirkland Lake where my Comanche was waiting. From Kirkland Lake it was a 90-minute flight to Sault Ste. Marie, and although there was not much daylight left, I decided to make the trip that night. About 20 miles out from the city, I called Sault Ste. Marie air traffic control to report my position. They returned my call to inform me that flying VFR (Visual Flight Rules) was not allowed after dark in Canada. It was, by now, very much after dark. I responded with a weak excuse for my predicament and waited for their response. And waited. And waited.

As I approached the airport, I called them again and asked for landing instructions. They let me "stew" for a while, but I had the airport in sight with no landing instructions. I knew the wind conditions and I was lined up for the correct runway. Finally, as I was lowering my landing gear, I got a call back.

"Piper 9264 Papa cleared to land. Runway one eight. Report to tower at landing."

The air traffic control officer was a lot nicer in person than he had been on the air and he accepted the "head winds" as my reason for being late. Jay and I spent the night in town and made the long flight home the next day with one fuel stop in St. Louis. Although Jay really enjoyed this trip together, he got the biggest kick out of telling Mom about Dad's butt-chewing in Canada.

The (Illegal) IFR Flight

On one particular trip I was returning to Alaska, flying up through Canada along the Alcan highway, and I had been moving in and out of good and bad weather for the whole journey so far. I had just departed from Watson Lake with a flight plan filed to Whitehorse, Yukon. It was pretty rough country between those two towns and the weather was not cooperating at all that day. Even flying through the valleys I could not get any lower than 6,000 feet because I would be running into the tops of mountains. I was a little nervous about those mountain peaks and I got to thinking about the training course on instrument flight, or IFR (Instrument Flight Rules), that I had taken several years earlier. With IFR, you fly strictly with reference to your instruments because you are in or above the clouds and cannot navigate by the seat of your pants like you do in regular VFR flying. I sure was glad I took that course, but I never actually completed it. I did not take my exam for an IFR rating because I never wanted to actually *have* to fly IFR, but I did want to know how in case I was ever forced to due to bad weather. During the course I gained about 10 hours of straight instrument time, enough to where I could keep the needle on point and stay on course.

I was about halfway from Watson Lake to Whitehorse when the ground fog began to rise and meet the cloud layer. I did not know at the time what was happening to me, but when I looked ahead everything was grey, like I was looking into a fog bank. All of a sudden, I was in a snowstorm—one minute I could see the clouds around me and the next minute I couldn't see anything. It was like being inside of a milk bottle; I lost reference to everything. When this happens—and you should not do it unless you are instrument rated—if you have some instrument training it can sure get you out of trouble, and it got me out of trouble that day. I was able to maintain my course, but in order to avoid the tall mountains I climbed up to an altitude of 8,500 feet. According to my chart, the tallest peak that I had to fly over was 8,000 feet, so I got up to an altitude I felt was safely above that and then tuned in to the VOR (VHF Omni-directional Range) station in Whitehorse. Then, I could just fly that beam on in. VOR has various vectors from 360° and you can fly any one of those radios that you chose by following the needle on your dash in an instrument that indicates whether you are coming to or from your destination, and whether you are deviating off course. I was already too deep in this weather to do anything else and I just quit looking outside. I kept my eyes on those instruments. When I got close enough to Whitehorse to reach air traffic control I called and gave them my position, which I was really just guessing because I could not see it. I gave them my estimated time of arrival and reported my flight plan.

Then, they asked me the question that I sure hated to answer.

"Give us a weather report. What's the ceiling?"

"The ceiling is about 7,000, broken," I answered.

"You *are* VFR?" they asked.

"Yes sir, I am VFR," I lied.

They stayed in touch with me and eventually informed me that I was on their radar and on course. They cleared me to land and I breathed a sigh of relief.

Anybody who is making a decision to start flying airplanes should definitely get some instrument training because you never know when a situation like this is going to be thrust upon you. I am not sure whether I would have made it that day if I had not known IFR. You should at least be trained in IFR to make a 180° turn so that you can just turn around and go back if you hit bad weather. I felt pretty secure in my ability to stay on course, and I did, but without that instrument training I would have been in big trouble that day.

I went up to the control tower and closed my flight plan. I also wanted to talk to the weatherman. My next destination was Anchorage and I was still a couple hundred miles from the border. The weatherman informed me that conditions were bad all the way to Northway where I would check in to customs.

"How was that weather between here and Watson Lake?" he asked.

"It was deteriorating behind me. I think I was flying out of it." I described the conditions so that he could use it in a pilot report, which is advice given to pilots from a controller within radio range that will inform them if another pilot has reported bad conditions. If you can be of any aid to someone else in the air you sure want to do it. I told him I would not advise flying VFR to Watson Lake. I never did tell him that I was skirting on the fringe of IFR flying.

Air traffic controllers frown on anyone stretching their luck, so I thought it best not to talk about it.

I spent the next two days in Whitehorse waiting for the weather to improve, all the time thinking that I had been stretching my luck too much on these trips. I vowed to myself that I was not going to do that anymore. When you are a younger pilot you think you can do anything and the good Lord will take care of you, but that is why we have search and rescue squadrons. They are needed all the time because someone like me stretched their luck a little bit too far.

After the weather finally cleared up, I flew VFR again all the way to Anchorage. I entered U.S. Customs at Northway and had a moose burger at the café they had on the field. I enjoyed that big moose burger. I never was sure whether they were actually moose burgers or not, but that is what they called them. I then left for Anchorage to complete my trip.

A little before I reached Anchorage I passed within 40 to 50 miles east of Mount McKinley, towering 20,320 feet into the skies. It was a perfectly clear day out, blues skies everywhere, and I got to thinking that I had never looked down on Mount McKinley from above—I was always looking *up* at it. I thought, *now is a good time to do it.* I called Anchorage control to let them know I was deviating from my flight path (I was trying to be a good boy now) and told them I was going to fly over Denali Park.

When I got to Mount McKinley I began circling and climbing and circling and climbing. I had altitude tested myself before in a pressure chamber at Fort Sam Houston in San Antonio. The test let me know my threshold for "losing it" at low oxygen levels in high altitude environments. I found that above 12,000 feet I would not be reliable to fly. When I went into the high pressure chamber to be tested I was given a pad and pencil, and after I got above the simulated pressure at 10,000 feet, the test administers started giving me instructions over headphones as if I were about to approach an airport. They gave me my approach directions and procedures and my altitude to fly, and I had to copy it all down on my notepad. After reaching the simulated conditions at 15,000 feet they depressurized. Then, I came out of the chamber and had a debriefing with the people running the test. What really got my attention was that I had written the first one or two letters of each word and then skipped the rest before moving on to the next. Nothing I had written made sense. I even swapped out letters, writing "v's" instead of "t's." My brain had been telling me to do something but my fingers were not following. That test sure let's a pilot know exactly what his limitations are, and I was glad that I had that experience because I might have gotten in trouble attempting to see the top of Mount McKinley from above.

I had to be careful, yet I was still looking up at Mount McKinley, so I decided to go up a little bit farther. So much for not stretching my luck anymore! I was flying a Piper Comanche and the plane wasn't having any problems at that altitude, so I went up to about 16,000 feet—but I was still looking up at the peak! I did not have oxygen on board and I knew what was going to happen to me if I kept going. I decided to stop my ascent and return to a safer altitude for flying. I did not get to the top of the mountain, and I still have not seen Mount McKinley from above.

The Urge to Breakaway

In 1973, I started getting a feeling in the back of my head about an adventure that I wanted to take. I had read about the North Country all my life, and for the past few years I had avidly explored it. Now, I started thinking about having my own cabin in Alaska. I wanted to find a location in the outback wilderness where I could build a cabin and, eventually, spend an entire year in it. Alone.

I spent two summers exploring and preparing for this project. I even took a six-week course at the University of Alaska to learn more about the wilderness of the North Country. Topics included climatology, wildlife, subsistence, natives, and anything else that fell into the Alaskan wilderness category. All scenarios had to be considered and worked out. Through my studies and conversations with the locals, I realized that it was not going to be any picnic living in the remote wilderness throughout the wintertime, but I was bound and determined that I would be successful and avoid any disasters that might arise. I was undertaking something that could turn out deadly if I was not prepared, so I kept in mind the Boy Scouts motto—"Always Be Prepared."

Because I was in the real estate business it was easier for me to block off time for a project like this. I made a few more trips up to Alaska inside of two years, studying the wilderness and looking for a cabin site with the help of Bill Howard. He thought mine was a neat idea, but everybody else was advising me against it.

"Do you know what you are getting yourself into?" they asked. "Do you really think you can spend the winter in Alaska all alone?" I was afraid to commit myself to this project for fear I might be committed! But my mind was made up. Many people proclaimed me an idiot for even thinking about such an undertaking, but that just made me more determined.

Back in Austin I made a deal with a Cessna dealer named Bobby Ragsdale. He was looking for volunteer pilots to ferry new airplanes from Wichita, Kansas back to Austin—a good opportunity to log flying time. I thought, *my gosh, he surely won't have any trouble finding pilots.* I volunteered right away.

Bobby Ragsdale had a Cessna 310 that could fly three of us up to Kansas. He always bought us a big steak dinner and we would stay the night. The next morning, we flew three new airplanes back home. In return for my service, I gained experience flying just about every model that Cessna built, including the 172, 175 (a plane I purchased), 182, 185, and the model with retractable landing gear, the 210. In a period of two years, I accrued hundreds of hours in flying time almost for free. And I loved it. We did not do it for money, we just did it for experience. It helped me to build up my flight log and gain experience in many different types of aircraft.

The in-flight experience I gained on these volunteer trips was invaluable to my flying career, and also to the adventure I was planning in Alaska. I returned to the North Country in late August of 1974 and stayed through the month of September. This time, my wife Edith came along with me. Edith wanted to see the North Country and visit with Vesta Howard, Bill's wife, and I wanted to use this trip as an opportunity to scout the Alaskan wilderness for a place to build a log cabin for my upcoming adventure.

Flying to Alaska is quite common, but I only recommend it to pilots who have been well-briefed on the course. It is quite an undertaking. For some reason or another, Edith did not fly back with me—she flew commercial instead. Edith seemed to have more sense than I did.

Edith and I left from Georgetown Airport and flew north to Cutbank, Montana where we cleared customs and entered Canada. We then flew north to Grand Prairie, Alberta. Just before Dawson

Creek we reached the start of the Alcan Highway which we followed for about 1,500 miles, just north of the Canadian Rockies. Flying in this area could be very problematic because there were no navigation aids. It was a lot of by-the-seat-of-your-pants flying, and the compass was constantly changing. Flying nearer to the north pole there is anywhere from a 30–40° compass deviation, so every 30 minutes I had to recompute my heading. It could get quite hectic, especially when coupled with bad weather.

We passed over Whitehorse in the Yukon Territory and entered Alaska at Northway where we cleared customs again and stayed the night. The next morning we left Northway and flew on to Anchorage. Because we had faced a lot of bad weather, it took us about 32 hours of flight time to get to Anchorage.

While I worked on my project, Edith stayed in Anchorage and toured around with Vesta. They visited places all over the lower part of the state, and I am sure Edith saw parts of the North Country that I never did. After a short trip, Edith returned to Austin, and I continued searching for the perfect site for my project.

One challenge I faced in locating a site for my project was finding an area where it was permitted by the forestry department to freely cut down trees, which would be necessary to build a cabin. Of course, there were regulations against this, but I eventually found some people who had a mining claim on the Post River that were open to allowing me to build a cabin there in exchange for their usage of it when I was away and they needed to make assessments of their claim. I thought this was a fair agreement so I flew to Post River to examine the area.

The Post River flowed northward, snaking its way between spiraling mountains on either side. I descended into the canyon for a closer look. The weather was my friend today. A light breeze out of the west gave me a margin of safety with no down drifts. Right at the confluence of a fast-running creek and the Post River I could see a gravel bar that looked long enough to land my Cessna 175 single-engine airplane. I circled back and slowed down to get a better look at the gravel bar. I decided it was worth a try. I began my approach about one mile north of the touch-down point I had selected, a spot marked by a drift log on the bank of the river.

With my heart beat increasing rapidly and adrenalin gushing, I began to throttle back and pulled full flaps to slow my speed. At about 10 feet above the rushing Post River, I gradually pulled back on the throttle, raising the nose of the plane slightly until I was literally hanging on the propeller and was on the ragged edge of a stall. *God help me if the engine should miss a beat!* With the stall warning screaming and my heart sounding like a tom-tom drum in my ears, it occurred to me what a position I was in: 100 miles from the nearest human being—alone—and nobody knew where I was.

I concentrated on landing as slowly as possible and at the same time keeping enough speed to maintain enough lift on my wings to stay in the air until the wheels touched the gravel. To my horror, I began to see that some of the gravel was not actually gravel but river rocks six to eight inches wide. Too late! The wheels touched down amid the sound of rocks flying up and bouncing off the wings. The strip now looked about the length of my driveway at home in Austin and was disappearing rapidly. Ahead, I could see the drop off of the gravel bar rushing at me. For a brief second, a scene flashed before my mind of an old western movie showing a covered wagon headed for a cliff and sure death and destruction.

I was jerked back to my present situation as the plane's wheels bounced over the rocks that lined the riverbank and the drop off ahead came speeding toward me. The brakes could not dig in and kept skidding under the wheels. I cut the master switch and prepared for a crash into the Post River. . .

At the last possible moment, I managed to stop the plane about 100 feet short of the drop off. I thanked God again for another save from a bad judgment call in an airplane. I sat in my plane for a few minutes as I gathered my wits back. After looking the plane over, I found only a few dents in the undersides of the wings and the leading edge of the stabilizer, and I realized just how lucky I was.

My "Post River International" Airport (also known as the gravel bar).

As I examined the Post River valley, I instantly knew that the site was perfect for my project. Post River was located roughly 200 miles northwest of Anchorage on the edge of the Alaskan Range. Approximately 100 miles northeast of this mountain range stands the United States' highest mountain, Mount McKinley, which reaches an altitude of 20,320 feet. The mountains surrounding Post River weren't nearly as high as Mount McKinley, but there were some peaks reaching elevations of 5,000–6,000 feet. One mountain peak about 10 miles from where I would build my cabin stood upwards of 9,000 feet. I determined that I would climb this mountain before my yearlong project was over.

In this part of Alaska, rivers drained to the north instead of to the south like they did in the Lower Forty-eight. The Post River flows into the Kuskoquim River which eventually flows into the Yukon River. The Yukon then empties into the Bering Sea. The Post River Canyon is surrounded nearly 360° by mountain peaks and a long canyon valley that is the flood plain of the Post River.

The site had all the resources I needed to build a cabin, and beautiful scenery for a new documentary film: the story of my year in isolation in the harsh Alaskan wilderness.

The Liard River Flight

I was returning home from my scouting trip in the Alaskan wilderness. A shiver ran down my back as I made the last of the pre-flight checks. I both loved and hated this moment on any flight. I was like a child on the night before Christmas: so excited about what was going to happen, yet feeling I would never make it through the eternal night. The pre-flight checks were essential, no matter how long they delayed me from getting back into the skies. I loved flying more than just about anything, and there was no way to compare the sensation of ultimate freedom with any Earth-bound experience. In the air, there was nothing else but God, sky, and mountains. Even persistent time seemed to relax, almost to a standstill. There are no distractions, save the occasional radio chatter. I found a few precious moments when my mind could forget all the phone calls and business lunches, the bills and deadlines of my regular hectic life in the city. I loved life. I loved my family and my businesses, and I loved meeting other similar-minded people who gave me a little energy in every personal exchange. But if I had to decide what was the best thing to do on any day, I would effortlessly find myself at an airport, making preparations for my next flight.

I had filed my flight plan, fueled my plane, and was intently finishing my pre-flight checks. I stepped back to do a 360° walk around the plane. As I was doing a final visual inspection, another chill shivered through my body. I was as ready as I was going to be, and the Cessna 175 was poised proudly, also eager to be back in the sky where it belonged. I was quite familiar with the Cessna. It was comfortable, like an old pair of boots that slip right on and make you feel better than you do without them. Some pilots turned their noses up at the 175 saying that it was not reliable. I knew this was because they had not learned how to fly one correctly. This plane utilized a gear-driven engine as opposed to the direct-drives that other pilots were familiar with. It had to be operated at higher RPMs to engage the engine-cooling system.

The engine had been modified and was larger than the regular models, giving it more power for shorter take-offs and landings. I knew I would call on this upgrade many times on my flights through the mountainous North Country. The STOL (short take-off and landing) kit installed in the plane would allow me to make easy off-airport landings and take-offs on any grass strip or shorter runway I may come across. A STOL kit is a modification to the airplane wing allowing it to fly and land more slowly and safely. If you have to put the plane down in a short, rough space, you can do so at speeds as low as 40 MPH. The modification kit also made the aircraft operate better in high altitude areas. I knew I had the perfect craft for the trip I was taking.

This morning marked the halfway point on my journey toward this project in Alaska. I had realized that city-living was wearing my soul thin and I had gotten the itch to get away. I had tried ignoring it for several months, but life had been a full on sprint for many years.

On the first day I flew as far south as Watson Lake, passing Northway and entering Canadian Country. I went down past Burwash Landing, Haines Junction, Whitehorse, and Teslin Lake, one of the longest lakes I have ever seen, which I estimated must be 100 miles long. From there, it was more or less a direct course to Watson Lake, where I landed around 4:00 p.m. After flying all day long, I was exhausted and needed some rest. I tied the plane down, refueled, and caught a ride into town to get a motel room. I got a good night's rest but awoke the next morning to an unwelcome sight: heavy, heavy rain. I could not see 100 feet past the motel window. I called out to the airport to double-check flight conditions. They said it was below VFR but that the forecast should be clear by noon.

A view from my flight down the Liard River.

I slept a little more, wandered around town, and killed time. I grabbed a bite to eat and met a couple of local bush pilots. We ended up talking for a while and I caught a ride with them back out to the airport. I frequently caught rides back and forth with the locals.

By the time I got to the airport the rain had stopped and the cloud ceiling was looking better, but I still had to wait. I checked in with the weatherman throughout the day, and around 2:00 p.m. he said he thought it would be safe to depart. I was looking at a 250 mile flight to Fort Nelson. At an airspeed of 140 MPH, heading 87°, I estimated about 1 hour and 50 minutes of flight time.

I was impressed by the network of rivers below me as I flew. Since visibility was decent (12 miles and improving), I did not follow the Alcan Highway. Instead, I charted a straight course to Fort Nelson. I was following the Liard River, "straightening out the curves" of the winding waterway that cut through the mountain range. As I entered the lower country, the weather had improved significantly.

Eventually, I reached the Sentinel Range and the terrain began rising. I was running out of sky as I had to fly higher to clear the mountains. Looking north, I saw that the weather looked even better so I made the decision to alter my course. I tried to contact Watson Lake Airport to inform them that I was deviating from my flight plan but I was unable to reach them on the radio. I then tried to radio Fort Nelson, but they also did not hear me. I was stuck between two airports. I saw high-rising mountains between me and my destination and I knew I would not make radio contact, but I continued flying with the intention of checking in later. I flew past Kohl River and the Liard River Hot Springs.

All of a sudden, the weather started rapidly deteriorating. I immediately decided to turn back toward Watson Lake and made a 180° turn, but I flew only 10 minutes before I ran into another wall of weather. Impassable. I made another 180° turn and passed back over the Liard River Hot Springs. Checking my map, I realized Liard River makes a confluence with the Fort Nelson River, which goes right by the Fort Nelson airport. I had passed over this area many times before and I knew that the airport was practically on the bank of the river.

I debated making what could have been a very foolish decision: to abandon my flight plan and go north where the weather looked a little better. It was clear that I was losing visibility and would no longer be able to continue on my present course. I saw that the Alcan Highway was going up into the mountainous territory—I would have no more luck following that route into the clouds.

I changed my course by about 30° to my left, headed northward, and began following the Liard River again. The river flowed and wrapped around several flood plains and I feared I might miss the correct route to the mouth of the Fort Nelson River. I knew I would be quite late on my flight plan and I still could not reach any of the radio stations. I had bottled myself up and had no other choice but to go forward.

I was flying through the canyon and it felt like a tunnel with the cloud cover overhead. I was down to only 3-miles visibility and, at best, a 300-foot ceiling. Most of the time I flew down below the walls of the canyon right over the water, berating myself for making such a stupid trip. But I was in it now, and the only thing to do was to keep going. The canyon was so narrow now that I could not make a 180° turn.

Had it not been such a dire situation this would have been an enjoyable flight. I was flying so close to the water I could see the salmon swimming and an occasional moose dotting the river's edge. I loved the wildlife on this route. Today, however, there was nothing to enjoy. The only thing I thought about was getting out of there safely.

When I reached the confluence of the Liard and Fort Nelson Rivers, I had doubts as to whether or not I had found the right spot. I was not sure if I was judging the topography correctly. The rivers circled around flood plains and it seemed that if I just kept going eastward, I had to hit the Fort Nelson River. I was correct; I found the river and continued down it as I had done before. . . but this river was smaller and the canyon walls were narrower. Again, I had no choice but to follow the course of the river, hoping that I was correct in my estimation of my location and the location of the airstrip. I scanned the river bed, hoping I might find a sand bar to land on as I had done in the past when necessary, but there was none to be found this time around. There was nothing but rocky canyon walls and no hope of landing anywhere.

I wormed my way along the river, following the canyon walls: left, then right, left, and then right, with no semblance of a straight path. Visibility had worsened, it was getting later in the day, I had deviated from my original flight plan, and I still could not reach anyone on the radio. I decided to climb a little into the overcast clouds, hoping to extend my radio range and reach air traffic control at Fort Nelson Airport. I thought at one point that I heard a scratchy reply on the radio but I could not make anything out. Just in case someone could hear me, I reported my situation and approximate location. I decided I would do so again every five minutes.

I felt trapped. I could only hope for the best. I thought, *only a pilot who has been in this situation before would know how this feels.*

The map definitely showed the Fort Nelson river flowing right past the airstrip—that was the hope I was hanging on to, tethering me to reality. It was the only thing I could count on. If I did not see the airport soon I would be in deep trouble. I had deviated from my course, but I believed I had enough in the tanks to make it to the Fort Nelson airstrip. Although I had meandered through countless canyons turns, I did not think I had burned up too much fuel. However, if I had miscalculated and overshot the airport, I had no hope. There was nowhere I could have landed that plane and survived.

I thought about all of the wonderful things that had happened to me in my life. I had lived a great life, full of adventures and great people. I had a healthy family and a prosperous business back home. *Yes, I'd had a good run.* But the next event in the cockpit of the Cessna was by far the best thing I could have hoped for. Fort Nelson Airport was calling me on the radio! It turned out that air traffic control had heard me calling. The transmission was garbled due to the mountains and cloud cover, but they had heard *something*. They, too, had decided to keep trying to make radio contact.

I reported my position. My best estimate put me approximately 30 miles north of their station, still navigating visually down the river. Fort Nelson confirmed that they had heard this part of my communication earlier. They also informed me that it was illegal to fly VFR at night in Canada. Visual Flight Rules may have been fine for a sunny day flight, but Instrument Flight Rules were not only the lawful way to make this journey, it was also the only sensible way to do it in these conditions. Instrument Flight would have left the navigation up to the instruments and other navigational equipment. Flying IFR, I would not have had to worry so much about the cloud cover and loss of daylight. It would have guided me to safety.

I waited for it. I knew what was coming next. I knew that they were about to scold me for doing such a stupid—not to mention illegal—thing. I was just like a kid who gets his hand caught in the cookie jar, even though he has been taught that it is the wrong thing to do. I waited. I was ready for it. I was just happy to have made radio contact with someone. *Anyone.* But I kept my course, and Fort Nelson station kept the comforting communication coming. Surprisingly, they did not say anything about my infraction. They did not tell me I should have known better. No one said that the officials were going to come down hard on me. Well, not yet anyway.

I rounded a bend in the river and canyon walls. I was flying southwesterly now. The map showed the airport to be appearing any second now. For miles I had been straining to see something—anything that was not rock. I had watched the canyon walls sail past me endlessly. The constant strain of this intense search had me feeling like my eyes were on stems, sticking out of my head. My brain was making rocky shapes look like familiar structures. I wanted so badly to see a hangar or a traffic control tower, but no luck—just more solid rock on either side of me.

Finally, after what seemed like hours of blind flying, I saw the beacon of the airport. I had found it. Less than three miles to go and about a minute of flight time. I saw a runway. *The* runway. I had done it! My map-charting and in-flight decision-making had been correct. I reported that I had the airport in sight and they cleared me to land.

This was the longest minute of my life. I did not blink for fear that I may open my eyes to more rocky cliffs. Finally, with the one thought of solid land beneath my feet, I landed the Cessna. When I touched down I wanted to relax my body, but it was still clenched tightly with the stress of my trip. I wanted to kneel down and kiss the ground.

Obviously, after this intense flight, I was not going to do any flying the next day. Or the day after that. But as it turned out, I did not have a choice in the matter. The bad weather continued to roll in and I found myself holed up in Fort Nelson for several days as the sky dumped rain.

I spent most of the next few days at the airport monitoring the weather. The coffee and conversation with the weatherman and the air traffic controllers were just what I needed to pass those few days away. At some point it occurred to me that they were going to let me off the hook for my flight violation.

It had definitely been a serious violation. Normal disciplinary action for a violation like this was dreaded. I recalled that on the night of this flight no one had said anything about my violation over the radio. Nor did they discuss ramifications with the authorities once I had landed. I had been ready for it, and in fact, I expected it. So, on the third rainy day, I felt that I needed to bring it up. I had gotten to know these guys and they had all been very friendly. So I asked.

The response was that they had deliberately chosen not to say anything about it on the air. If they had done that, there would have been an official record of my violation and an investigation would have ensued. Basically, they said I was damn lucky! Lucky as hell that they were not reporting me for this violation. I have said before that some of the friendliest people I have ever met were those living along the Alcan Highway, and that the best ones were at the airports! I have never before mentioned a word of this incident out of respect for the guys who spared my license that night. However, enough time has passed that the ground crew who helped me are now long gone. Their help, along with a huge helping hand from God, got me out of trouble that night. I never would have made it without their help, and I do not feel bad about revealing this story now.

I was really just loving life. The only thing that continued to bother me was that I had left all my family at home. Edith had made one trip with me to Alaska, but she just did not like it at all. It was too cold for her. Things were getting a little bit strained at home, and my wife and I were having some problems. I am sure a large part of it was because of the time I spent away in Alaska. Eventually, we decided to divorce. My children were grown so it was not as bad as it could have been, although any divorce in a family is hard on the kids. Edith and I parted as friends, and we have remained friends to this day.

I was alone again—I was at a crossroads in my life—and now more than ever, I felt drawn toward the wilderness.

Part IV
Year in the Cabin

Preparing for a Year in the Alaskan Wilderness

I more or less promised myself that before I turned 60 years old I was going to have my great adventure in Alaska. I would build a cabin in the remote wilderness, spend a year in isolation living off of the land, and make a documentary film of my experience. This great adventure would test both my will power and a lifetime's worth of acquired survival skills. I was approaching my 51st birthday.

It takes an awful lot of planning to do what I was thinking about doing, and I took countless measures to prepare for this adventure in the months before the start of the project. I had to plan for my food and clothing for survival and protection in the harsh Alaskan winter, and I determined what percentage of my subsistence would actually come from living off of the land—a ratio that is not always easy to figure. I would need to maintain a healthy balance of protein, carbohydrates, fat, and other nutrients, keeping in mind the effect of the bitter cold on my body.

In the area where I would build my cabin a large variety of fish and fowl were available to hunt, and one of the prey that I counted on was the ptarmigan, a bird about the size of a pheasant. For almost everybody who hunts for their subsistence in the North Country, the ptarmigan is an essential part of the diet. In addition to the fish I knew I could acquire from Post River, and the ptarmigan I knew were living in the area (I had already scared up several flocks before beginning my project), there was also an unbelievable abundance of berries. My favorites were the blueberries—of which I had hundreds of acres—but there were also cranberries (both low-bush and high-bush), currants, and soap-berries. The soapberry, as it turns out, is aptly named—I did not eat those.

Finally, there was game meat. Rabbits and Dall sheep roamed all over the mountainside, and when winter came and I needed to replenish my food supply I took a moose. When I came out of the canyon the following spring, I carried a considerable amount of that moose with me. As you might imagine, it would be hard for just one person to eat an entire moose, and I had friends in Anchorage who received the meat very happily.

I would never have to worry about refrigeration during the frigid Alaskan winter. I would, however, have to worry about keeping my food out of reach of the animals. To prevent animal pillage, I built a food cache high up off of the ground—a structure common among people living in the wilderness. My food cache stood about 12 feet high on hand-cut four-post logs. I also cut up some 5-gallon square cans that I had used to transport fuel and wrapped the legs of those posts with the metal to prevent animals from climbing up them. This technique worked surprisingly well.

Over and above what I could take from the land, I carried in several slabs of bacon. I just did not want to give up my bacon and eggs. The eggs I brought to the mountain lasted until I was able to harvest a few eggs from some sizeable birds that flew up and down the river. Oddly, these birds looked like large seagulls, but I was 150 miles from the nearest sea. When these birds nested, I would "borrow" a few of their eggs.

In addition to the bacon and eggs, I brought sugar, flour, shortening, a variety of seasonings, and a sourdough starter given to me by a friend in Anchorage. I could make biscuits, pancakes, cinnamon rolls, and loaves of bread—just about anything! And I loved sourdough. After a while, I got the hang of the sourdough starter. I kept the sourdough going by using the starter often; if you don't, the bread gets too sour. That is the secret to good sourdough: you replenish the dough with new ingredients each time you use some.

My sugar was also very important. Living in isolation for a year, I could not do without something sweet every now and then.

In the fall season the blueberries were just about ripe and I was able to make delicious blueberry cobbler in an old antique wood stove I installed in my cabin. I would also make pies from a combination of blueberries, currants, and cranberries all mixed together. When you are living in the remote wilderness you can't run down to the corner bakery and pick up a pie, so you have to work with what you've got. Although there was not a large variety of pies I could make with the resources I had, the ones I did make tasted pretty good!

Again, this type of project all falls back on planning. You have to plan, you have to study, and you have to do whatever else you can to educate yourself and to plan correctly. No detail can be neglected. When I went into the wilderness, I also took with me a broken tooth repair kit. My dentist gave me some tools in case a filling should come out or a tooth crack, and he showed me how to mix up the concoction to fill a gap. The filling would not be permanent, but it would last until I could get home and have the tooth properly fixed. As it turned out, I *did* have to use the dental kit. I did not lose a whole tooth, but I broke a large chunk out of one. I followed my dentist's instructions, mixed up the concoction, and was about as amazed as I could be. It actually worked! I did not do a great job—the filling was not smooth and I could constantly feel it in my mouth—but I sealed that tooth up so that nothing could get to a nerve.

Perhaps most importantly in preparing for this type of experience, you have to figure out how to negotiate loneliness. I had been on lone excursions of various kinds before in my life, but this would be entirely different. Naturally, everybody advised me not to do this. They said I did not know what I was getting myself into. Even old-timers up in Alaska whom I had become acquainted with told me the same thing. I had been adequately forewarned of all the dangers, but I felt that I was prepared for the adventure. That is simply what it all boiled down to: preparedness.

The Post River Cabin

On the eve of my departure for my adventure in Alaska, I had a barbecue evening for all my kids and grandkids. It is hard to say goodbye when leaving for a venture that could lead to all sorts of peril. You have to be able to look into each other's hearts and touch where they live. Jay was the only one who could not be there, but I had discussed this project with him before, and his only comment was that he wished he could do it with me. It was kind of a sad night. The older kids understood what I was doing, but some of the younger grandkids left me feeling some remorse that I had not felt before. Goodbyes are a little complicated with young children. They thought this meant that I was going far away and would not be coming back. I had not expected this and had a little trouble explaining that I was not going to be gone forever. My mind drifted back to a time long ago when I last saw my Grandpa Collison. This made me more aware of my own grandchildren's feelings, but it was still hard. I would recall these last moments with my family many times in the frozen tundra of Alaska. There is nothing better to warm your heart. As for my six brothers and sisters, they were never surprised at what I did.

When I arrived at Post River in July of 1975 to begin my project, I put my many preparations and survival skills to work. My first and most vital task was to build a cabin that could not only withstand the harsh Alaskan winter, but could also keep me safe within it. I did not waste any time—as soon as I arrived I started construction of my cabin.

Arriving at Post River.

To describe a typical day as I built my new home, I would get up in the morning, put on a pot of coffee, and have breakfast. After my eggs ran out, my breakfast mostly consisted of sourdough hot cakes (I would mix some of the pancake flour with the sourdough because I wanted that sourdough flavor). After breakfast I went out and cut wood. According to the journal that I kept, I cut 87 logs to build my cabin. However, this did not amount to a total of 87 trees because some trees provided two or more logs. I used all of the tops of those trees for firewood, some of which I split up into smaller pieces to use in my antique wood cook stove. I also brought a Franklin fireplace to install in my cabin.

Whatever wood I could not burn for heat or for cooking I piled on top of the stumps where I had cut the trees. If you went up to my cabin today you would not be able to find a bare stump sticking out of the ground. Furthermore, whenever I cut a log, I never cut two in close proximity to one other. I love nature and the wilderness as much as the next man, and I believe God gave us these re-

My skills with an ax put to work as I chop down logs.

sources to make use of when necessary, but not to waste. I feel that I did not waste anything.

I used a variety of techniques to move those heavy logs in order to build my cabin. On my last trip into Anchorage for supplies, I went to a junkyard and got two bicycle forks and two wheels. I welded a little saddle in between them and attached short lengths of chain; I could lay a log upon the saddle between those two wheels and move a pretty big load. The main reason I used bicycle wheels was because of their larger diameter. The tundra that I had to work on was soft and mossy and a small wheel would just get buried up in it, but a larger bicycle wheel would roll right through.

I had a lot of work cut out for me. Incidentally, I cut my first log on the Fourth of July, 1975. By October of that year, construction was complete, and I was living in the cabin.

As I erected the walls of my cabin, I rigged up a system to lift the logs. I had two poles that extended from the ground to the top log, forming a sort of ramp. I would lay a log at the bottom of those

The wheels I rigged up worked well to move the logs.

poles, anchor a rope at the top, and then bring the rope down under the log and back up to the top. I would get inside of the cabin walls, pull on the rope, and roll the logs up that ramp, lifting them into place. With this system, I could move logs weighing several hundred pounds.

The log that gave me the most trouble was the ridge log, or ridgepole, that is placed at the top of the cabin. Including the porch I built out front, my cabin was a little over 22 feet long, and I wanted that ridgepole to extend all the way from the rear of the cabin to the front of the porch. I will admit, I had some trouble with this. Any log long enough to extend across my cabin would have a pretty large butt end on it. The small end of the log was about 6 inches in diameter, while the butt end was about 14 inches in diameter. And this was a heavy log! I had to rig up some A-frame scaffolding out of even more logs before I could actually lift the ridgepole one end at a time, moving it just a few feet with each lift using a winching device called a come-along. Keep in mind that I was working all alone. I had to figure out how to move this log in such a way that I did not get hurt. What was I going to do if I hurt myself?

Knotching the logs to fit.

Fortunately, other than a bad ankle sprain, I did not sustain any serious injuries while living on Post River.

I wanted my cabin to be as comfortable as I could make it. The major issue I had been warned about was how cold it would get in winter, and believe me, I was not disappointed. To keep myself warm, I constructed my cabin with insulating material. I brought with me a roll of bat insulation that I cut up into strips about four inches wide. Where each log would join the next, I scribed them with a foot adz until they were flat, and before I rolled the next log on top, I laid down a strip of the bat insulation which would compress and seal up any spaces between the logs. There were no cracks in this cabin. The old-timers used a mixture of mud and moss to caulk their cabins but I went a little more modern with my bat insulation and really sealed that cabin up well. Knowing that the insulation would be so tight, I figured I would have trouble with the draft in my cabin from my little fireplace and my wood stove. To solve this problem, I took

Peaceful Peak is framed under my legs.

some three-inch-diameter stove pipe and ran it underneath the cabin and up through the floor close to the fireplace. I installed a damper that I could turn on and off, and that is how I controlled my fire.

Next, I had to make shingles for the roof. I had tools with me that I had saved from my childhood. My dad, uncles, and grandparents had all used these tools, and now I was using them to build my own shelter. I had a foot adz, a broad axe, a regular lumberman's axe, a drawing knife, and a fro to split shingles, among other tools. With these tools, I was able to trim the shingles and set them in place.

The door to my cabin was about 32 inches wide and just over six feet tall. I am only 5'9" and I was not expecting any visitors that winter, so a smaller door opening would help retain the heat within the cabin. I made the door out of two-by-twelves, each six feet in length, that I brought into the canyon with the rest of the supplies in my Comanche.

One of my colder days.

I also installed windows in my cabin—one in front and one on each side—so that I could observe what happened outside the cabin walls. I called my windows a version of the poor man's thermo-pane. I purchased windows with wooden frames from a lumberyard in Anchorage that sold used equipment. The windows were solid and in good shape. As I installed the windows, I put a heavy coat of wood glue around the edges of the glass panes before placing them into their window frames. Then, on each window, I placed another glass pane, weighed it down, and sealed it, giving me double-paned windows. These windows helped turn back some of the cold during the winter, even when temperatures dropped below zero in the rough Alaskan climate. I kept a thermometer outside one of the windows and in the month of February I recorded a temperature of 41° below zero. Now that's cold! The best thing about these windows, however, was that I had an incredible view looking several miles up the Post River valley. It

The completed cabin and food cache.

was a beautiful sight to greet me every morning while I sat there with a cup of coffee looking out at the river.

I built my cabin on a high point above the confluence of a small creek and the Post River, giving me an excellent view of the flood plain. The moose and caribou liked to travel up and down that river because it was an open area and there was less resistance from brush and rough terrain. They could also see when a wolf was attacking, which they frequently did. I witnessed all sorts of wildlife and I spent a lot of my time just watching nature through my window. It was just like a television screen to the world as I sat watching the wilderness life unfold. On clear days, I could look out of my cabin window and witness the beautiful, majestic scenery. I called it my picture window view. On rainy days, I could see only a half-mile beyond my cabin, but even these days were beautiful to watch. Sometimes it rained for several days at a time, but my cabin was strong and sturdy and protected me from the outdoors. No matter the weather, the view outside was breathtaking.

I built a loft for my bunk at the back end of my cabin high enough to walk under. I also built a ladder out of poles. There were several purposes for having a loft. It is always warmer up above because heat rises and the cold settles on the floor. Also, if I was asleep and a bear were to break into the cabin, I felt I would be in a much better position to defend myself if I was looking down at that bear, rather than the other way around. Fortunately, I never had a problem like that. I liked my loft so much that I built another one at the other end of the cabin to store all my junk. And what kind of junk would you have out in the wilderness in a log cabin? Believe me, it accumulates. It was not long before I had that thing full.

The reason I felt so well prepared was because I heeded the advice I received from so many friends and acquaintances who knew this country so well. They all meant well in giving me this advice and I remembered it and used it as much as I could.

The Otter Salvage

Back in Austin, one of my neighbors, Charlie Hunter, had a son named Wally who was about 18 years old. Before I left for Alaska, Charlie and I had discussed the possibility of letting Wally come visit me at my cabin in the wilderness. We did not make any definite arrangements, and I did not encourage or discourage him, but about halfway through the summer I got a letter from Charlie wanting to set up a date for Wally to come visit. The mail that I was receiving from home was brought to me at Post River by Les Risley. Les had a flying service that came into the Post River area, and every so often he dropped me my mail from the air. When Les delivered the letter from Charlie, he messaged me on my ham radio about a project he had undertaken recovering a crashed airplane at a site about 100 miles north of Post River. Les had a side business salvaging aircraft that had gone down in the bush and he wanted to know if while Wally was visiting we would consider coming along to help him salvage the airplane. I still had some extra fuel so I could justify making the trip to give Les a hand. I let Les know that we would help him out. Once Wally arrived and I told him about the project, he was excited about getting involved in the venture.

It turned out that the airplane was a de Havilland Otter. De Havilland made several airplanes that were excellent in the bush. They manufactured the "Beaver," a single-engine airplane that could carry heavy loads and get in and out on short airstrips, as well as the "Otter," a single-engine aircraft slightly larger than the Beaver. The Otter we were salvaging had crashed near Lake Minchumina.

Les used an H-21 helicopter (one of those big banana shaped twin-rotors) that he had bought surplus from the government and rebuilt himself. Les could pick up quite a load with this helicopter. When a plane went down in the bush, Les would bid on the aircraft with the insurance companies and could often purchase it at a very low price, but it was up to him to pull the plane out of the bush and rebuild it. Les was the only guy I ever heard of up north who salvaged airplanes this way. Ordinarily, when a plane went down in the Alaskan wilderness, you would just forget about it. It was rare for someone to go through the trouble of salvaging the aircraft. Thus, with little competition, Les had a pretty good business going and easily won the job of salvaging the Otter on Lake Minchumina.

On the date that we arranged to meet Les, Wally and I jumped in my Comanche and took off. The flying conditions were not great that day but they were not bad either—it was typical Alaskan weather. However, about 15 miles south of our destination, the weather started to deteriorate and we ran into ground fog. I could see the edges of the lake ahead of us with fog forming over it, but I could not see the airstrip. I throttled back, went up and down the lake two or three times, and called out to Les—or anyone else that I could reach—over the radio.

A man named Ray answered. Ray had flown into the area with his Super Cub also to help Les salvage the Otter. I told Ray my situation.

"Yes, we hear you flying over," he said. "Visibility is less than half a mile here. We can talk you in but it doesn't look too good."

"It doesn't look at all good to me either," I said. "I can see the lake but I can't see the airstrip."

"There are actually two strips, and one is on high ground about midway up the lake. It's all dirt but it is a pretty good strip and it is long enough for you to land your Comanche."

Ray then explained that the second strip was just a few hundred yards south of the first on lower terrain. This strip was at lake level and was shorter in length—only about 1,200 feet. I made a few more passes up and down, got to the end of the lake, and told Ray to describe to me the location of the second airstrip. The lake kept appearing and disappearing through holes in the cloudbank and I decided I would get down on the edge of the fog. Suddenly, through one of the openings in the clouds, I caught a quick glimpse of the smaller airstrip. I made a 180° turn and went back south. I slowed down, lowered my gear, and put about 40° of flaps on the wings. Flying about as slowly as I possibly could, I got right on the edge of the lake, searching to find the airstrip again. Ray told me that the strip came right up to the water, but as I got down to 100 feet above the lake I had a visibility of only a couple hundred yards ahead of me, at best. I got closer and closer to the edge of the lake and at the last second located the strip. I hooked a left, pulled full flaps to slow me down, and landed on the airstrip using only half of the runway.

Ray came up to meet me and helped me taxi my airplane down a smooth trail.

"Follow me right this way and we'll tie your plane down," he said.

There was a lodge midway down the lake where fishermen bunked and Les had made arrangements for all of us to stay there. Ray was going to prepare our meals. We had about a week's worth of work ahead of us to attempt to make the crashed airplane airworthy.

The crashed Otter before we repaired the wing.

We learned that the pilot of the Otter had come to the area to drop off two moose hunters in the bush. He had dropped them off in a float plane at another lake about 10 miles away from Lake Minchumina and made arrangements with the hunters to return later to pick them up. On the agreed-upon date, the pilot returned to take the hunters home, but this time they had a moose with them. The hunters had field dressed and butchered the moose but their new cargo weighed several hundred pounds. As they took off in the Otter the pilot gave the plane full throttle, but by the time he reached the end of the lake he was still on the water, headed straight for the shore banked with trees, some standing 30 feet tall. At the last moment the pilot got the Otter into the air, but not high enough to crest the tallest trees. The plane went down, breaking off the left wing strut, and there it sat in the trees. Fortunately, nobody was hurt. Shortly after the crash Les went out to the site to examine the airplane and a month later our team was there ready to salvage the Otter.

Wally and I hung around the camp for a day or two while Les and his crew got their things together. Then, we all got in Les' big helicopter and he flew us out to the crash site. It was a mess! That beautiful airplane had its left wing hanging down and bent toward the back. Luckily, Les already had a plan. He brought in chainsaws and we began cutting down trees in a big circle around the aircraft. Then, we spent the next few days making repairs to the Otter.

We were about 200 yards from the edge of the lake and we decided that it would be safest to wait until the lake froze over before we ever attempted a take-off. We certainly did not want to mess up the plane again, and it would be better to take off on top of ice rather than water, even with the floats. I had never seen or heard of anyone taking off from ice on floats, so I was very curious to see how it would be done. Les explained that the seam at the bottom center of the floats where the metal was welded together would ride like ice skates over the frozen lake.

The decision was made that Les and I would return later in the year to complete the salvage. Les would stay in touch with the owner of the lake lodge who agreed to inform Les whenever the lake froze over. At that, Les went back to Anchorage and Wally and I returned to Post River. For a few days Wally helped me with the construction of my cabin, then I dropped him off in town and he returned home from his vacation in Alaska.

It was mid-October when Les showed up to my cabin in his helicopter.

"We're ready to go!" he said. "The lake is frozen over."

Les had already picked up Ray, so I buttoned up the cabin and climbed in the helicopter, and the three of us flew back up to Lake Minchumina. On the way there, Les let me fly co-pilot in the big H-21. In fact, I flew most of the way there, but Les took over to land the helicopter once we reached our destination. It was late in the day and there was little sunlight left so we spent the night at the lodge. The next morning, the three of us flew out to the Otter and it was just as we had left it.

Repairing the damaged wing tip on the Otter.

It was a good thing that we had another man with us because we had trouble shifting the plane around and breaking it loose from the snow. The Otter had nearly frozen to the ground after sitting there for so long. To speed up the process, Les got in the plane and started the engine. As it warmed up, Les revved the engine and used the controls to rock the plane back and forth while Ray and I stood outside at the ends of the wings pushing the Otter. Finally, we broke the plane loose from the ice. Les taxied around in a little circle and moved the plane down toward the edge of the frozen lake.

"Walt, you are going to have to fly the helicopter back," Les said.

"Les, you know I haven't been checked out in that thing," I replied. "I think I can fly it but I don't know whether you should turn me loose in it just yet."

"You can fly it all right. We've got two aircraft to move and I have to fly the Otter."

"Well, maybe I can fly the Otter and you can bring the helicopter in," I suggested.

"No, it's too risky," Les said. "We've still got a problem with that wing strut. If it doesn't hold and we lose a wing, whoever is in that airplane is going to be in a mess." I was convinced. It was decided that I would fly the H-21 back to Anchorage and Les would fly the Otter.

Ray opted to go with Les in the Otter, so I had to make this flight by myself, but I actually felt better flying without anyone else on board. Although I did not have a rating for this type of aircraft, I had flown it before and did not feel that it would be too much of a problem. The flight to Anchorage would be about an hour and a half.

Les let me take off first and I hovered around above the lake until Les got the Otter in the air.

"I'd sure feel a lot better with you flying along with me," I told Les over the Unicom. "Why don't you just throttle that thing back?"

The Otter was considerably faster than the helicopter but Les agreed to stay with me and we got to Anchorage without any problems. I had no trouble flying that helicopter, but if an emergency had come up, I am not sure how things would have worked out.

When we flew into Anchorage Les reported in for both of us and gave our positions, and we were cleared to land. Les let me touch down first and then I watched as he prepared to bring the plane down. Those floats were amphibious on that Otter. Les had practiced letting the wheels up and down along the way and was convinced that they would land. If the wheels did not extend through those floats then he was just going to land in the lake, but he preferred to land at the airport so that he could taxi up to his hangar. The tower reported that Les' wheels were down and he also landed with no problem. We decided after the successful recovery project that Les owed us each a big steak, so away we went to a popular steakhouse in town. We thoroughly enjoyed our dinner and congratulated each other on what we had done.

The Dry Ice Runs

After recovering the Otter, Les asked me if I would consider staying in Anchorage for a few more days to help him with his dry ice program. I was not familiar with this program so I asked what it involved. When visibility was zero on the ground at Anchorage International Airport due to low-lying clouds and heavy fog, long delays and backups in the landing schedule resulted. Heavy transport airplanes, commercial airliners, and Flying Tigers frequently complained about these landing backups and the expense of circling Anchorage as they waited to come in to the airport. If the runway could be cleared, the planes could fly right in, so Les came up with a business plan based on the dry ice system that he developed. Les would take blocks of dry ice up into the sky in his Beech twin-engine D-18, drop the dry ice in an electric hopper, grind it up, and fly over the airport spraying the dry ice into the clouds. Within minutes, the dry ice would disperse the clouds and actually make them start snowing! For just a short period of time, it would clear the runway.

The process was almost like magic. The first time I saw it done, I could not believe my eyes. I looked behind me and could see a clear streak of open skies, all the way to the ground. The process worked tremendously well.

The dry ice program was an intricate procedure and it would have helped Les to have a co-pilot, but mostly he flew by himself. Les had a helper in the back whose job it was to remove the dry ice from the boxes, grind it up, and spray it out of the plane. Then, Les made parallel passes over the runway separated by a few hundred feet. All the while, Les is flying blind, using only his instruments.

Les asked for my help on this particular occasion because the man he normally employed to assist him in dispersing the ice had gone on vacation and would not be back for a week. Les' contract with Anchorage International called for him to be available at a moment's notice, but he did not have anyone else in mind to help him. Since I was already there and he knew I would be able to do

Austin business man. . .

. . . six months later, Alaskan wilderness man.

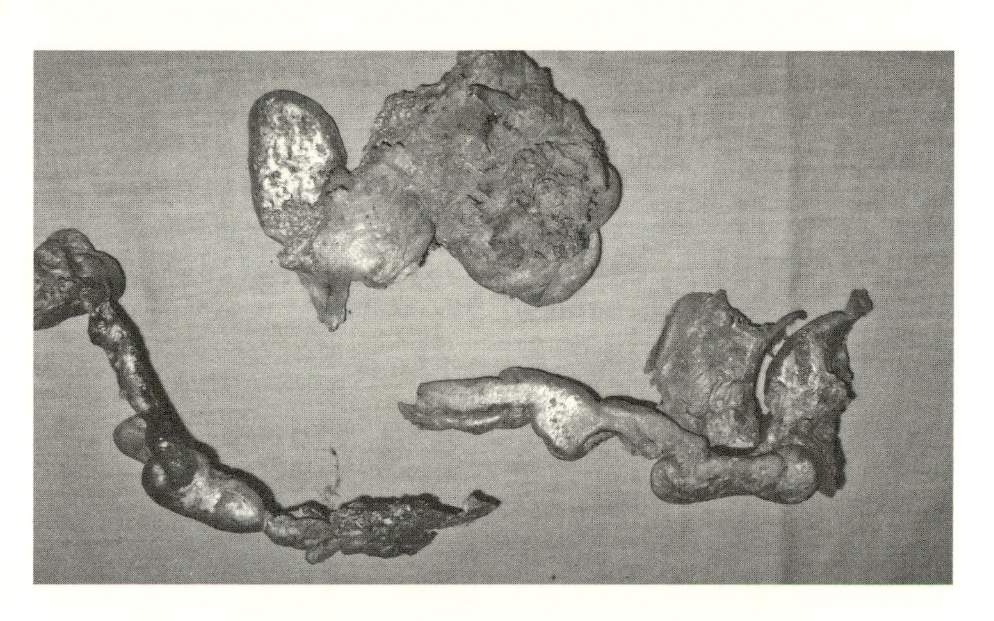

Molten sculptures formed by melted metal from burning helicopter falling in water.

Lunch break on Post River.

Where flying is King.

The repaired hole on the right side of the valve cover caused engine failure during helicopter flight over Shelby, Montana.

One of my neighbors on Post River.

Corporal Hawkins of the Royal Canadian Mounted Police.

it, Les asked me if I would consider working with him for a few nights. Most of his dry ice runs were made after dark.

Les had helped *me* so much in the past that I gladly agreed to do it. We practiced in the hangar and Les showed me how to grind the ice. I needed a good pair of gloves because I had to pick up these chunks of dry ice and drop them in the hopper.

It was around midnight on the first night when Les rolled me out of my bunk.

"We've got to go," he said.

We loaded onto the D-18 and took off. Les was probably as good an instrument pilot as there ever was. At first I was a little uneasy about flying in the poor weather conditions, but after a few trips it did not bother me. We flew back and forth over the runway while I ground up the ice and shot it out of the chute into the clouds, opening up the skies. Then, we circled over the city, waiting to be called for the next run.

If there was not much wind we could make three or four passes over the runway to clear it and it would remain clear for 15 to 20 minutes. When a big plane came in, the clear skies allowed for much safer landings. Of course, these pilots had instrument landing to aid them, but with zero visibility they often did not see the runway until their wheels hit the ground. As well as increasing safety, the dry ice procedure saved the heavy flying aircraft a lot of money in holding patterns.

Les got paid for the number of hours he stayed in the air. He had a six-hour range on his tanks, and whenever we went up I knew we would stay up there for at least that long. I never did know how much Les got paid to make these dry ice runs, but whatever it was, I guarantee it was well-deserved. Les took his life into his own hands to make it safer for other pilots to fly. Of course, Les would get tired, so I flew co-pilot in between runs, which I really appreciated because I gained a lot of twin-engine practice time that I would not have acquired otherwise. That Beech D-18 was just a pleasure to fly. I never attempted instrument flying on those trips, I just circled the city, building up time in my log book, but Les could fly just about anything, and in any condition. Les reminded me of James Cagney who remarked on his flying skills in a movie: "What do you mean 'can I do it?' I can fly the crates that they come in!" I believe Les Risley was one of those pilots.

Circling the city at night was a beautiful sight, and I could see the glow of the city through the clouds. Although the flights were pretty tiring, I never tired of the view.

When a call came in from air traffic control that a Flying Tiger or an airliner was approaching the airport, I woke Les up and returned to my post, and we would make another pass dropping dry ice over the runway. It was challenging work, and picking up those blocks of dry ice was hard on my back, but the really mean part about these runs was that by the time it came our turn to land, we nearly always had run out of dry ice. Les had to make a completely blind landing. I would sit in my co-pilot seat with my head out the window and my eyes sticking out on stems. As soon as I spotted a marker or approach lights on the runway, my job was to let Les know because he could not take his eyes off of those instruments.

Those blind landings used to really worry me. Here I was, my head sticking out the window, freezing cold—even with a fur parka on—and I am looking for those lights. Whenever I hollered "Lights!" Les throttled back on the engine. I could see nothing but the approach lights passing by us, and often I did not see the runway until we were on it.

Les Risley was a Jack of all trades. He even purchased surplus World War II aircraft from the government. One plane he bought was a B-25 Mitchell that had zero time on the engine and which he rebuilt himself. Les flew this plane for the Alaska Pipeline Company, which at the time was building an oil pipeline across Alaska. In the mountainous town of Valdez, a community along the path of the pipeline, the snow was late to melt making installation of the pipe much more difficult. To solve this problem, Les flew in with his B-25 and dropped 10,000 pounds of coal dust on the snow, speeding up the melting process. The jobs Les worked paid good money, but all of them came with high risk.

Les also took part in several air shows. Every year there was a big show in Anchorage, and Les flew that B-25 and performed all sorts of aerobatics. He even flew over the crowd with one engine cut. I thought, *what in the world would he do if that thing doesn't start up again?* But Les was just that good—he could fly that airplane with one engine as well as he could with two.

Les was a master at rebuilding aircraft. In fact, he rebuilt the H-21 twin-rotor helicopter that we used for the Otter recovery. Les bought three helicopters of the same model, none in flying condition, and he took the good parts from each to make one that worked perfectly. Les went to Tucson, Arizona to a huge aircraft bone yard, bid at an auction on the helicopters, and then had them shipped to Anchorage. He spent well over a year rebuilding the helicopter, but Les had a knack for projects like that.

After helping Les with his dry ice runs I was really anxious to get on back to my cabin. I had other projects there that I wanted to get started, so Les flew me back to Post River. When we got back to my cabin I pulled out some frozen stew that I had in my food cache, warmed it up, and made some biscuits for Les and me to eat. Then Les was gone and I was back to my regular routine, alone again.

There was only one thing at my cabin that I noticed had been disturbed. I had stretched out the skin of a sheep I killed earlier and hung it on the side of the cabin to dry out. I was not exactly sure what I was going to make out of it but I did not want to throw away a nice, big sheepskin. Unfortunately, a bear had come upon it and shredded it to pieces, but I was glad I was gone when it happened. In all the time I spent in Alaska I never had to shoot a bear, but I may have been forced to shoot one in self defense if I had heard this bear scraping on the side of the cabin.

Flight—Make that *Fright!*—To Post River

By October of 1975, I was knee deep in my project and winter was fast approaching. It started snowing on October 1st, dropping about six inches of snow, and from then on, the ground would stay white until May. The most severe snows would come in November and December with the snowfall on the ground averaging four feet deep.

With my birthday approaching in late October, I realized that it would be the first time in my life that I'd be spending it alone. When the day did come, I almost forgot it! I celebrated with some "snow ice cream," chocolate syrup that I poured over a snowball.

Now that construction of my cabin was complete, I began thinking of the coming winter and how I would keep an airplane at my camp on Post River in case of an emergency. I certainly was not going to leave the Comanche out there on wheels throughout the winter because you cannot operate wheels on snow, so I got in touch with Bill Howard and he came up with the best plan. Bill co-owned a Piper Cub that he kept in Alaska, but he was being transferred back to Houston and would be leaving Anchorage in a few short weeks. He suggested that he fly my Comanche home to Houston and arrange for me to have his Cub at my campsite during the winter. This sounded like an excellent plan to me—the only problem was that the plane needed to be put on skis, but Bill told me that he would help me locate a pair that I could install on the plane. He found some that needed repairing, but it wasn't something I could not take care of myself. With everything in place, I left Post River and flew to Anchorage to exchange airplanes.

Les Risley helped me to winterize the Cub. A Cub must be winterized because it has an open cowling to the engine, exposing it to the air. Gas cannot vaporize in freezing, sub-zero temperatures, and consequently, the engine may quit in flight. However, the plane can be modified so that the cooling vents are more or less closed off and the cowling sealed in. This allows the engine to retain the heat that it produces and keep the plane running.

Once the skis were installed and the modifications to the plane complete, I felt that I was ready to fly the Cub back to my cabin on Post River. I watched the weather for a few days, waiting for good conditions to fly, but at the same time, with the engine winterized, I could not fly in temperatures that were too warm. Not yet in the deepest throws of winter, the temperature was lingering around 32°.

After a couple days of waiting I finally decided to go. The weather was mostly clear but the temperature was still averaging 32°. I was slightly concerned about flying in this warmer weather after winterizing the Cub for sub-zero conditions, but I decided to go ahead anyway. I was anxious to get back to Post River, so I departed Anchorage and set my course northwest over Mount Susitna, also called the Sleeping Lady. From a distance, it is amazing how the mountain actually appears to be a lady in repose on her back. Mount Susitna was a good landmark for people coming and going from the area, and my course carried me right over it.

Shortly into my flight it became clear that the Cub did not like the warm weather and the engine began to overheat. I had not been flying 30 minutes when the engine temperature gauge neared redline. I was cruising at about 1,000 feet but decided to climb to 5,000 feet so that the temperature at the higher altitude would cool the engine.

At 5,000 feet and still near redline, I concocted a new plan: I would cut the engine to about 1/4th the power and slowly glide on, descending while the engine cooled. The engine temperature would drop and then I could increase the power and climb again, repeating the process.

The first glide brought the temperature down slightly, so I climbed again until I hit the redline, then cut the power and descended while the engine cooled. The plan was working but I was not sure how long the Cub was going to accept this treatment. I sweated blood as I watched the temperature rise, wondering how much of this the engine could take.

I was flying over a vast wetland crisscrossed with streams and lakes, and no place to land on skis—the ground was covered with brush. As I climbed to 3,000 feet I still had good visibility ahead as I approached the foothills, but I had to reach 7,500 feet to start my descent. My nerves were on edge and thoughts of having to put the plane down in this terrain did not help any. I had about 50 miles to go before reaching the entrance of Rainy Pass, the engine was still overheating, and my glide ratio was about 5–6 miles to each 2,000 feet in altitude. As I pinned the redline, I hoped that maybe the gauges were giving me some leeway, but that could have just been wishful thinking on my part—we are all taught in flight school to believe our instruments.

I decided that if I could make it to Rainy Pass I would land by the lake and wait for colder weather. Rainy pass was now just 20 miles ahead of me and the terrain below was approaching 4,000 feet. I hoped that the colder air at the higher altitude might cool the engine, but I was now at 5,000 feet and still redlining at the apex of my climb. With my eyes sticking out like stems I strained to see that lake.

This time I descended to a few hundred feet, cooling the engine a little bit more, and the needle dropped just a *bit* off the redline before I had to start another climb. I knew I would not be able to continue this way much longer, if at all. In the distance, I strained to make out the lake at Rainy Pass Lodge, located in a valley between two mountain ranges. Everything below me was white. The only dark forms were the cliffs and rocky slopes on either side of me.

I started another climb, stretching it to the limit this time to make it to that lake. At 7,000 feet, the needle was not quite in the

The Cub on frozen Post Lake.

red when I ran into turbulence that shook the little Cub violently. I looked at the temperature gauge, tightened my seatbelt again, and kept my eye on the needle. *It is not in the red. . . still not in the red!*

Maybe it was just more wishful thinking, but I believed the needle was dropping. I said a little prayer, continued climbing, and kept my eye on the gauge. I could not believe it, the temperature *was* dropping! I also started getting colder—in fact, I was freezing. It had not dawned on me that the turbulence I just met was a cold front. I had a kitchen thermometer taped to a wing strut and again I could not believe my eyes. The outside air temperature was showing 18° and dropping.

What was happening was an answered prayer. Although visibility was dropping, I could still see about five miles ahead of me. I thanked God and Mother Nature and abandoned any thought of landing at Rainy Pass, glancing again at the thermometer. I kept a constant eye on it.

Eventually the temperature dropped to 10°, which the plane could easily withstand. I continued my flight, went through Ptarmigan Pass, flew over Post Lake, and then followed Post River to the gravel bar where I had built my cabin. Before I left Post River to retrieve the Cub, I improved the gravel bar for landings by cutting the tops off of some small trees so that I could make a better approach. I determined now that I would be able to land my Cub on that gravel bar.

I landed on the gravel bar in about 18 inches of snow and tied the Cub to a log that I had prepared earlier for this purpose. Then, I got a fire going in my cabin and put on a pot of coffee. I sat there thinking how lucky I was that I had run into that norther—and at just the right time—because I do not think that engine would have stood much more of the treatment I was giving it. I really should have waited for colder weather to hit Anchorage before making this flight, but that might have brought with it low ceilings and poor visibility, preventing me from leaving at all. I do not know if I was shaking from the cold or the frightful flight, but I was shaking like a leaf.

Surviving the Wilderness

One project I took on that winter, primarily to occupy my time, was to build a dogsled using nothing but a pocketknife. I made the dogsled out of sapling and small spruce trees that were abundant in the area, and I built it in the same way that the Eskimos built their dogsleds years ago. First, I took the raw hide from the moose I hunted and cut it up into quarter-inch strips to make string. All the wooden parts of this dogsled I fit together by whittling out joints that nested into each other; there were no nails or screws. I then drilled a little hole through an upright that I had fastened together and strung the wetted raw hide through the runner, the skid, and the little hole, tying it tight. In some places I would crisscross the hide, or string two strands through the same hole, in order to make the sled stronger. When the raw hide began to dry it tightened up, almost like steel. There was no way that you could get a tighter joint, even if you used screws or bolts.

For the runners of the sled, I cut two spruce poles that were a little less than two inches in diameter at the big end and about three-quarters of an inch at the small end. Runners on a sled have to bend upwards in the front in order to glide across the snow, but bending wood can be a slow process. Earlier in the season I built a jig out of the stumps where I had cut these poles. I placed the poles into the jig and bent them to the shape that I wanted, holding them in position with a log laid on top. A few months later, when I was ready to make the dogsled, I pulled the runners out of the jig. By then, the poles were seasoned and the curves held on

My sled with emergency gear over frozen Post River with movie camera mounted on front.

their own. I took my drawing knife and whittled the bottom of the blades to be semi-flat, removing all the bark from the surface so that the sled would run smoothly over the snow. I then fastened the crosspieces, uprights, and runners into one solid unit. Finally, I built a basket around the sled that would carry my equipment. Again, the biggest tool I used was my pocketknife, other than an axe and a drawing knife to cut down the poles.

When I went on my little jaunts through the wilderness, most often to check my trap lines, I took my sled with me. The sled came in handy when I caught a wolverine or a fox because I could carry the animals back to my cabin in the sled. Several times a week I put on my snowshoes to explore the flood plain of the Post River, and after the water froze over and was snow-covered, I had a big, white, open area to travel that seemed to span in every direction. I carried a sleeping bag and any emergency supplies that I might need in case I got stranded out on the trail and I pushed that sled along with me wherever I went. You would be surprised how easy it was to push that sled through the snow—there was very little resistance.

On one of my exploring trips, I actually did become stranded when I got caught in a blizzard about 17 miles up the river from my camp. Fortunately, in the area where I was, there were large spruce trees with limbs that fanned out all around the bottom like skirts, creating a sort of enclosure. You could part the bows of the limbs hanging down and crawl inside the enclosure and you would have yourself a country tent. When this blizzard blew in, it was snowing and sleeting so hard that it felt like BB's hitting my face. I decided that I did not want to make the long trip back to my cabin in that weather so I crawled inside the tent of one of those big spruce trees, carried my sleeping bag in with me, unrolled it, got inside, and stayed in that enclosure for eight hours waiting for the storm to quit. The snow was considerably deeper on the trek back to the cabin and I was thankful that I had my snowshoes with me or I really would have had trouble getting back home.

For food on these little forays, I packed a "portable stew." Back at my cabin, I whipped up a stew mixture that I let freeze in a large pan. Then, with a knife, I made brick-sized score marks in the frozen stew, broke them up into little blocks, and wrapped them in tin foil. When I went out on these jaunts on the trail, I took one block of stew with me, a little pot to melt snow for water, and a concoction of flour and seasoning that I mixed up to make a dough. I would then cut a stick from a tree, wrap the dough around the end of it, and hold it over the fire to cook until it got crispy. There I was, deep in the wilderness, with hot tea, hot stew, and hot bread for lunch. Now that is living high off the hog! I still remember the meals I had on the trail and how much I enjoyed them. I actually gained weight in the wilderness that year, and I was in just about as good of shape as I could get because I was clamoring up and down those hills nearly every day. I overcame all the obstacles that arose while living off the land just by taking advice from others, thinking, and planning.

Ice Fishing

The small toboggan sled I used when ice fishing.

Fish is one of the primary subsistence items available in Alaska, and ice fishing was an essential part of my plan to live off of the land. Post Lake was about five miles south of my cabin, a pretty good trek in the winter—especially when the snow was nearly up to my waist. I had to walk on snowshoes, which could be a little awkward. I had to fall down and dig myself out of the snow a few times before getting the hang of the snowshoes, and once I did get used to them, they were still very tiresome because they demanded use of muscles in the legs not normally required for walking. Despite the challenge, I would walk to Post Lake in these snowshoes about twice a month to do some ice fishing.

I usually planned my fishing trips a day or two in advance, and anytime I left the cabin for more than just a short distance I always left a note as to where I was going and what I was doing in case something should happen to me. I was well aware of the fact that I was at least 100 miles from the nearest human being and I thought it unwise not to leave word of my whereabouts because something *could* happen to me. If I left a note, at least someone looking for me later would know which direction I had gone and where to look.

I had studied the trail from the cabin to the lake before the winter season, but once three to four feet of snow had fallen, everything looked considerably different. Fortunately, I had mapped out the path through the Post River flood valley before the snow arrived and managed to figure out where I was going. My cabin sat on the west side of the Post River, and Post Lake was located on the east side. However, Post River did not run straight, it snaked its way throughout the floodplain, and so I had to cross it several times on the trek to the lake. Crossing the river turned out to be the biggest challenge in reaching the lake. During winter the river froze over but in the deeper channels there was still running water beneath the ice. Sometimes I did not know whether to trust the ice or not. On my map I had marked out some crossings where the river was shallow in case the ice should break, and I trusted the map to keep me on the safest route, but I always exercised extreme caution whenever I crossed the river.

Living without a busy schedule, whenever I came across anything of interest on my journey I could stop and observe it for as long as I wanted. It was just like being in an outdoor classroom, everyday of the year. One of my "lessons" came from a beaver that I encountered on the way to Post Lake. There was an abundance of beavers in the Post River flood plain, and they worked tirelessly chopping logs and building dams. Several creeks fed into Post River and nearly every one of them had a beaver damn built on it. On this occasion, I stood and watched a beaver cut down a tree eight inches thick. It took the beaver about an hour to tip the tree, but as soon as it fell, he immediately started cutting off limbs, just like a lumberjack would do. I finally understood the expression "busy as a beaver." Working his way backward, the beaver chopped the trunk into chunks small enough to drag. These beavers looked like they averaged around 35 pounds in weight, but it seemed like they could easily drag a 100-pound log.

Once I finally reached the lake, the first job was to get through the ice, which was over a foot thick. The first time I went ice fishing was in the latter part of December and the lake had probably been frozen since October. *Maybe I could just ask for fish for Christmas,* I thought. Unlike an experienced ice fisher I did not have an ice auger, a hand-operated tool that drills a hole about six inches in diameter down through the ice. Instead, I carried an axe with me on these little sojourns and literally chopped my way through the ice, which does not sound like too much trouble until you get into the act. I was taught to drill a hole the size of the fish you expect to catch, but it is not such a simple task. Chopping at the ice with an axe, the hole gets wider at the top and smaller at the bottom, and on this occasion, my hole was three or four feet wide at the top and narrowed down to eight inches. What's more, I was out in the middle of the frozen lake, and who knew how deep the water was? After working at it for a while and still not hitting water I started to think, *what would happen to me if all of a sudden I fall into this hole that I am chopping? What if the whole thing goes falling through and I go with it?* Those thoughts reminded me that I had to be extremely careful, but finally, after quite some time, I broke through the ice.

Trapped beneath the frozen surface of the lake, fish cannot feed on flying insects during the winter, so I assumed they were probably hungry. I used a piece of foil wrapped around a hook for my bait, a technique I did not devise myself. From the conversations I had with local Alaskans, I learned different methods that could be used to bait fish when you are caught without food and have to scrounge up something to eat. Because the foil is glittery, it attracts the fish when it is dropped into the water and jiggled up and down. Using this technique, I felt fish pulling on the line in no time.

I went ice fishing at least half a dozen times that winter and I never failed to catch a fish. There was no shortage of fish in that frozen lake and I had no trouble getting them to bite. The fish I caught in Post Lake were mostly whiting and brown trout, and I caught about half whiting and half brown trout each time I fished. Both types of fish averaged about 18 inches in length, but every once in a while I caught one considerably larger. The fish never got wise to the tin foil. I knew how to use my rod and lure, but I think anything bright and shiny would have lured those fish. I experimented with other baits just to see what those fish would grab. I had a red and white plastic "gimme" pen in my pocket that I fastened to a hook, and when I dropped the line into the water, I caught a fish just as quickly as I did with the tin foil. There must have been nothing in that water for the fish to feed upon because whenever they saw something that looked like food, they grabbed it.

After fishing for a while I would stop and warm my hands by a little fire that I'd build. Curiously, you can build a fire on top of ice, but even with a down-filled parka and the aid of a fire, I was still cold. I wore thin gloves under large mittens but I had to take both off whenever I did anything with my hands, so it really felt nice to stop every few minutes and warm my hands over the fire. The fire would eventually burn down to the ice and melt out a shallow depression, but it never burned all the way through.

After catching four or five fish, I wrapped them up, put them in my sled, and started back home. Back at my cabin, I placed the fish in my food cache, or what I liked to call my outdoor freezer, but I always fixed one fish right away. I had various ways of preparing the fish and I experimented with different spices and seasonings, but my favorite was to batter and deep fry. I dipped the fish in a batter that I made out of pancake mix, sprinkled on some sesame seeds, and then fried them in oil. There was no better eating!

Animal Trapping

In keeping with living off the land like the old-timers did, I obtained some steel traps for catching animals. I had a trap line that I had to run everyday: once you set a trap, you have to attend to it. You do not want an animal dying a horrible death because it can't get out of a trap, so I carried a .22 Magnum to dispatch the animals after I caught them. Many people object to trapping, and to a certain extent I agree with them, but I was trying to relive the life of the people who first settled this country. When our pilgrims landed on the east coast of the United States, there was no country store that they could run to in order to buy what they needed, so they trapped for food and animal fur. They had to live off of the land. One of the things I set out to prove on this venture is that we are the same people today that we were in the frontier days, and I wanted to make a statement that we are still capable of taking care of ourselves in the wilderness. I am proud to say that I did it.

I primarily trapped for wolves, wolverines, and foxes, as well as other various smaller animals. My toughest catch was a wolverine that had outwitted me several times by getting into my food cache. I vowed that I would catch him. I found where this wolverine was ranging about three miles up the creek from my cabin by following the tracks he made in the snow, and I laid a trap line in the area.

I never will forget that first wolverine I caught. On the third morning after setting my traps, I scouted the area of my trap line and noticed that the ground was disturbed and the snow I had used to cover my traps was gone. For a moment, I was at a loss as to what had happened. Then, I figured it out. The wolverine had been caught in a trap, but in the midst of fighting to try to get out of it, he had disturbed the area considerably. When he realized that he could not get out of the trap, he curled up in a little ball of fur to keep warm a short distance from my trap line. Once I spotted him, I walked up and disturbed him.

If wolverines were just a little bit larger they could rule the world because they are some kind of fighters. A full grown wolverine only weighs around 60 pounds, but it is capable of taking down a 300-pound caribou. I know this because I witnessed it with my own eyes. There were five caribou in a group travelling down the river, but one was straggling behind the others. All of a sudden, a wolverine leaped out of the snow and went straight for the straggler's throat. Wolverines are like pit bulls—when they latch on to something, their jaws lock and they keep their pray until it dies. It took about five minutes for that caribou to thrash around and die.

Despite their vicious strength, wolverines are not dangerous until they go into defense mode. Of course, when you've got a wolverine trapped, it feels defenseless and is going to attack. Fortunately, when I set the trap I attached it to a small chain about six feet long and anchored it to a log because some of the animals I caught earlier had run away with my traps. On this occasion, the chain came in handy for a different reason: the wolverine jumped straight for my throat, but the chain ran out about six inches from my face and jerked him back. If it had not been for that chain he would have had me.

I had to shoot the wolverine three times in the head before it died because the bullets just glanced off his head. Later, when I skinned and cleaned the wolverine, I could see where the bullets had hit but not penetrated the skull.

I caught several foxes in my trap lines. Foxes were physically much easier to catch than wolverines, but their intelligence and cunning was tough to beat. I learned that foxes are trap-wary—they could smell the steel and they associated that smell with danger. I used bait and set the traps around trees to confuse the foxes, but to no avail. When they smelled the steel they expected my traps. The foxes would work around a trap with their paws until it was exposed and then throw the trap without getting caught. They learned that there was a pedal in the middle of the trap under one of the jaws that they could touch in order to set off the trap without getting hurt. This happened time and time again. I would go check one of my sets and a trap would be sprung, but there would be nothing in it but the fox's tracks.

With time, I figured out how to outwit the foxes by setting more than one trap in close proximity to one another. The fox would throw one of the traps and mistakenly think he was safe. He would become careless and jump on the tree to get the food that I had set for bait. Then, as he went for the food, he would step in one of the other traps.

Wolves were another tough catch, although they were not so difficult to track. I learned that the wolves nearly always travelled the same circuit while on the hunt for food. With snow on the ground it is easy to observe the habits of the animals, but the wolves left the most distinctive tracks.

One wolf in particular, like the wolverine, had been trying to raid my food supply. I thought it would be a good contest between a wolf and a wolverine to see which animal was the tougher adversary. To catch this wolf, I used scraps from a Dall sheep I had hunted as bait. The sheep had provided me enough meat to last nearly all winter, but I saved one of the leg shanks for just such an occasion. I took the bait and secured it to a tree with a twenty-penny nail so that the wolf would have to work to get to the bone. Then, I surrounded the baited tree with traps. After three days, I finally caught the wolf, and he is hanging on the wall in my den today.

I set some snares for rabbits whenever I found their trails. It was amazing how many rabbits I caught, but I would only set the snares whenever I wanted to change my diet for a day or two. When a rabbit gets in a snare and realizes that it cannot get out, it just sits there. It does not jump or jerk or bounce. Every rabbit I ever trapped I had to dispatch because they were just sitting there waiting for something to happen when I found them. The rabbits I caught were brown during the summer and white in winter. I thought it was an amazing thing that these animals could protect themselves from their prey by camouflaging in this way.

This was the extent my trapping. I did not trap to accumulate fur (although I did use some beaver skin to make a hat), or because I thought it was fun. I trapped because it was what we used to do to survive off of the land. I felt for these animals that I was killing, but it was a part of living life in the wilderness. Later, I spoke on a radio talk show in Austin and told some of my trapping stories. It was not long before I was engulfed by animal rights activists calling in to the show. Many people were quite unhappy with me, and

I really felt bad about it, but I just do not think they understood what I was doing. I was not killing these animals because I enjoyed it; in fact, I thought it was a really miserable thing to do. I was living the way those did who settled our country. Today, we do not have to use techniques like trapping, but I wanted to prove a point that we can still survive in the wilderness, and I am satisfied that I more than proved it.

For me, it came down to some primal base of nature to see if I could still live off the land, but as in any endeavor, in order to be successful, you have to want to do it. I have seen so many people start projects and then quit saying, "It's too hard. I don't want to do it anymore." I had to teach my own kids that you just do not quit unless some physical impairment forces you to. I hope I have taught my children to look at life that way. I believe I have.

The Iditarod and the Buffalo

Throughout the year I spent in Alaska I often listened to an Anchorage radio station on my little portable radio. In the dead of winter, it was broadcasted that an Iditarod dog sled race would be passing through Rhone Station, which was within 10 miles of my cabin on Post River. Each year the sledders and their dogs would stop at Rhone Station to catch a little rest. While I listened to the broadcasts, I tracked the location of the sledders as it was announced on the radio. On the day I heard that they were passing through Ptarmigan Pass, I knew they would be spending that night at Rhone Station.

You have to keep an airplane engine fairly warm in weather that cold, so I rigged up a little wood heater with a stove pipe directly underneath the cowling of the plane to heat the engine. I would also drain the oil from the engine and keep it in my cabin in a large bucket to prevent it from freezing. When I got ready to start the Cub, I put the warm oil back into the plane and there was never any problem starting up.

View from the air of two dog sled teams on the Iditarod trail. Note the snowshoes attached to the Cub's wing struts.

The day the dogsleds passed through Ptarmigan Pass, I packed up my camera, fired up the Cub, and took off toward Rhone Station. When I reached Rhone Station, there they were, dogs and dogsleds everywhere. Rhone Station was a small log cabin, and I probably could have landed my plane in the snow, but I did not want to take the chance of getting stuck. Instead, I circled overhead and took pictures as they prepared to depart. I got some great shots of the sleds taking off up toward the Yukon River. I followed them for a while and just enjoyed the show before turning back toward Post River. I then landed on my riverbank, secured my plane, and returned to my cabin.

The riverbank was fairly flat for about 200–300 feet. At the end of the flat bank the tree-covered mountainside began to rise up, and this was where I kept the Cub. One of the beauties of this spot was that it protected the Cub from the heavy winds that often blew through the Post River valley. I had to do everything with careful consideration of the weather, and every once in a while, a really *willy-wah* type wind would come through the canyon that could damage the plane. I had to be sure that something as light as a Piper Cub was very securely tied down. Because the plane was on skis, I parked it on a platform of logs running crosswise to the skis to prevent them from freezing to the ground. I also fashioned a couple of poles about three feet apart to rest the plane upon before anchoring it down.

On another flying adventure, I flew over a game reserve to scout a herd of wild, roaming buffalo. Before I started my project, Bill Howard told me about a friend of his who was attempting to get a buffalo herd started in Alaska. A few years earlier he had turned loose several buffalo in the game reserve, and after hearing that I would be living on Post River that winter, this man asked if I would check in on the herd and report back to him with a buffalo count. I agreed to help him. I may have counted some twice, but I recorded 47 buffalo. They started as a herd of only two dozen, so it looked like the buffalo were doing all right. If they kept on that way, this man was likely to have a buffalo season soon.

I had to keep in mind my fuel supply when I went on these flying excursions through the area. During the summer I was going back and forth to Anchorage to pick up various supplies, and when I had room I threw in an extra 5-gallon can of aviation fuel. In the winter, however, I could not replenish my supply. The fuel was contained in square 5-gallon cans that were common up north, and at one point I had built up a supply of nearly 100 gallons. Still, to be safe, I did not fly the Cub as much as I wanted to, and it was reassuring to have that supply on hand.

Despite my precautions and preparations, however, I learned first-hand that on a very cold day the engine may still die on you. One day, I was coming in to land at a spot I had picked to camp out for a few hours for some hot tea and frozen stew. The temperature was below 0°, and when I throttled back to land the engine promptly quit. It was no serious problem because there was plenty of flat snow in front of me and I was already prepared to land, but it did worry me. In response to this incident, I developed a technique I would use from there on out: rather than chopping the throttle to land, I would land with power. The technique worked as long as I kept 1,500–1,800 RPMs instead of cutting the throttle to make a full-stall landing. I was constantly learning and adapting in my flights through the North Country.

As I became more familiar with the Cub I also learned more about flying skis on snow. There were dozens of places in the Post River valley where it appeared I could easily land the Cub in the snow and I was anxious to practice. On my first practice run I found a nice, smooth area over frozen water that looked very inviting, so I proceeded to make my approach. I did not realize just how deep the snow was. I landed in about four feet of snow and immediately sank down into it, coming to an abrupt stop. There I was, stuck in the snow, and my engine was not powerful enough to pull the plane out of it and take off again.

Once again, the tips and advice I learned from the bush pilots with whom I had become friends came in extremely handy. They taught me to always carry plastic garbage bags with me in case I should ever get stuck in the snow. Thankfully, I had heeded their advice. I pulled out a couple garbage bags, dug down in the snow, and slipped them over the skis. This was no easy job considering the weight of the airplane, but after about an hour I got the garbage bags in place. I then tramped up and down in the snow for about 100 yards in front of the airplane, packing it down into a sort of ramp that I could use to pull out of the hole. When I was done, I fired up the plane, gave it full throttle, and slid right out of the snow on those garbage bags. The plane just took off something wonderful. Of course, as soon as I got in the air the wind tore off the garbage bags and they fell to the ground. I suppose I was one of the first people to litter in the Alaskan wilderness because those garbage bags were gone.

The Glaciers

Some of the most amazing sites I saw were the glaciers. I often flew over an area just filled with these frozen rivers which could run anywhere from a few miles in length to 100 miles through a canyon. I suppose they dated back to the Ice Age.

The glaciers were constantly moving and sliding down as millions upon millions of tons of ice were added during the winter. All the weight is compressed into the glacier, pushing it downward and sometimes breaking pieces off. Most of the glaciers had a lake at the bottom that the broken-off pieces—the icebergs—floated upon.

A couple times I was fortunate enough to observe part of a glacier breaking off. It was a spectacular sight to see! A huge chunk of ice the size of a 10-story building suddenly, and seemingly slowly, broke loose from a glacier. As the iceberg struck the edges of the jagged glacier, it tumbled and broke apart before finally hitting the water in the lake below it, sending a huge plume of water shooting skyward. Although it happened in a flash, it felt like slow motion. It was as if the falling iceberg stopped in time, suspended in the air as I watched it. It was a beautiful sight and I was able to see this phenomenon happen twice.

As I explored these glaciers I noticed all the intricate features and changes in the terrain. I truly believe I discovered how it was at the beginning because what I observed in the movement and surroundings of the glaciers were phenomena thousands of years old. I pulled out my chart and identified one glacier as the Agazas of the Bagley ice field. I used this glacier to examine the surrounding topography of the ground from the face of the glacier to about four miles down-terrain.

Right at the edge of the glacier I saw nothing but desolation and barrenness—just grey, wet sand and ice. There was no vegetation or wildlife, just dead, grey earth. A couple hundred yards down I came to some small tufts of moss-like growth that were not quite green but a greyish-green color. Farther down-terrain the amount

Collecting glacier ice—thousands of years old—for drinks.

of moss increased and rock and gravel began to appear. I guessed that this gravel was formed by thousands of years of constantly tumbling ice grinding up the rock. The rocks varied in size—some were large and some were ground into a fine grey sand that filled in the cracks and crevasses in the earth. There was still no wildlife in sight, but as I moved farther downhill the moss grew heavier and soil started to appear beneath my feet. I hypothesized that the soil was formed from millions of years of decaying vegetation. I could see the soil line increase as I moved farther down the terrain.

Approximately one and a half miles from the face of the glacier I began to see new types of vegetation. There were weeds and small tufts of growth that resembled buffalo grass, and it grew abundantly in the area. A little farther down the way I spotted the first signs of wildlife: a hoary marmot (a small squirrel-like animal), some parka squirrels, and some birds.

Continuing farther down, the brush started growing heavier and I spotted signs of glacier bear tracks. I never saw a glacier bear in the wilderness, but I had read about them in books and seen them in museums. This species of bear was about the size of a black bear but was blue-grey in color and lived on and around the glaciers. I also saw signs of fox, wolf, and wolverine, and spruce trees about 5–6 feet tall started to appear. The underbrush began to thicken and I observed more bird life.

As I examined the topography, I believed I was witnessing the process of forestation. The farther I moved down the terrain, the taller and more densely populated the trees grew. I could see how the forest had grown as the glacier slowly receded, and it was spellbinding to stand there and see how life itself was formed. This whole country was once covered by ice, and this slow process of forestation has given us the earth we have today.

Cabin Life

Many times a man can get lonely, but I never did. I was simply alone, and there is a difference. I enjoyed the nature provided for us in this world, and this enjoyment overrode any apprehensions I had about being alone in the wilderness. I felt that I was communing with nature first-hand, and it gave me goose bumps all the time. Plus, I had a good, solid door on my cabin and I felt safe from any threats from the outdoors. I enjoyed every day that I spent in the Alaskan wilderness that year.

I learned throughout this project that I had to stay busy. Whenever I mingled with people who lived in the most remote areas of Alaska, the subject of cabin fever always came up. Living in isolation, you can find yourself sitting and staring at a wall but your eyes are focused several feet on the other side of that wall. Jack London experienced cabin fever, and I had read about it before moving to Post River, but what it boils down to is keeping busy. Fortunately, there was always something to do living in the Alaskan wilderness, and any spare time I had I spent reading. I have always been an avid reader and I carried in to Post River about 50 pounds of books on different articles and subjects that I wanted to increase my knowledge.

I did not have to worry about light to read by until deep into the winter. Located only a couple hundred miles south of the Arctic Circle, daylight could last until two or three o'clock in the morning in the spring and summer seasons. However, throughout winter it got very dark with only four hours of daylight, so I brought in Coleman lanterns to read by. Sometimes I read adventure stories for enjoyment, but for the most part I read non-fiction for knowledge.

Christmas on Post River.

I came out of the wilderness with a better understanding of life and maintaining oneself in the world today. I believe I got my Masters in Life out on Post River that year.

I also made use of my radio to keep my mind active. I was a ham radio operator and I brought with me to the wilderness a small portable rig. We used phonetics when hamming around on the radio to get our call letters right. My call letters were W5UKC; phonetically, Walter's Five Ultra Kitchen Coverings. I was also Uncle King Charlie. Inside my radio I used a battery out of the airplane that I charged with a small Honda generator and I worked mostly on CW (continuous wave) using Morse code. *Da da da da, dit dit dit, da da da, dit, da da da.* I had to focus and concentrate to communicate in Morse code. After a while, using code just comes naturally, but it was a useful activity to keep my mind sharp.

I can honestly say that I was never bored, and if I did get to feeling restless, I would put on my cold weather gear, strap on my snowshoes, and explore up and down the Post River or through the canyon leading up to the mountain. I was curious to see what sort of animal life I would run into with all the snow, and I often thought about how much harder it was for the wildlife to make their living in the harsh winter than it was for me.

How about this, sourdough cinnamon rolls!

Although I never felt lonely, I did long to see my family again, and missing my family made Christmas an emotional day. I had been away from home on Christmas before, but never alone. On Christmas morning that year on Post River, I went out and cut myself a nice Christmas tree. I had millions to choose from. I even shot some footage of myself trimming the tree. Despite my isolation in the wilderness, I actually received gifts that my grandkids sent. Les Risley had dropped them from the air a few weeks earlier. I recorded this on film, as well, as the package came floating down to the ground in the twilight sky. How could I keep a dry eye on a day like that? In that package was a voice recording on tape of all the kids wishing me a Merry Christmas. I played it over and over as I decorated my tree. That day changed me and the way I saw my family for the rest of my life.

There was so much to learn out in the wilderness that I never would have had the opportunity to learn in the city. Living in Alaska was a constant learning process for me, but I truly came to know the land well. With time, I could predict the weather—I always knew when a storm was coming. I even noticed that the snow changed. In the dead of winter, when everything was already covered with a thick layer of snow, the sky would fill with tiny ice crystals floating down to the ground. And there was silence. It was so quiet that I felt I could *hear* the quiet. It felt like sitting in a completely sound proof room and hearing the blood rushing inside your head. That was the kind of life of quietness I led.

Throughout the winter season I had a lot of snow clearing to do around the cabin, extending all the way back to my wood pile. I cut 11 cords of spruce wood. After chopping a log, I cut most of the remaining tree into fire wood. Spruce is similar to Pine and burns fast, so I used a lot of it to cook and to fuel my Franklin fireplace. In addition to my wood pile, I kept a stack of chopped wood on my porch. I liked to keep a supply of wood sheltered on my porch so that when it snowed I would not have to dig it out in the morning.

I did not create much garbage, but the trash I did produce had to be thrown away. Way down the riverbank, several hundred yards from my cabin, I dug a deep hole in the sand and gravel. I carried all my garbage down to this hole and dumped it in, shoveling a few piles of dirt on top every time. I also had to empty my dishwater into the creek, which was a big hassle. I thought, *if I ever do this again, I am going to bring in a supply of paper plates.* I did not leave any odors around the cabin that would attract bears. Leaving odors can be very dangerous in the wilderness, and people often become careless about throwing out their waste. If those odors linger, they will very easily attract a bear, and if that bear detects that the odor is coming from within the cabin, it is going to get inside one way or another. I was extremely careful about my housecleaning and made sure that I did not leave anything out that could be taken as food.

Despite the sub-zero temperatures that I had to withstand, I also brought with me to Post River a hand-cranked ice cream maker. As cold as it was, it may seem odd that I would want to eat ice cream, but I was intrigued by the idea of making ice cream without any ice. Using powdered milk, I mixed up a batch of the necessary ingredients, put on my down filled parka and heavy mittens, sat down out on the porch of the cabin, and started cranking that ice cream. In a temperature pushing -15°, I made myself some very good ice cream. The ice cream provided a change in diet that I was grateful for because I was getting tired of eating beans all the time.

Even as time passed, I still could not completely absorb everything that I was seeing. Some of it was just too unbelievable, but every incredible experience taught me something new, and often unexpected. For instance, I learned that bears do not actually stay in hibernation all throughout the winter. In fact, if the temperature warms slightly, a bear will leave his den and range around the area. One winter day, the temperature had warmed to a cool 20°. I was exploring up the creek when I came upon some bear tracks that crossed my path. They almost looked like human tracks. I thought, *this can't be possible,* so I decided to investigate. I followed the tracks over a small embankment and down a slope, and there lay a big, cinnamon-colored bear. He must have come out of his den to find food. I did not want the bear to see me and be disturbed so I quickly made my way out of there. When I looked over my shoulder, I saw that the bear *had* been disturbed but, fortunately, it was moving away in the opposite direction.

Another amazing feature of the area was that there were very rich silver deposits in the mountains surrounding Post River. However, there was no way to properly mine the silver because no roads could be built through the treacherous terrain in order to come in with machinery and haul out the ore. The ore could not be flown out of the area either because the silver's carrier was lead, and even the concentrated ore was too heavy to lift out by air. On a few occasions, I went up the mountain with my own little prospector pick and was able to retrieve some small chunks of solid ruby silver from one of the veins. Years later, the land was brought under the Natives Claim Act, making it even more difficult to do any mining, but if we ever urgently need silver for the national treasury, we will know where to find it! Prospecting for silver in the mountains around Post River planted the seed that would later lead me to an extensive career as a gold miner.

The Climb of Peaceful Peak

In the spring of 1976, as the winter climate slowly waned, temperatures dropped, and nature became kinder, I knew the most challenging part of my year in the wilderness was over. I had made it through the harshest winter I had ever faced, and my sense of confidence and trust in my survival skills became stronger. I had proven to myself that I could still live off of the land in one of the least forgiving wilderness environments I had ever known.

I was nearing the end of my yearlong experience in my cabin on the Post River. Everything was green and the snow was beginning to melt atop the mountains that surrounded me. Over the course of the winter everything had iced over and there was still quite a bit of ice and snow in the riverbed. I measured that the ice had built up to as much as four feet thick, but in a few short weeks, it would all be gone.

Once again it was the Fourth of July and I had made it through a year on Post River. That afternoon, I was sitting on my cabin porch about to pop. I was so full of homemade ice cream that I could hardly move. I wanted to uphold the tradition that I had always had of cooking barbecue and making homemade ice cream on the Fourth of July, and living in the wilderness was not going to stop me.

I pulled out my ice cream freezer and mixed up the ingredients. Then, I acquired some ice from Silver Creek where it was still frozen in large chunks. I chopped off smaller pieces of ice with an ax, crushed it up, and packed it around the freezer can. Finally, I sprinkled table salt over the ice and waited for the ice cream to

Table manners training with the squirrels.

freeze. Periodically, I removed the lid and stirred the mixture with a wooden spoon, scraping the frozen ice cream off the sides of the can. The whole process took only 30 minutes and I had myself a large can full of fantastic ice cream! I threw some blueberries into my bowl and it was just too good to stop eating, but after I was done I sat there feeling miserable because I had eaten so much. Despite the discomfort, I was happy to have kept up my Independence Day tradition.

As I sat on the porch, one of my pet ground squirrels started scratching on the door. I had been so busy fixing barbecue and making ice cream that I forgot about my little buddies. I had gotten used to feeding those little rascals and I thought they were becoming dependent on me—I was afraid that when I left they might starve! But if they were going to eat my food, they were going to have to learn some manners. I whittled the little critters a squirrel-sized table and a set of stools where they could eat their snacks, and by the end of the year, I had trained them to sit politely at the table!

Over the course of my year on Post River I shot hundreds of feet of film footage. Now that the year was over I was ready to start editing my film, but I was still thoroughly enjoying the peace and quite of the solitude that came out of the mountains. Before my time in the wilderness was over, I wanted to climb the 9,600-foot peak just west of my cabin with my camera equipment in tow in order to film the experience. I knew that as I climbed the mountain and reached higher elevations I would have fantastic views of the surrounding terrain which I hoped to capture in panoramic shots.

The only thing holding me back was the rotten snow at the top of the peak that still had not melted. At that time of year big chunks of ice fell from the peak and I had already seen several avalanches. Needless to say, I wanted to wait for safer conditions before I made my climb.

While I knew the footage from the top of the peak would be excellent for my film, the main reason I wanted to make the climb was to place a time capsule at the top of the mountain. Before I left Austin I prepared a bottle with a message and a few other odds and ends inside, and I used a torch to melt and seal the bottle opening. In my message I wrote down Walter Yates' formula for happiness. I hoped that one day in the distant future somebody would stumble upon my capsule and, perhaps, it might help them find the same peace and happiness that I found on Post River.

There are thousands of peaks along the Alaskan Range and they are just too numerous to all be named, but this one was so outstanding with its magnificent spires towering so high above the rest that I decided it needed its own name. I chose the name Peaceful Peak, and I do not believe any other name would be as befitting as that. The peak had been a peaceful inspiration to me all throughout the winter that I spent looking out to it through my cabin window—it was just utterly beautiful.

On July 10th I woke up early to a pretty day and decided it was time to climb the mountain. I packed my lunch, camera equipment, and audio recorder to chronicle my trek up the mountain.

My baggage weighed about 30 pounds, so I knew before I reached the peak I would have to unload some gear.

I left my cabin and took off downhill toward the creek. From there, I planned to hike up the Post River canyon to the base of the mountain. The water in the creek was crystal clear and flowing strong. As I walked alongside it I wondered if there was water as fresh and pure as this anywhere in the Lower Forty-eight. There was just a little bit of ice left in the creek bed, but it would all be gone in only a few more days. About a mile into the canyon, however, the ice was still up to three feet thick.

In 72° weather wearing a khaki shirt, I was sweltering hot as I meandered through huge chunks of ice. It was a surreal feeling. By the time I reached the base of the mountain, at a confluence of two creeks, I was already winded. The first 300 feet up the mountain seemed to rise straight up out of the ground like walls before leveling off into a gradual slope that I would not have any trouble climbing, but first I had to get past that steep, vertical wall. I could have scaled this part of the mountain but I did not want to bother with ropes or risk taking a serious fall, so I decided instead to go around it.

I kept telling myself that I was in excellent shape, but when I started up that mountain I wondered if it was true. Nevertheless, I enjoyed the physical exertion—it gave me a good, healthy tiredness. When I reached an elevation of about 4,000 feet, 2,000 feet above my cabin on Post River, I stopped to shoot some movie footage. At this elevation I could not yet see my cabin but I could almost make out the far side of the Post River canyon bed.

The mountains just east of my cabin across the river were absolutely spectacular and I was happy I had caught a day when the sun was shining to capture them with my camera. The sun shone onto the mesa and the mountains behind me as I made my way up to the peak, and the different refracting colors and rock formations were absolutely beautiful.

About halfway up the mountain the green timber and vegetation ceased to grow and all that was left was brown and grey earth.

Peaceful Peak, still snow-covered.

The mountain itself was only about 6,000 feet in elevation but there were still many patches of snow. As I looked toward my destination, I almost got a crick in my neck trying to catch a glimpse of the top of the peak. And the closer I got to it the rougher my hike became. I knew it would not be easy to summit the peak.

Looking downward to the valley below I could see where Silver Creek ran out of a box canyon. As the creek flowed down around the mountain, another small creek to the south of the mountain cut in and joined it, along with numerous other small streams. I stopped here and shot footage of this panoramic view down the canyon. I also sat down and took a rest. I had climbed approximately 1,500 feet since my last stop and estimated that I was at an elevation of about 5,500 feet. I was almost level with another mountain just east of my cabin and I used it as a guide to gauge my elevation.

Soon after resuming my climb I heard a noise in the canyon and stopped abruptly. Then, all of a sudden, I saw a rockslide coming down off of Peaceful Peak. The sight was absolutely spectacular, but my movie camera was still in my pack. It would have taken me several minutes to set up my camera equipment so there was no way I could have filmed it. I was disappointed that I had missed the shot—there were literally tons of rock sliding down the side of the mountain—but I realized I needed to be extremely careful as I continued forward and was thankful that I had not been in the rockslide's path. In the fall and spring, water seeps down into the crevasses between big rocks high upon the mountain. In winter, the water freezes and expands, cracking and loosening the rocks. The result of these rockslides can be seen in the piles of shale and tumbled rock down below the mountain. This process has been taking place for millions of years: freezing, expanding, breaking.

I picked up my belongings and continued on my hike. The wind blew harder the higher I climbed up the mountain, and by now I was moving a little slower. I knew I needed to take it easy as I ascended the mountain—I could feel it sapping the strength out of me.

At 6,000 feet I came to what I would call a humpback ridge that gradually sloped steeper and steeper as it reached the mountain peak. I guessed that I had 2.5 to 3 miles left to reach the summit, much of which would be traversed across three steep patches of shale that were slippery and difficult to cross. It was like trying to climb a huge pile of gravel—not *too* dangerous unless I lost my footing, in which case I would take a steep fall.

I was tired, but the temptation of the nearing 360° view of pure, awesome, raw beauty kept me going. The nature of the country had a special effect on me, and so I kept climbing. All around me were mountains, but by now the smaller ones had receded and no longer felt so massive. The most spectacular peaks were beginning to appear and I knew I would only see more once I reached the top of Peaceful Peak. Many of the peaks were cone-shaped and looked like ice cream cones flipped upside-down. The tops of those peaks were white and covered with snow but began to streak out where the snow had melted into brown, grey, and purple hues. I was about

Traversing the shale slope.

as deep into the Alaskan range as I could be, and joked to myself that in any direction I traveled I'd be leaving.

At 8,000 feet I stopped and unloaded some of my equipment. I did not need to carry everything I had with me to the top of the peak, but I did take my movie and still cameras. I also left behind the 30.6 rifle that I brought with me in case I crossed a bear because I knew there would not be any at this elevation. I could now see the full Post River canyon and its wide flood plain covered with serpentine streams that branched out, came back together, and then branched out again.

I reached the point in elevation where I had just a ridge to walk upon. I had one foot on the right side and one on the left as I walked, straddling the mountain. Ever more tired, I nestled into some rocks sticking out of the ridge and took another short rest. Then, I got up, resumed walking, and climbed the last stretch of the mountain to the summit of Peaceful Peak.

When I reached the top of the peak I triumphantly declared aloud, "I hereby proclaim this mountain Peaceful Peak!" I was going to christen the mountain with a can of orange juice, but in my thirst I decided to drink it instead. I stacked up a pile of rocks about three feet high and underneath it I buried my time capsule. In case of the unlikely event that somebody should find the capsule too soon, I scratched a message into a piece of slate-shaped rock about six inches square asking that the capsule not be disturbed prior to the year 2000. I wanted the capsule to remain unopened until the 21st century.

Once the capsule was buried I allowed myself to sit down, relax, and take in the amazing view. *Oh my god,* I thought reverently. The sight was utterly fantastic. I was surrounded 360° degrees by mountains and in the distance I could even see Mount McKinley towering 20,320 feet high. I was so overwhelmed I had to hold back tears. I had never had anything grab me like this mountain did that day.

I could finally see my cabin and I discovered a lake nestled in the mountains only about 10 miles away from it that I had never seen before. The lake was blue-green and surrounded by trees—I could even see a grazing herd of caribou through my telephoto lens. I believed I was standing where no man had ever stood before and I was truly moved. As a fellow once said, I thought, *I am glad I now know what I know now.*

I knew that the first 1,000 feet of descent would be worse than it was coming up it, so I allowed myself plenty of rest. However, it had been a long day so far and I had a long trek back, so I knew I could not stay too long. Before I left, I scratched my name and the names of some of my closest family and friends on a rock to be forever immortalized on the top of Peaceful Peak in the Alaskan range.

I reached the bottom of the mountain by four o'clock in the afternoon. Just above where the creeks forked, I stopped to watch a mama bear and her cub a half-mile below me. I was not sure if I should wait until they left before continuing down the path, but I decided I would work my way closer, keeping the mama bear in sight at all times.

The wind was blowing down the canyon and the mama bear caught my scent before I could reach her and startle her with my presence. As soon as she saw me she left the area, probably to protect her cub. With the path cleared, I made my way down the creek and headed for my cabin.

Once I was safely back at home, I knew my project was complete. I had spent a year—four vastly different seasons—in the Alaskan wilderness living off the land, and I had planted my time capsule at the top of Peaceful Peak. I sat down and wrote a letter home announcing my return to Austin by the first of August—but I had one last adventure planned before leaving Alaska.

The Arctic Circle and the North Slope

"Anchorage approach. This is Comanche 9264 Papa. I'll be penetrating your traffic corridor 10 miles east of Anchorage Airport. Altitude 4,500. Heading 270°. Requesting radar surveillance through the traffic area. Over."

I had just taken off from Campbell Airstrip about 10 miles southeast of Anchorage International and the skies over the city were filled with traffic. Anchorage International's traffic corridor intersected with part of the military's corridor, so the skies could get pretty congested. I had landed at Campbell because it was less busy, but I had to cross Anchorage International's traffic corridor to get out of town. This required communication with air traffic control to avoid any serious incidents.

I needed to return to my cabin on Post River in the Alaskan range to pick up a few items of survival gear. Rain was drizzling and the weather was deteriorating so I planned to stay the night on Post River and leave for the Arctic Circle early the next morning if the weather improved. When I got back to Post River, I landed on the gravel bar and hurried to my cabin to start a fire and put on a pot of coffee. It was only 54° but I was cold and wet. I pulled out some groceries that I had left in the cellar under the floor and warmed them up for my dinner. I could not help thinking, *anybody who hasn't eaten a big plate of red beans, potatoes fried with onions, and biscuits, just hasn't eaten!*

It was just after midnight and still light outside. At that time of year I had about 18 hours of daylight at Post River. The rain had stopped and I was excited for my flight the next day so I climbed into my bunk and went to sleep.

The next morning I woke up early, loaded up the plane, and prepared for my trip. I filled my fuel tanks completely full, giving me a six-hour range. Depending on the wind factor, I could fly between 1,100–1,200 miles. With the amount of fuel I had, I believed I could make it back to Fairbanks after circling the Arctic Circle. If not, I would have to pay the horrendous gas prices charged at the refueling station at the North Slope.

The weather was not as good as I had hoped with drizzling rain and low ceilings, and I was sad to leave my cabin—I had been happy here—but I knew I had to get going. I shut the cabin door for what would be the last time for quite a while, but I knew I would return the next summer for vacation. I latched the door shut but I did not lock it. There was enough food in my shelter to last a man a good while, and if someone should wander by in need of food and shelter, I wanted that person to be able to use my cabin.

As I made the short walk from my cabin to the gravel bar I ran into two old friends—a pair of seagulls who had nested on Post River. Like me, they were also leaving, heading back to the coast for the warmer summer season.

Back in my plane I warmed up the engine before taking off. You never want to attempt a take-off with a cold engine. I was almost at gross load with 90 gallons of gasoline on board the aircraft. At six pounds per gallon, that comes out to 540 pounds of fuel, and I had just as much weight on board in equipment and gear. I was not worried, though. My airplane had always performed well and I felt comfortable taking off from my gravel bar.

I made a smooth take-off and headed for the western coastline of Alaska in the direction of Norton Sound. Once there, I flew over the bay and steered my plane toward Moses Point, passing about 30 miles north of Nome. By the time I reached the bay the weather had improved and visibility had increased to 25 miles. The rain also seemed to be tapering off.

I passed through the southern slope of the Bendeleben Mountains and flew over Davidson's Lodge and Coffee Creek. The Bendeleben Mountains were not nearly as high as the mountains surrounding my cabin and appeared to be on average about 3,000 feet high. Still, I was glad that the ceilings had risen and that I could see the mountain peaks clearly in the distance.

I flew directly in the direction of Teller and Point Spencer. From there, I followed the coast north to Wales. The farther I flew the more the weather improved, and visibility grew to about 40 miles. The temperature had also dropped to 37° and the heater in my plane was set to full blast.

Due to the circumstances of this particular trip I did not file an official flight plan. I was not sure just how long I would be gone or to what airstrip I would return. I did, however, give Les Risley in Anchorage an informal flight plan summarizing the basic route I intended to follow. We agreed that I would call him long-distance the first place I landed that had a telephone so that he could keep track of my whereabouts.

When I got to Wales, the excitement really began—I would now fly straight out over the ocean and head for Little Diomede. The weather was clear enough that this tiny U.S. territory was within my field of visibility. I would have cancelled my flight out there had the weather not been clear enough to see the island from Wales; it would not have been worth the risk of accidentally straying across the border into Russian territory.

The view from the air was beautiful. I flew over ice floes in the strait that were so tightly compacted I could not imagine how any boat could pass through them on their way to drop of supplies to the oil fields at the North Slope. I estimated that I was only about 35 miles from Little Diomede and after only a few minutes Big Diomede came into view. Big Diomede, a Russian territory, was home to the city of Nunebruk, which I hoped to see if I could get close enough.

Then, as if out of nowhere, I could see the eastern coast of Siberia! It was just fantastic, but also eerie. I was only 10 miles from the border between the United States and Russia, flying due west, yet I saw no signs of life. There weren't even any other aircraft flying in the skies. Only five miles north of Little Diomede and four miles east of the Russian border, I debated whether or not to penetrate any further. It was carefully pointed out on all the charts that any U.S. aircraft that accidentally strayed over the border was subject to being shot down without notice. As it would turn out, the decision whether or not to press further was soon made for me.

All of a sudden, three McDonnell Douglas F-4's passed only two miles to my left on what I *thought* was the U.S. side of the border. The three planes made a big circle southward, came back around on my right side, then crossed in front of me and returned to their original course. The message was clear: these were U.S. military planes and I had flown too close to the Russian border. I received no radio signal from them but I knew I needed to get out. Immediately, I headed due east, flew away from the border, and watched as the F-4's continued their flight south.

Once I was certain I was at a safe distance from Russian territory (about 10 miles east), I turned north and flew parallel to the border. I was due east of the eastern-most point of Russia. I calculated on my chart that I had passed the towns of East Cape, Naukan, Uelen, and Dezhnevo, and I determined that I was now about 60 miles below the Arctic Circle. I set myself on a course that would take me just north of Shishmaref and across the coast into Kotzebue Sound. Then, I would fly northwest up the coast to Kivalina and Point Hope. I realized on this flight that this was one of the greatest experiences I had ever had and I was thoroughly enjoying every second of it.

I flew past no less than 22 large tugboats carrying supplies up to the North Slope. They looked like they were bogged down in the frozen ice on top of the water, but there was a ship in front of them breaking up the ice and creating a path for the rest. Flying at an altitude of 1,000 feet I approached Espinburg, making my way closer to the Arctic Circle. According to my map, Espinburg was situated directly on the Arctic Circle. I was about to pass through.

The water below me was completely packed with ice. I glanced at the clock and at 2:15 p.m. local time I crossed the Arctic Circle. I noticed no difference in the surroundings, just more ice! I had caught a terrific tailwind of nearly 50 knots and there was no turbulence, so I felt assured that I would not have to refuel any time soon. I estimated my ground speed at about 230 MPH, which was terrific for an airplane that normally cruised at 185 MPH. Five miles west of Kivalina I flew over some Eskimo villages with names I could not pronounce, such as Ungayookot, and I finally spotted another sight I was hoping to see on this trip: seals! The ice pack was totally solid beneath me, and there were seals everywhere. I guessed that there were several hundred, and every once in a while I would see one jump into the water through an opening in the ice. I noticed that the nearer I flew to them the more rapidly they jumped into the water—I must have scared them. I snapped a few still shots before continuing on.

I was right at the edge of the Chukchi sea, a part of the Arctic Ocean, and I was skimming along only a couple hundred feet above the ice. I was hoping to spot a polar bear but I never did see one. By now, the weather had deteriorated slightly—the skies were grey and the ceiling had lowered to 4,000 feet—but I still had excellent visibility. I continued to fly in a northeasterly direction and eventually rounded Point Hope, Kapalawa, and Cape Lisburne. Every once in a while I passed a small village but it was difficult to distinguish one from another amidst the vast, icy backdrop. In fact, I could hardly distinguish the land from the water. Everything was white. One village, however, reminded me of Padre Island back home in Texas. There was also an inland bay just off the coast near Talageek that looked like Matagorda.

As the weather deteriorated more, I decided I better move to Icy Cape and proceed directly to Point Barrow, the northernmost point of the United States. I had a visibility of 20 miles but the ceilings were getting lower and I still had to make my way back across the North Slope and the Brooks Range, so I did not want to push my luck.

When I reached Barrow I passed over the Wiley Post monument at Briarville. This monument stands at the site where Wiley Post and Will Rogers had their fatal crash on an exploring expedition to the north. I took a picture of the monument but with the grey weather it did not turn out well. The photo had bad contrast and, later, hardly anybody could tell what I had taken a picture off. I circled the monument a few more times but did not stay long because I needed to make sure I had enough fuel to get to Bettles, the town where I decided I would stop and refuel.

"Point Barrow radio. Comanche 9264 Papa. How do you read? Over."

I had some trouble getting in touch with air traffic control at Barrow for a pilot's report but we finally made contact. They reported to me that a Learjet had come across some bad weather but had passed through it, and that another pilot had just flown through the Brooks Range and landed at Bettles with no incident. With this information I was confident that I could make a safe landing as well.

By the time I landed at the Bettles airstrip I only had about 40 minutes of flight time left in my fuel tanks. Bettles was a desolate place, even for a man who had spent a year in isolation in the wilderness. There were a handful of buildings, a lodge, and a restaurant where I ate a late lunch, but other than that there was nothing. With no reason to hang around, I refueled my airplane, got back in the air, and flew south. It was time to return to Texas.

When I was back in the Lower Forty-eight and on my way home from my fantastic adventure, I was sad to see the project come to an end, but also thankful for everything I had gained. I was especially thankful for the personal growth and the gift of inner peace that I found in the northern wilderness. I knew I would continue to travel and take on new adventures but I was sure I would never have another experience that could equal the year spent on Post River. As I flew home, returning to my family, I thought about an old poem by Gill Robb Wilson called "The Airman's World." I had learned the poem many years earlier and thought it expressed just how I felt about flying:

Not one who plows upon the blue is free from threat of storm,
And none there are who do not know the dreaded anvil form.
Where blow on blow is forced to soar of lightening stride a blade
To cleave the sky and blind the eye and make thee heart afraid.
Yet for the heavens, always clear, the winds forever fair,
The cockpit where I sweat my sweat, were but a rocking chair.
Where I should wither in my soul, fret my life away,
Untempered by my daily toil to meet a judgment day.
I cannot know what he will ask who totes the great white book,
Of what I selfless gave to life or what I selfish took.
But this much I will hazard him when asked if I'm afraid,
Aye, sir, but fear has served me well. I've walked where storm is made.

Gill Robb Wilson

Producing *Breakaway*

Before I left for my year in Alaska in 1975, I got in touch with Ivan Bigley who ran Texas Motion Picture Service. With a little help I thought I could produce a really interesting documentary about my year in the wilderness, so before I even started my project I set up a partnership with Ivan. While I was on Post River I occasionally sent film footage back to Ivan to start editing, and when I returned from my year in Alaska, I spent quite a bit of time with Ivan in his studio producing the movie, quickly realizing that making a movie is no easy task.

"You really need a director," Ivan said. "You need somebody who can help you put this together because you've got a really good story here."

"Would you recommend anybody?" I asked.

Ivan told me about a good friend of his who had worked with him on some other films and said he might be able to help me.

"What's his name?" I asked.

"Warren Skaaren."

I told Ivan to give Warren my phone number so that we could discuss the project.

A few days later I got a call from Warren and he told me he wanted to meet up to talk about the documentary. Over lunch, Warren decided this was a project he would really like to work on and I realized he would be a big help to me, so we reached an agreement and he became the director of my film.

We made plans for four of us—Ivan Bigley, Warren Skaaren, a man from the film studio named Loyd Colby, and me—to go to Alaska to shoot more footage. I flew the men from Anchorage to Post River in my Piper Comanche and they got the thrill of a lifetime flying through the mountain passes deep in the wilderness.

We started work as soon as we got to my cabin. I had shot a tremendous amount of footage by myself during the winter but we needed to film background shots and other scenes that I could not capture myself. We also needed footage of me climbing Peaceful Peak, and this was not going to be easy. I told Warren that the climb was rough and that I did not know how far they could go with the camera.

"We've taken care of that," Ivan chimed in. "I brought along an 800-millimeter lens. We will go as far as we can and then we'll be able to follow you with the camera."

We loaded up with the camera equipment and Warren, Ivan, and I started up that trail. It was four miles from my cabin to the foot of the mountain and, having been up it before, I knew at about the 4,000-foot mark there was a bench where we could stop and set up the camera equipment. From there, the guys could follow me with the camera as I climbed the rest of the way up the mountain.

It was a nice little trek going up that trail, and because it was a warm day, we stopped periodically to take a drink out of the creek. The great thing about being in the wilderness of Alaska is that any mountain stream you come across has crystal clear water, and it is certainly good when you are thirsty.

It took us about two hours to get to the bench, trudging through the shale and loose rock. Warren and Ivan set up the camera equipment and we got some nice shots of the Post River flood plain. There were also some sheep ranging on the mountain below us and we shot some footage of the white specks they made on the landscape. I looked through the telephoto lens a few times and I was amazed at how it brought in the mountain. It made you feel like you were there.

I left Ivan and Warren and started up the mountain, but when I got to the steep parts of the climb I really had to slow down. We had hand signals so that I could show them which direction I was going. When I made it to the pinnacle I took in the view and let them film me at the top of Peaceful Peak. I checked on my bottle and it was still safely tucked away, waiting to be discovered.

Coming down the mountain was a lot more difficult than going up it because I ran into loose rocks and if I was not careful before I put my weight on my foot it could slide out from under me. I was over 9,000 feet up and it would have been a long way down if I slipped. It took me another two hours to get back down to Ivan and Warren and we congratulated each other for the climb. Warren told me they got some terrific footage and that they were able to follow me all the way up the mountain.

We got back to the cabin around 10 o'clock that night and discussed what we had done. After a few more days of filming at Post River we flew back to Anchorage, but this time we followed a new route to see some different scenery. I took them by an active volcano that we could look down into and see the steam rising. We were flying along, singing, and having a ball. That night, we slept at Les Risley's—he let all these guys stay with him, he had a heart as big as a watermelon—and the next day we got our gear together and flew back to Austin from Anchorage.

While I was home that year working on my film, I ended up falling in love. The woman's name was Tracy Pustjovsky and we had known each other for a long time from the real estate business, but now my feelings for her were growing strong. I really did not like the single life and I missed having a wife, so one day we just up and got married. Tracy and I have been happily married for 33 years now. Want to know the secret? Communicate. Know and respect each other's needs. Of course, there have been a few bruises along the way, but they heal.

Tracy had a 15 year old son named Gregory, so the marriage increased my family to four children. Greg and I got along really well. He enjoyed the outdoors and we took many deer hunting trips together. Greg was a quick learner. I had the joy of being with him for his first eight-point trophy buck, which he bagged in one shot. I always hoped my son Jay would follow in my footsteps by becoming a pilot, but he was more interested in the mechanical aspects of aircraft and made that his career. Greg, on the other hand, loved flying, and with a little encouragement from me he soon became a pilot. He still has his pilot's license today, but when his own family grew by two children, a boy and a girl, he was forced to shelf his flying career as flying is not cheap.

Greg began observing my work while I was still active in the real estate business, and although I was not aware of it at the time, he was very interested in getting into real estate himself. I encouraged Greg to follow this path and he took to the real estate business like a duck takes to water. By the time he was 22 years old he had his broker's license and he was in it with both feet. I helped Greg get started. I was still developing land at the time, so I let Greg sell the lots. Greg has a good personality and communicates well with others, yet he is not high pressure. I thought it was great that he picked up on the real estate business because it fit his personality so well.

Greg had a steady girlfriend named Lisa, a beautiful redheaded gal with a great personality. It was obvious that they were meant for each other, so the date was set and they got married. We rented a big meeting hall and there were at least 200 people at the wedding. It was jam packed. Everyone danced and visited, and Greg and Lisa passed around a boot for each guest to put in a little money—an old custom that I had never heard of before. When the party ended that night, Greg and Lisa had a boot full of money, which was a nice send off for the newlyweds. They soon added to the family with a little boy named Luke and a little girl named Lauren. Lisa sure raised those kids right. She is a tremendous mom. And I'll tell you, Luke and Lauren are two siblings that just flat out get along with each other. If one does something, the other one has to do it too, and they do it together. It got to the point where if one had a birthday, we had to give a present to both of them! They were just that close, and still are today.

Back at Texas Motion Picture Service, I spent a lot of time with Warren editing and splicing the film. Warren was very enthusiastic about the project—we *all* were. When the film editing was nearly complete, Ivan made arrangements for us to go to Hollywood. Warren knew several people at Consolidated Film Industries so when we got to California we rented out a splicing room and continued to work on the documentary every day for two weeks.

With Warren's expertise and the accommodations of this film company we did a good job putting the movie together, but Warren thought something was missing.

"What we really need is a well-known actor—and there are quite a few of them out here—to narrate this film for us," he said.

Warren got in touch with Hal Holbrook. We told Hal about our film and he agreed to come by Consolidated Film Industries to see the movie. He sat there all the way through our 90-minute film and we could tell he enjoyed it.

"Let me give this some thought and see what my schedule is like. When did you need this job done?"

"We are just about wrapped up," I said. "We need to make the final print just as soon as we can."

When Hal left I asked Warren, "Do you think he'll call?"

"Oh yeah, he will call."

The next day Hal called me at my hotel and said he did not have time to do the project for another six to eight weeks. On top of that, he quoted a fee that shot us out of the saddle. Even if he could have done the job that very day I could not have justified paying what he was asking. In the end, we did not get Hal Holbrook to narrate the film; instead, Warren narrated most of it himself and I thought he did a great job.

I decided to call the film *Breakaway*. The documentary tells the story of a man truly breaking away from the daily rat race that we are all caught up in and going into the wilderness to rediscover himself. Warren and I had a lot of success with *Breakaway*. We four-walled the movie at theaters across the country and won "The

Award of Excellence for Outstanding Documentary" from the Film Advisory Board. The plaque sits on my mantle today. While we were in Hollywood I met a lot of Warren's friends in the industry and I realized how lucky I was to have him working on my film. Years later, Warren went on to produce Top Gun, and he wrote the screenplays for Batman, Beetlejuice, Fire with Fire, and Beverly Hills Cop 2. Skaaren tragically died in 1990 from bone cancer, and his collection of screenplays, films, and other materials are now archived at the Harry Ransom Center at the University of Texas.

Movie poster for Breakaway.

Part V
Goldmining

Flight School Again

You can't go to Alaska without getting involved in gold. Nearly everybody and their brother is a prospector and it was not long before the gold fever rubbed off on me. The problem was, I always heard the same cautionary tales from retired miners: they ran out of grub before they found any gold. I was bound and determined that if I got involved in mining, this would not be my story.

I spent the summer of 1978 researching mineral rights in Alaska and prospecting sites throughout the state, kicking off a gold mining career that would last over a decade. At the end of the summer I returned home to Texas, the desire to mine still strong, but I realized that the only way to prospect the remote areas of the North Country was by helicopter. After giving it a lot of thought, I called a helicopter instructor.

My instructor, Don Peck, taught me on a Bell 47, the kind of helicopter seen on M.A.S.H. For the first few hours of training, I was just about ready to quit. I just could not get the hang of it, but Don encouraged me to stay with it.

"That's the way we all are when we first start," he said. "It just takes a while to get comfortable handling a helicopter. Pretty soon you will get the feel for it."

Don convinced me to continue with my lessons, and after a few weeks I had my breakthrough—all of a sudden I could hover the helicopter, keeping it within an area about the size of an acre.

One day, after nine hours of instruction, we landed on the edge of the runway and Don said, "You take it around now!" This caught me by surprise but I did not have time to question him, so I got back in the helicopter and fired up. Don Peck was a pretty heavy man, probably weighing around 240 pounds. My average weight, on the other hand, was only 150 pounds. When I took off again without Don riding passenger, the helicopter shot up like a cork out of a champagne bottle. I did not loose control but I wobbled around a bit until I got myself stabilized. Then, I did as Don instructed and took the helicopter around the field. As I came in to land Don waved for me to go around again, which I did another three or four times. This really boosted my confidence in the helicopter.

Don had to leave Austin for about ten days but he left the helicopter in my hands at the Georgetown airport.

"Fly the helicopter whenever you want," he said. "There is a meter in the helicopter that will tell me how much time you flew, so just practice all you can."

I went up in the helicopter every day that Don was gone. I am sure everyone in the neighborhood was going crazy as I practiced landings, quick stops, and the many other maneuvers Don had taught me. I practiced everything alone but an auto-rotation landing—I wanted to wait until Don could be there with me to perform that maneuver. It was a tricky procedure and I just was not ready to try it by myself.

When Don returned I received my private rotorcraft rating. I now knew how to fly a helicopter, but I still needed practice. I started looking in *Trade Plane* magazine, a publication that listed aircraft for sale, for a used Bell 47 that I could afford, and eventually I found one with pretty good time left on the engines and blades. At the time, I thought the price of the helicopter was tremendous, but considering how much helicopters cost today, I was practically stealing it. I borrowed $24,000 from the bank, bought the Bell 47, and flew it every single day. I practiced, practiced, and practiced some more until I thought I was ready to go a step further and get a commercial license.

There was an organization in Houston that taught police helicopter pilots, but it also checked out private pilots for commercial ratings. They too taught their students in a Bell 47, so when I flew with the instructor I was very comfortable with the aircraft. My instructor tested me on every possible maneuver, including autorotation, engine-out, tight-spot, and pinnacle landings.

After about three days of testing—and they really wrung me out—my instructor brought me into the hangar, sat me down, and started filling out papers. When he was done, he looked up and said, "You passed your exam, and you are now a commercial helicopter pilot." I flew home, feeling great, and started thinking about the upcoming gold prospecting season in Alaska. I continued to practice flying my helicopter every day and made arrangements to return to the North Country. The following spring of 1979, I would fly my helicopter to Alaska to continue prospecting for gold.

All the while, my good-natured family was putting up with all this nonsense.

Gold Prospecting

In the spring of 1979 I hopped in my helicopter and made the long flight north to Alaska. I had traded in my Bell 47 for a newer model, the Bell 47J2A, and I flew the helicopter all the way to Anchorage from Austin. The flight was quite an experience, and there can be many difficulties flying a helicopter nearly 5,000 miles, but it was probably the most spectacular and beautiful trip I have ever made. The reason for this was simple: I flew lower and considerably slower in the helicopter than I ever could in an airplane. Over the past decade, I had probably made ten trips to the North Country in an airplane. I had always thought that the country was fantastically beautiful the whole way there, especially through Alaska and the Canadian Rockies, but I had always flown over it at a considerably higher altitude and at a much faster speed than I did in the helicopter. Although it was beautiful as a whole, I missed all the details. This time, flying at an average altitude of 500 feet, and occasionally as low as 200–300 feet, I saw so many new and indescribable features in the nature, particularly the wildlife. I saw moose, caribou, sheep, and a few bears, often near the remote rivers and lakes I passed over in my helicopter.

There was one particularly remote lake that I had flown over many times before in an airplane that I always wanted to visit, but I had no place to land the plane. This time, I was bound and determined to do it since I was in a helicopter. When I reached the lake, I stopped and spent about half a day exploring. I set up camp, fixed lunch, and fished in the lake. For a few hours I just rested and mused and enjoyed the complete solitude of this remote lake where I could see no signs that any human being had ever been there before. Once I was good and rested, I departed again in my helicopter.

Let me describe the plain, hard facts of flying a helicopter such a long distance. I want to go on record right now and say that I do not recommend it. I think anyone would be better off just shipping the helicopter or pulling it on a trailer. Nevertheless, this was an experience I wanted to have, and I am really glad I have it behind me now. Although I gained valuable experience flying a helicopter in the North Country, I encountered some serious problems during my flight, including two forced landings due to engine problems.

My flight lasted seven days, but two of those days were lost due to the engine problems. Theoretically, a pilot could fly a helicopter from Texas to Alaska in five to six days, weather permitting, and if he has the stamina and willingness to keep going. It gets awfully tiring flying a helicopter for hours on end, and it really took it out of me. On my longest day I spent 11 hours in the air on the cyclic stick. That was by far my hardest day.

My route from Austin sent me due north through Oklahoma, Kansas, Nebraska, South Dakota, and across a corner of North Dakota. The reason I went straight north instead of angling northwest was to get as far north as I could before encountering mountainous country. I figured that by the time I reached Canada I would be more familiar with the Bell 47J2A as I had not flown this particular machine more than 20 hours since I bought it. The lengthier route gave me a chance to get a little more accustomed to how this model flew.

A major problem during that first leg of the flight was the heat. Travelling through hot weather, I had trouble with the engine overheating, not to mention my own discomfort spending such long hours in a hot bubble. Fortunately, by the time I reached North Dakota the temperature outside had lowered to a degree that both the helicopter and I could handle.

In North Dakota, I turned west and flew through Montana on my way to Cut Bank. I was making good progress when all of a sudden, flying over the small town of Shelby, about 40 miles south of the Canadian border, I experienced my first engine failure.

I had a tremendous stroke of luck on this one. When the engine failed, I was directly over Shelby's little airport. The first indication that I had trouble was when I lost all my oil pressure. There was nothing to do but shut the engine down and put the helicopter on the ground, which is really not as serious of a maneuver as I thought it was the first time I had to do it in a helicopter. Once I got the aircraft on the ground, I discovered that a part had broken loose on one of the rocker arms that rotate the valves, knocking a hole in the rocker arm cover and leaking out my oil. The rear section of the helicopter looked like it had been dipped in engine oil—it was completely covered. I was horrified when I saw what had happened, but a nice gentleman working at the airport managed to get a mechanic out to help me. It did not take the mechanic long to determine what had caused the problem and make the repairs, and by the end of the day he said my helicopter was in good shape.

I flew to Cut Bank and spent the night in town. The next morning, I departed again and entered Canada at Sweetgrass, a small town on the U.S.-Canadian border. I landed at Sweetgrass to check in at customs and then I flew past Lethbridge and Calgary. At Red Deer, a small town between Calgary and Edmonton, I cut northwest and intercepted the Alcan Highway. From there on, I followed the Alcan Highway up through Fort St. John, Fort Nelson, Watson Lake, White Horse, Teslin, Burwash, and then Northway where I checked in to customs again to enter back into the U.S. at the Canadian-Alaskan border.

My cruising speed was about 100 MPH. Sometimes I could reach slightly higher speeds with a tailwind, but of course, the reverse was true when I had a headwind. In order for me to be able to make this extended trip in a helicopter, an aircraft with a relatively short fuel range, I installed a ferry tank in my Bell 47J2A. A ferry tank is an auxiliary fuel tank made to fit underneath the rear seat of a helicopter so that it sits at the center of gravity and does not affect the flight characteristics. My ferry tank held 44 additional gallons of fuel, and combined with my main tanks, I was able to make it to all points along my route where I had planned to stop and refuel. Most of the legs of my journey were easily within range of my next fuel station, but I had to make short stops between stations because I could not transfer the fuel from the ferry tank to the main tanks during flight. After about 2.5 hours on the main tanks I had to land and make the switch manually. This was always a good excuse to take a break from flying, and when I could, I would pick out a really pretty spot, sometimes along a river or a creek, and a few times out on the prairie, as I flew through the northern United States. With a hand-cranked pump, I would transfer the fuel out of the auxiliary tank into the mains, rest for a few minutes, and then get back in the helicopter and continue on my way. These stops broke up the long trip and made it more enjoyable.

Prospecting trip. Note the shovel attached to the skids.

I was really lucky weather-wise on this seven-day journey. There were a few light showers along the way, but no real storms or heavy rains. When faced with rain in a helicopter, you can normally slow down and work your way through it, or just ground the aircraft and wait it out. Still, the rain can be a little bit nerve-wracking because it has a tendency to stick on the helicopter bubble and does not roll off like it does on the windshield of an airplane. Visibility can drop to practically zero, particularly if it is just a light rain. In my Bell 47J2A I could lean out the window and look over the side of the bubble, but it was not the best way to fly.

Perhaps the biggest challenge on this flight to Alaska was staying awake! Although I was enchanted by the natural landscapes and wildlife that I witnessed along the way, the continuous drone of that engine would nearly lull me to sleep. With someone to talk to I might have stayed more alert, but with all my prospecting equipment and survival gear, it was too crowded for anyone to ride along with me so I made the journey alone.

When I finally made it to Anchorage I decided to look for a business partner who had gold prospects that he could not get to by car or foot. I would make a deal with this prospector to fly him to his sites in my helicopter and we would prospect from the air. I ran an ad in the Anchorage newspaper and got *boocoos* of replies, but I took a liking to a man named Earl Foster. In addition to being a prospector he was also a gemologist, an expert on gems and assembling jewelry. Earl had worked a government job a few years earlier surveying remote areas of Alaska. On his surveying trips, he went out on his own to sites along creeks that he thought were promising prospecting sites and panned for gold. Any place he found color he recorded in his journal to return to at a later date. The only problem was that he could not get back to these sites by himself. He had flown into these areas on government helicopters and needed to find a way to get back to them on his own.

Earl and I met up and we prepared ourselves for a season of prospecting. The first place we went was in western Alaska near McGrath on Granite Mountain. We found color in the creek just like he had before, but no nuggets. It looked like it would be difficult to set up a placer operation at this site so we decided to move on to another location.

Panning for gold.

We flew to a promising site on a mountain about 80 miles north of Mount McKinley. The site was close to a small community called Colorado Station on a very pretty lake, but like the previous site, it was not good enough to strike out with our equipment.

We then moved about 100 miles east to a canyon where there was already a big mining operation in place. We could see the sluicing apparatus and mining equipment from the air. Earl had checked the mineral records and found a site near this mining operation that had not been claimed yet, so we landed and spent another day prospecting. We moved up and down the creek along the side of the mountain and found all sorts of outcroppings of minerals, and we knew gold had already been found only a mile down the creek. We went and visited with the other miners and they were friendly with us once they realized we were not trying to jump their claim. They showed us some gold nuggets they had recovered and Earl and I were very encouraged. We marked this site as number one on our list.

Before we made our final decision, Earl suggested we visit a friend of his who lived in the Yukon Territory and ran a successful mining operation on Squaw Creek.

"I'm ready!" I told him.

Earl and I drove to Haines Junction in the Yukon Territory and I was introduced to Heinz Eckervogt at his home on Dezadeash Lake, located 30 miles south of town. Heinz was an immigrant from Germany who had homesteaded in the North Country. Heinz was a personable fellow and he showed Earl and me a jar of nuggets he had acquired mining, some of them weighing as much as an ounce—that is some kind of good nugget! I could already feel the gold fever growing stronger. Heinz mined on Squaw Creek, a placer gold mine in southwest Yukon Territory near the Tatshenshini River, one of the wildest rivers in North America. Averaging 200 feet wide, it was too deep to ford except in early spring and late fall. The river ran swiftly and deeply throughout the summer. The Tatshenshini was a popular river for rafters, and in time the rafters would be instrumental in stopping all mining in the area. I often met rafting groups preparing to head out, and sometimes they looked down their noses at us—they had no use for miners. Still, I would have loved to take a rafting trip with them.

After meeting Heinz I went to the local library to read up on the history of Squaw Creek. The creek got its name from the Native American Squaws who first found gold in the area. They found some nuggets after trapping for animals in the springtime. As the waters came rushing down the creek, gold nuggets appeared in the exposed gravel and they used them for trade. It had been called Squaw Creek ever since.

The creek had only been pan-mined since the late 1920s, thus only the surface gold had been recovered. We were interested in going down to bedrock. Using heavy equipment, we could do in an hour what it took a miner a week to do 50 years earlier, and we could dig down to the gold that they were unable to recover by panning. Earlier miners had only hand tools to work with and it was nearly impossible to reach the bedrock below. Many claims on

Squaw Creek had been worked very successfully by panning years earlier, but I believed they could be successful again if worked with modern equipment, uncovering even more coarse gold.

Heinz had several claims on Squaw Creek and offered to lease one of them to us for 10% of any gold we recovered. Earl and I snapped up the offer right away and Heinz drew up a lease. We signed and then returned to Anchorage.

Earl had another friend named Ed Spencer who he had done some prospecting with in the past. Ed was an adventurous character too and he wanted to join us in our gold mining venture, so the three of us formed a partnership.

Later that summer, my son Jay and his friend John drove up to Alaska from Austin to visit me on a prospecting trip in the western part of the Yukon Territory. Jay and John drove up in my little Subaru Brat carrying equipment and supplies. Our first destination was near a beautiful alpine lake nestled between two mountain peaks in the Noisy Range. We were a little over 4,000 feet in elevation in a huge valley surrounded by breathtaking mountain ranges that looked like giant mounds of chocolate ice cream with marshmallow streaks running down the sides. The snow had not yet completely melted.

I am sure I disturbed the wildlife a little when I landed the helicopter, but they got used to me. A bird kept squawking at me that really did not like my presence, but on the other side of the lake, a huge bull moose only curiously looked up at me. It did not seem too worried that I had arrived.

Jay, John, and I were exploring a new area not far from Kluane National Park in Canada and Saint Elias Park in Alaska. Both of these parks had been declared international reserves. We were prospecting just above the confluence of the Tatshenshini River and Low Fog Creek. I took Jay and John about eight miles up Low Fog Creek and pointed out various spots that looked encouraging to prospect for gold. The boys were very excited and optimistic. Jay just *knew* we would find a creek full of gold; it was like being a kid again on an Easter egg hunt. I told Jay that anything was possible but that mostly he should be out there for the fun, recreation, and excitement of prospecting.

The system I taught the boys had worked well for me in the past and Jay and John picked it up quickly. In the bottom and sides of a 5-gallon plastic pale I drilled quarter-inch holes to create a sieve. We dug into the bank of the creek trying to locate a spot where bedrock was exposed and shoveled about ten mounds of sample dirt into the pale. Then, we took the pale into the creek, immersed it about a foot deep in water, and shook it vigorously over our pan. This mixed up all the material and caused the finer concentrate—hopefully with some gold in it—to settle in the pan. We then washed the material in the pan and looked for any signs of color, flakes of gold, or larger nuggets. The beauty of this process is that we could do in five minutes what old-time prospectors would have taken two or three hours to do in the past, and we got a much better sample at a given spot along the river. If we did not find any pay dirt in a hole, we just moved elsewhere on the creek and dug another. It was a process of repetition.

Jay and I did a lot of exploring on this prospecting trip. I believe we found some of the most amazing sites in the North Country because we were able to fly through it in a helicopter. Some of the areas we explored were completely inaccessible with anything but a helicopter—even by foot! The undergrowth and brush were so thick that we literally had to cut our way through it, and there were clouds of mosquitoes and other small bugs that could drive a man insane. We were using what seemed like a gallon of insect repellent a day, smearing it all over our bodies and our clothes. Even then, the bugs still buzzed around us nonstop, but eventually we got used to it.

The country we were traversing was completely isolated and remote, unless we judged by the bear population. I have never seen so many bears in one place; they seemed to be everywhere. I counted between 15 and 20 a day. These bears behaved as though they had

My son Jay performing a pan test.

never seen a human being before, and most of them did not get skittish and run away like other bears I had witnessed in the wild. Some would look at us curiously, catch our scent, and realize we were unfamiliar creatures, then slowly scatter off. The bears gave us no trouble, and they did not bother our camp.

One morning Jay woke up before I did and crawled outside the tent, but he immediately turned around and came back in.

"There's a bear out here," he said.

I thought he meant that there was a bear down the hillside. Our tent was pitched on a high point above the creeks so that we had a good view of our surroundings and we could watch for animals in case any should bother us. Half awake, I stuck my head out of the tent to see where Jay was pointing, but he did not have to point. The big old bear was standing in our camp about 20 yards away, just looking me in the eye. The bear stood there for a minute sniffing the air and then got down on all fours, walked around, stood back up again, sniffed the air some more, and then calmly trotted away.

If there had been people in this area before us, they left nothing behind because we found no signs or remnants of human activity. It is hard to describe the complete, utter awayness and aloneness that you feel in an area like this when you realize that you are somewhere that only a few people, if any, have ever been before. I always got a strange feeling about it, but I loved it, and apparently some of this must have rubbed off on Jay because he seemed to be in hog heaven out there as well.

Jay and John spent two days working their way down Low Fog Creek while I waited for them to cut across the ridge and meet me at the lake farther down the mountain. While they were gone, I caught up on some fishing and relaxation time. I could see the fish in the lake from the air as I hovered over the water and I was almost certain these fish were rainbow trout.

I pitched a pup tent and caught some fish for a nice supper. I really had to watch myself because the catch was so good up north it could ruin a man! Those lakes really spoiled me—the fish would grab at anything thrown into the lake. I caught about 15 beautiful rainbow trout but I released all but one, which I ate for dinner. The rainbow trout in this lake averaged about 18 inches in length. In other areas of the country I saw rainbow trout as long as 36 inches, and I guessed that the fish in this lake were limited in size due to competition for food. I was curious what the fish actually ate. Sometimes I saw them slurp up bugs off the surface of the water then disappear in a swirling splash, but there certainly were not enough bugs on the lake to feed the entire fish population. To solve the mystery, I checked my dinner trout's stomach when I cleaned it and saw something I had never seen before. The fish was full of small, black snails about an eighth of an inch in diameter.

After my dinner I sat at my campsite by the lake and enjoyed the view. The bull moose was still grazing across the lake, completely undisturbed, and the bird whose alarms I had set off had finally quit squawking. He must have decided I was not going to hurt him. I did feel just a little guilty coming into such a remote, undisturbed area. The lake was uncharted on the maps, and I am not sure a helicopter had ever landed in the vicinity. I saw no signs of campfires, shelters, or any human disturbance to the landscape. The lake was only about 300 meters long and about a third as wide, and at this elevation it was not a good spot to land a float plane. The only way a human could get to the lake was by helicopter or by foot. I marked the location of the lake on my own map and hoped to return one day to wet my hook again.

Jay and John eventually drove back to Texas, and that was the last time my son saw me before my helicopter crash in British Columbia. By September, Earl, Ed, and I had spent the summer prospecting, but it was too late in the season to begin our mining operation, so the three of us made arrangements to return the following year and start mining on Squaw Creek. We had done just about everything we could to prepare for next year's gold mining season, so on September 1, 1979, I loaded up my helicopter and prepared for the arduous flight back home to Austin. Little did I know just how arduous it would be.

Returning to the Scene of the Crash

On September 2nd, 1979, I crashed my helicopter flying home from my prospecting trip to the North Country. It was a traumatic experience, but it did not change my love and fascination of Alaska and the Yukon Territory. A few months after recovering from my injuries, I wanted to return to the crash site in order to see it from a better position than I was in while it was all happening. On a trip back from Alaska with Tracy and Greg, I went to Fort St. John to find a helicopter pilot to fly me to the crash site. There were several helicopter operations at the Fort St. John airport so I just picked one at random, walked inside, and introduced

Recovering the door I used to make a shelter.

myself to a man named Trevor Grimshaw. I told him what I wanted to do.

"I've got the coordinates and everything on the map," I told him. "I can tell you exactly where it is."

"Oh, you don't have to do that," Trevor said. "I was involved in the search and rescue for you. I know exactly where it is."

I thought that was amazing. At one time while I was waiting to be rescued, I recall hearing a helicopter flying two or three miles away from me—who knows, it may have been Trevor.

We flew around the site and I took some pictures from the air, but there was hardly a place to land a helicopter. The search and rescue team had not even landed to pick me up during my rescue, they just hovered over the site, lowered a line, and brought me up in a basket. However, we were about 100 yards from a small lake, so Trevor hovered around the edge of it and spotted a couple of sunken logs in some water about a foot deep that he thought he could land on.

"I am going to try to set us down on those logs," Trevor said. "We are going to have to wade through the water to get out but that is about the only place I can land."

Trevor got right down over the water and I stuck my head out the window—I wanted to be sure he was right about those logs because if he was wrong we might just sink. Trevor was a good pilot, though, and he knew what he was doing. He slowly set the helicopter down and the skids went under the water, but then I heard a thump and we stopped on top of two logs. Trevor sat there for a few minutes without cutting the power, shifting the helicopter around to see if it would settle, but the logs were solid and we did not sink. Then, he shut down the helicopter and we climbed out. Boy, the water was cold! Of course, I should have known what to expect because I had lain in it for two weeks. We had to wade about 50 yards to the shore in order to get out of the water, and then we walked up the cut to the wreckage. I took more pictures, including one of the little shelter I built using the helicopter door that had flown off of the aircraft before it burned.

I retrieved something that I only then recalled hiding away while I was stranded. In Canada you were not allowed to carry a handgun, but I always kept a .357 Magnum pistol with me underneath the seat when I flew. After my crash, when I was recovering items from the wreckage, I looked around and found the burned up pistol and rifle. They were ruined, but at the time of my crash I thought, *my god, if the Canadian authorities find out that I had this gun in the helicopter, I am going to be in trouble.* Of all the things to worry about! There was a little pool of water close to where I crashed and I took that pistol, pushed it down under the water, and left it. Now, I remembered what I had done and had no problem finding it in the mud. When I started rooting around in the water, Trevor asked me what the heck I was doing.

"I hid something here," I said. When I dug the gun out from the mud six-inches deep, Trevor laughed.

"Well, we don't have a permit for that. I hope you don't get me in trouble back at the airport!" he joked.

I still have that burned .357 Magnum today, as well as my 30.6 caliber rifle that I recovered from the wreckage. From the crash site, I also took with me the tail rotor and tail rotor drum assembly because Trevor had enough room in the baggage compartment of his helicopter. I wanted to have the parts analyzed to find out exactly why the helicopter had gone down. When I got back to Austin, I took the parts to a professor at the University of Texas named Mel Wilcox. He took x-rays of the metal and found that part of the tail rotor gear box was not an official Bell helicopter part—it was a phony bootleg part that someone had installed, and it failed. So that mystery was solved.

After the trip back to the crash site, I got to be really good friends with Trevor. On one of my trips north he invited me to stay at his house. I spent the night and visited with him, his wife, and two boys. Trevor's family also visited me in Austin. It is strange the ways we meet new people and become friends. That helicopter crash disaster led to another friendly family for me to know in Canada.

The First Mining Season

In March of the following year, 1980, it came time to start my first gold mining season on Squaw Creek. I knew better now than to make the journey north in the helicopter, so instead, I loaded my new Bell 47 G4 helicopter onto a trailer that I pulled behind my truck. I removed the blades, put them in a box beneath the underbelly of the helicopter, and strapped everything down to the trailer. Then, I pulled the trailer carrying my helicopter all the way to Seattle, Washington. Despite the serious injuries I had sustained in my helicopter crash, and the difficult recovery period I had endured, I felt strong enough to carry on with my mining plans. I enjoyed driving up and down the Alcan Highway and I was amazed at how friendly the people were at every place I stopped. I became acquainted with a few people whom I always made sure to visit whenever I passed through the area, and they always invited me to stay a night in their home. To this day, I still have friends living along the Alcan Highway who would always open their doors to me. In fact, they would be offended if I did not stay the night with them on my travels.

One of my neighbors had convinced me to let him ride along on the drive to Alaska. He was not going to mine, he was just along for the ride. This was my first experience driving all the way to the North Country—I had always flown in the past. I saw an awful lot of scenery flying in my airplane, and even more in the helicopter, but travelling on the ground I could stop and explore whenever I wanted. Once we reached Seattle I went to the ferry port and reserved a space for my truck and trailer. The ferry would be departing for Alaska in two days. I spent part of that time visiting a friend of mine named Andy Andersen who lived across the bay at Sequim, Washington. Andy was a retired bush pilot from Alaska and I had flown with him many times.

The ferry trip took three days and I really enjoyed it. The trip along the coast was beautiful, and I recommend it to anyone touring the area.

When we finally reached our destination, my neighbor continued on to Anchorage while I went to Heinz Eckervogt's house on Dezadeash Lake in the Yukon. Heinz and his wife Katy welcomed me with open arms and gave me my own room to sleep in. They told me I could stay at their house anytime I was in Haines Junction, and if I had a friend with me he would be welcome too.

I spent about six weeks getting ready for the gold mining season. I had a bunch of equipment but I had never sluiced for gold before, so I relied heavily on advice I got from Heinz. Earl Foster had never done any real sluicing either, so we had a lot to do to prepare ourselves. We acquired an old dump truck bed to use for our dump box and welded a trough-like apparatus out of steel for our sluice box. Fortunately, welding was a hobby of mine and I was able to build the apparatus myself. I also forged riffles out of angle iron that I bent at a slight angle and then welded together. Water would run over the riffles and any gold—which is 19 times heaver than country sand—would fall into the spaces between the angle irons.

With Heinz' help, Earl and I also rigged up a huge 25-foot four-wheel trailer that had been abandoned in the area many years earlier. All we had to do was fix the tires, put some sides on the trailer, and load up our gear. We learned to make do with whatever we could get our hands on while working on Squaw Creek.

Finally, Earl, Ed, Heinz and I all went in as partners and bought a D6 Caterpillar bulldozer. We rigged up a trailer hook on the back of the Cat and used the bulldozer to drag the big trailer 12 miles up the mountain to our claim on Squaw Creek. We also obtained a 2000-gallon fuel tank that could fit on our trailer, filled it up with diesel, and carried it with us to the creek. Finally, we brought in

The aluminum boat crossing the Tatshenshini river on a cable.

plywood and lumber to build a cabin shelter. Heinz and his two sons Thomas and Martin, as well as one other miner, were also getting ready to work a claim a few miles above us on the creek, so we all rode in together. It is best to stick together when doing something like this because all sorts of things can, and *did*, go wrong.

Just getting to Squaw Creek was an adventure in itself. The creek was located 20 miles west of the Haines Highway at an elevation of about 5,000 feet. With all our equipment in tow we had to cross the Tatshenshini, a rough river to negotiate. The water could rise very high, and many vehicles and lives have been lost attempting to cross the river. The unlucky ones would find themselves out in the middle of the river stuck in deep, swift water and would be washed away. Fed by glaciers, the river was still frozen up with a layer of ice from the previous winter, but we had no problem breaking through the ice with our heavy equipment and we crossed the river.

When we got to the other side, I noticed an aluminum boat just up the river that was docked on the bank and attached to a steel cable that stretched 150 feet across the Tatshenshini. The cable was anchored on each side of the river to two cottonwood trees. By tilting the bow of the boat into the current, the water would pull the boat and its passengers safely across the river.

"I'll have to remember that boat," I said to Heinz.

"We will be using it a lot this summer," he answered.

The Tatshenshini River flows through the Noisy Mountain Range and joins with the Alsek River. It then flows out from the Alaskan coast at Dry Bay about 45 miles south of Yakutat. Not far from where we crossed the Tatshenshini, at a spot where the old-time miners used to cross the river, sat the old Dalton Post. Jack Dalton, founder of Dalton Post, was somewhat of a desperado in the late 1800s, and the Dalton camp was built on an area of level ground a couple hundred yards from the river. The camp consisted of five cabins, two of which were almost completely intact when I explored the site. The rest were rotted and falling apart.

Jack Dalton had been a notorious ruffian in his day. He set up this camp and, according to the tale, charged people to pass through on the trail he established. The story goes that he bought the trail from the Indians and charged everyone who wished to pass through to and from Haines. It is also purported that one man who refused to pay Dalton's fee was hung beside the trail to warn others of the consequence of disobeying. Jack Dalton was making good money and did well enough to establish a small community, but when the Canadian government found out about Dalton's dealings, the Royal Canadian Mounted Police built a cabin next-door to the post and stationed a man to subdue any squabbles between Jack Dalton and the people he was extorting money from.

According to an old miner in the area named Charlie Ross, the story about Jack Dalton was true. According to Charlie, some shreds of rope were still present at the site many years later, but Jack Dalton left the country and fled to South America. Heinz had even talked to Jack Dalton's son who visited the area, and he also insisted that the stories were true.

After our crew crossed the Tatshenshini I spotted what I guessed was our trail to Squaw Creek, but this "trail" would require a pretty rugged four-wheel drive vehicle to traverse it. It took us three days on the trail to travel the 12 miles up the canyon to the creek. We left the bulldozer running at night because the weather was still so cold that we knew it would not start up again the next morning if we shut it down.

The trials and tribulations that a man goes through when he catches the gold fever are something else. We were trekking up a canyon to reach our gold claim on Squaw Creek, and the terrain we were negotiating was nearly impossible to traverse. We had to cross two large creeks and a steep mountain on a makeshift trail hacked out of the side of the mountain, a mile-long stretch of which was along the edge of a cliff. Normal men—those without the fever—probably would not think of doing something like this. There we were, dragging heavy equipment through a wilderness canyon, with the possibility at any minute of losing everything by falling over the side of the cliff. But the lure of gold is strong.

Even when I was in grade school on the mountain in Arkansas I read books about prospectors mining for gold in the north, inspiring dreams of taking my own adventures one day, travelling cross-country on a sled with a team of dogs, hollering "Mush!" I never thought I would actually end up seeing these dreams become a reality, although in truth, it is more romantic to dream about gold mining than it is to actually do it. Traversing the terrain of the North Country is extremely challenging.

We crossed the first stream and inched our way up the mountain, pulling the big trailer and the D6 Caterpillar behind us. It was a bad place to run into a frost boil, but that is what we did. A frost boil is an area where warm water seeps out of the ground, and although it may freeze over on top, it is soft like quicksand underneath. The D6 Caterpillar got stuck in a frost boil and was buried all the way to the top of the tracks. The man driving the caterpillar was wiggling around, moving it back and forth, and digging it deeper into the ground.

"Stop!" I hollered. "You're just making it worse! Let's figure this out."

Heinz looked the situation over and suggested that we take the blade, operated by hydraulics, and push it as far under the Cat as we could to raise the tracks and then shove some logs underneath. We cut up some logs with a chainsaw, lifted the tracks with the blade, and shoved the logs beneath them to give the 'dozer some traction. For the next two hours we crisscrossed logs along the path about 100 feet ahead of us, building a bridge over the mud. Everybody pitched in and helped, otherwise we would have lost the bulldozer.

Once our log path was placed we fired up the bulldozer—it is a wonder that the engine had not been sucked full of mud. Right away it was apparent that we were going to have trouble with the fan blade because it was jammed with mud, so one of the guys got in there and just removed the whole fan belt altogether. Once again, we fired the 'dozer up and, lo and behold, our log bridge worked! The Cat crawled up those logs and made it to solid ground.

After this ordeal travelling up the trail to Squaw Creek, I began thinking that it would be a good idea to come in with a helicopter and search for a new trail that was not pervaded by frost boils. Sometime later, I took a roll of binder twine, picked out a route with Heinz that we decided was a good detour from the current path, and strung the string out behind us as I hovered over the trees with my helicopter, marking a new trail from the air. We then followed the string by foot, cleared a new path, and built a road.

Mining on Squaw Creek with Earl and Ed was a learning process for all of us. Earl had prospected before, but he had never sluiced and did not know how to run the equipment. Ed had worked with heavy machinery in the past but had never done any mining, either. Of course, it was my first time too, so we really depended on Heinz to guide us through the process. Fortunately, we were all fast learners and it was not long before we hit pay dirt.

Earl was not the type of guy that could do hard labor everyday so Ed and I did all the mining on Squaw Creek while Earl took care of everything else. There was assessment work to do and permits to acquire, and Earl was pretty good at managing those tasks. Before we got too far into the season we had to build a cabin shelter because it got mighty cold in the canyon at night. We had brought in plywood and lumber on our trailer, and as soon as we finished building our sluice box we went to work on the cabin. Our cabin was small, only 8 x 12 feet, but we added a lean-to on one side that jutted out another 8 feet where we built our bunks.

Of the three of us, I happened to be the only one who knew how to cook, so right away I was appointed the cabin chef. Normally I enjoyed cooking on my camping trips, but it got to be quite a drag preparing meals three times a day on top of all our heavy mining. Eventually, we decided that we would eat only two meals a day to save time. Every morning we woke up early, worked for a couple hours, stopped for breakfast, and then went back and worked some more. Between 1:00 and 2:00 p.m. we ate again and then worked late into the night. Sometimes we even skipped the noon meal, but we lived by a pretty rigid schedule. We were all so anxious to sluice that none of us could stay away from the mining equipment. The enthusiasm we had imagining gold underground kept us going and we worked until our bones ached.

In our second or third week at Squaw Creek we had our first encounter with a bear. Apparently, we had not done a good enough job keeping the smell of our foodstuffs from the animals. We built the cabin a couple of feet off the ground to have space beneath our shelter to store tools and other equipment. By mistake, we had also stored some of our food there, including several dozen cartons of eggs and a slab of bacon, and it was not long before a bear came and found it. We were awakened in the middle of the night by a racket that sounded like someone tearing off the side of our cabin. Half-asleep, I did not have the slightest idea what was going on, but Ed figured it out right away.

"I think we have a bear after our food," he said.

Ed grabbed his shotgun, threw open the door, and sure enough a bear's butt was sticking out from underneath the cabin. He had the box of eggs out in front of him, eating what he could and breaking all the rest. Ed fired the shotgun into the air and scared the bear off. We learned a good lesson that night about protecting our food from the animals. Protecting our food meant protecting ourselves.

We had a gas-fired refrigerator with us that we had not hooked up yet, but after our bear visit, we did not put off setting it up any longer. I was amazed that a refrigerator could burn propane and turn heat into a freezer. Everything that was not dried or canned we stacked in the refrigerator and we had no more problems with animals getting into our food stash.

Mining for gold is a multi-step process. First, with the front-end loader we gathered huge piles of gravel, rock, and sand and dropped them into the dump box to be sluiced. Then, we dammed up the creek so that water would run through a pipe that we had fed from the creek to the dump box. We put a wooden gate at the end of this pipe so that we could shut off the water as needed. The water then broke apart the dirt and gravel and washed it down another tube connecting the dump box to the sluice box, a welded structure about 40 feet in length. The material flowed through the riffles and settled into Astroturf carpet that lined the bottom of the sluice box. The carpet caught almost all the fine gold and black sand before it flowed out the end of the sluice box and back into the creek.

After two or three days of sluicing we shut off the running water, removed the riffles from the sluice box, and washed the carpet in a huge, oblong-shaped tub about half-full of water. We flipped the sections of Astroturf upside-down, shook them back and forth in the tub, and washed out any nuggets or fine gold that had accumulated in the carpet. We acquired more black sand than anything else, but we also recovered a fair share of fine gold and, periodically, some nuggets.

If you are going to mine for gold in the North Country, it is important to know that perhaps one person out of a hundred will discover a paying gold claim—one that will yield real returns. It is certainly a lot of fun going out and prospecting, and I did hope that my efforts would pay off, but I mostly mined for the sheer enjoyment of being out in the wilderness. I loved working hard in the outdoors, and to have a purpose and a goal like I did only increased my enjoyment. While I did not have any illusions about finding buckets of gold, I also thought, *who knows?* Other people had succeeded, and everyone believed that there was more gold in the ground yet to be found than had ever been discovered.

There were two types of mining operations in the North Country: the first was what you would call the "mom and pop" operation, or the family operation, in which individuals went out to their claims for two or three months out of the warm summer season, worked the land by hand, and made fair money. There were many mom and pop operations all over the state. These were folks like me who loved the wilderness and living off the land. They thoroughly enjoyed the experience and probably covered their expenses, even making some extra money on top. It's just great recreation. I know I certainly loved it. The other type of operation was the big mining company. These corporations had every conceivable piece of equipment you could imagine. They were serious miners and they made serious money. A lot of people get anxious and stand on their heads when they hear about the big mining companies and their machinery because they think they are destroying the natural environment, but I never saw any place up north where the big mining companies left the nature looking worse than it was when they started. They took care of their surroundings. It is true, they did muddy up the stream while they worked it with a dredge, but it cleared up quickly.

I often met with miners who worked for these large operations and they really were proud of their country. These fellows were very conscientious of their surroundings and I appreciated them for that because I loved the North Country and wanted to enjoy it too. Those people were out gathering the natural resources that our country needed and it provided many hard working men and women with jobs that they might not have had otherwise. To those who protested I always said, "The more power to them, let them go."

Equipment Repair

Working a placer mine as we were on Squaw Creek, the only way we could even hope to have some success was by using heavy equipment. We were working in grit and sand—abrasive conditions all day long—and so we used a bulldozer and blade to stock pile materials from the cuts that we selected to sluice. We also used a front-end loader and the D6 Caterpillar bulldozer to aid us in the process. With the bulldozer we dug out and piled up the dirt from the creekbed, and with the front-end loader we scooped up that dirt two or three yards at a time and dumped it into our sluice box. We then sluiced the dirt for gold.

Under the rough conditions that we had to work, our equipment was breaking all the time. Fortunately, I could make most of the repairs by welding. I was just a "Shade Tree" welder, as they called them, when I first started mining, but before long I got to be pretty skilled with the torch. We had a gasoline-powered welder, and occasionally *it* would break down as well. We were usually able to make any equipment repairs ourselves onsite, but this was not always the case.

On one particular occasion I was operating the 'dozer and pushing up a pile of dirt as big as my house. I was really cutting into the ground. If you asked me to explain the difference between good ground and bad ground, about the only thing I could say is that good ground has gold in it! The vein I was working had been yielding some pay dirt and I was trying to dig deep enough to get in a good week of sluicing. Then, all of a sudden, the Caterpillar's right track became slack and halfway slid off the machine.

After examining the track I realized that the problem was worse than I originally thought: the idler gear had broken. We were working with used equipment that we had bought at an auction, and we had used our best judgment in choosing good machinery, but it was difficult to judge the condition of the underpinning and rollers that the tracks rode on beneath the bulldozer. Apparently, ours was not the sturdiest.

Removing the broken idler gear for repair.

On either side of the bulldozer is an idler gear, which is a large, solid-steel wheel anywhere from 20 inches to 2 feet in diameter and 5–6 inches thick. Axel and all, our wheel weighed nearly 200 pounds. The track rests upon the idler gear, allowing it to roll back and forth while in operation, but the wet, gritty sand wears down the rails on the bottom of the track, which in turn puts pressure on the idler gear as it rolls back and forth. Eventually, the idler gear becomes so worn down that the wheel splits in half, and that is exactly what happened to ours. Fortunately, I was on level ground when the wheel broke and knew how to remove the idler gear from the bulldozer. I located the master link pin in the track and drove it out using a sledgehammer and another pin of a slightly smaller diameter.

Ed and I managed to get the wheel off the track and we saw that it had split two-thirds of the way around. There was just a thin layer of metal holding the wheel together. If it had been just a small crack I could have welded a bead back and forth across the crack with hard-surface welding rods and repaired the break. In this case, the wheel was broken beyond any repair I could make in the field, so we decided that I would have to take it into Whitehorse.

Whitehorse was a little over 200 miles away. I had my Bell 47 G4 to make the trip, but I had to figure out how to safely haul that big wheel off of the mountain, down through the canyon, and on over the Heinz' house where I had a pickup truck waiting. I did not think the weight of the wheel would be a problem—it would be just like a 250-pound passenger—but it was so unwieldy and oddly shaped that I needed to secure it to the helicopter in such a way that it would not shift around during flight.

Ed cut down a couple of small spruce trees about 4 inches in diameter and made two poles about 7 feet long. I laid the two poles crosswise a foot apart on the helicopter skids and secured them to the helicopter by triple-wrapping them with the heavy-stranded wire that we had used to rig up the sluice box. Ed and I then managed to roll the wheel down to the helicopter and place it on the logs with the axel sticking up vertically directly under the main rotor shaft and engine so that it would sit at the center of gravity. Using more of the strong wire, we secured the wheel to the log poles in four different places so that it would not budge. If it shifted out of balance during flight I could easily lose the helicopter. I checked and then double-checked the wheel, finally deciding that it was safe to go ahead. Our mining operation would be shut down until I got the machinery fixed, but fortunately the stock piles of material that I had been working on were large enough to keep Ed busy for a couple of days while I was in town.

Early the next morning I woke up, fired up the helicopter, and practiced lifting the aircraft off the ground. Ed watched closely as I took off two or three times to make sure the wheel did not shift. At an elevation of 4,000 feet the helicopter was a little sluggish coming off the ground—the higher the altitude, the less lift you have in a helicopter—but I was able to get it in the air. Since I would be descending in altitude to the base of the mountain I felt that conditions would only get better as I went. Ed and I put together a list of groceries and other items we needed from town, and then I fired the helicopter back up, told Ed I would see him in a couple days, and took off.

I followed the creek down the canyon, but as I neared the Tatshenshini River, I felt something bothering me. The helicopter was not performing well and was requiring more and more right cyclic stick to keep it level. I sensed that the load had shifted so I leaned over as far as I could to try and look underneath the helicopter, but I just couldn't see anything. I spotted an open area on the riverbank below me so I landed the helicopter. It was a good thing I did; one of the logs had shifted and the idler gear had moved nearly a foot forward. This slight shift threw the helicopter out of balance, pushing the center of gravity forward and to the right. I had difficulty holding up the nose of the helicopter as I landed and I had to pull the cyclic stick all the way back in my lap to keep it level.

I got out of the helicopter to move the log and wheel back in place when I realized I had made another mistake: I had not brought the roll of wire with me. Fortunately, I remembered that about a quarter-mile from where I landed the helicopter a miner named Doug Buset, who had a claim above mine on the creek, had parked his truck. I walked down to the truck to see if there was anything in it I could use. I guess all miners must carry the same stuff because he had a roll of the same kind of wire lying in the back of his truck. I grabbed the wire, returned to my helicopter, and laced the wheel back up using the wire cutters and heavy-duty pliers that I always carried with me on my flights.

Again, I practiced a few take-offs and the helicopter seemed to pick up without problem. By now, I was hovering in the bottom of the flood plain of the Tatshenshini River. I had to ascend about 1,000 feet to get out of this flood plain and continue on my course, so I knew as soon as I took off I was going to have to climb. This time, I had no trouble flying; I safely made it to Heinz and Katy's house and landed in their yard. Heinz came out to see what was going on and chuckled at the way I had rigged up that wheel.

Heinz helped me get the wheel off the helicopter and into the back of my truck. From there, it was about a 160-mile drive to Whitehorse. Heinz invited me to have dinner with his family and spend the night, but I was in too big of a hurry to get the wheel fixed.

"Thanks, Heinz," I answered, "but we are shut down until I get this thing fixed. I am going to drive on into town today."

Heinz asked me where I was taking the wheel to be fixed. I told him I was headed to a fellow named Jacobson in Whitehorse who owned a machine shop and whom I had visited several times for various equipment repairs in the past. Heinz knew Jacobson and agreed that he would certainly be able to do the job.

I took off in the pickup, stopping only in Haines Junction to eat a hamburger. It was nice to have a store-bought hamburger for a change. I arrived in Whitehorse late that afternoon and presented my problem to Mr. Jacobson. He told me that he normally had old idler gears lying around that I could exchange for my broken one, but he did not have one at that time. We called around to other heavy equipment dealers in town to try to locate an idler gear but we had no luck.

"We can rebuild your idler gear," Jacobson said, "but it is going to require six to eight hours of welding."

"Well, I've got to have it," I said. "And I've got to have it as soon as I can."

"I close at six. We can get a little done today and then I will get a man back over here in the morning."

"I just really need it now," I persisted. "Do you have a guy who would work late? I'm happy to pay overtime."

"If he does work, you *will* have to pay overtime because that is what he'll charge."

Jacobson had an employee named Ivan Igotsky who I had met once before. Everybody called him Iggy. I asked Iggy if he would be willing to work late that night to fix my idler gear. He agreed, and we decided that I would stay and work there with him.

At ten o'clock that night I said to Iggy, "I haven't eaten supper and I know you haven't either. Let's take a break and I'll buy your dinner." Iggy took me up on my offer, so we went down the road a couple of miles to a popular restaurant in town and arrived just before closing. We had a good meal and we each had a slice of cherry-rhubarb pie.

An hour later we returned to the shop.

"Iggy, how about letting me help you weld?" I asked. "I know you've got another welder lying around here and there's no one around to see us."

"I don't know," Iggy said. "I don't want to lose my job. You being a Yank, you can't work up here."

"Well, I'm not working for anybody, I'm working for myself!"

Iggy finally agreed to let me help him weld. We found another hood and stick welder and we both worked on the wheel from opposite sides. Repairing this wheel was no easy job. After putting the two sides together that had split apart we had to lace metal back and forth all the way around the wheel about a half-inch thick. Every once in a while we had to stop, rotate, and roll the wheel around. I tell you, my back was just killing me from leaning over that thing, but I sure was not about to complain to Iggy. I wanted to get the job done.

I checked my watch around 2:30 in the morning and realized we still had about a third of that wheel to go.

"Iggy, I just really have to have this thing finished by morning. I sure would appreciate it if you stayed a little longer. I'll pay you a bonus."

"Oh, you don't have to do that, I'll help you," Iggy said. He really was a nice guy. He understood my problem and was going to do everything he could to help me.

We finished repairing the wheel at 5:30 a.m. that morning. Boy, was I beat, and Iggy was beat too.

"I guess you're going to go home and get some sack time," I said.

"No, I have to get back to work in about thirty minutes," Iggy answered. "I'm going to put in another day of work."

I paid Iggy and prepared for the trip back. Before leaving Whitehorse I stopped at the grocery store, filled my bill of groceries, gassed up my truck, and took off down the highway. I drove back to Heinz' house on Dezadeash Lake and, fortunately, he was there to help me unload the wheel. Heinz admired the handiwork and I told him Iggy had made the repair.

"If Iggy did it, you know it's been done right," he said.

Heinz told me I was going to have to rig up the wheel in a different way for the trip back. He had some two-by-fours that he used to anchor the wheel. Heinz did most of the rigging, and I was depending on him because he really knew what he was doing.

"You better get out of here before an inspector comes," Heinz said. "What you are hauling is not a legal load."

"Yeah, I know. I should get going!" We went inside for a quick cup of coffee and Katy packed me a sack of sweet rolls to take back to my camp. Then I fired up the helicopter and took off for Squaw Creek.

As I approached the Tatshenshini River the clouds began to lower. I had a ceiling of about 3,000 feet and it was misting a light rain. I was a little concerned about this weather because I had to climb up to at least 4,000 feet to reach my claim and I did not know what I would run into along the way.

Squaw Creek runs down the canyon for several miles and then flows over a waterfall, dropping about a hundred feet. It then continues to follow the lay of the land and eventually flows into the Tatshenshini River. Rather than follow the trail to my cabin, I decided to fly over the creek because I knew there was a small bluff near the waterfall where I could land if I ran into any trouble. That is the good thing about flying a helicopter: if you get into a sticky situation you do not need a runway to land, but you do need a flat, open space, and there weren't too many of those around Squaw Creek.

I slowed down to a ground speed of about 60 MPH but when I came to the waterfall I could not see past the fog to the top of it. I hovered for a few minutes and thought, *I know what's above the waterfall, and there aren't any trees in the middle of this creek to get in my way.* So I went for it. Very slowly, I climbed straight up the face of the waterfall to the top of that cliff and then I continued to follow the creek. The ground fog covered everything and I could see only 50 yards ahead of me. Believe me, that is like flying in a milk bottle. It took me a good 30 minutes to move five miles up the creek, but I felt secure. I did not think I was stretching my luck *too* much, which I occasionally did.

Ed told me later that he heard me coming way before he ever saw me. I landed the helicopter in front of our little cabin and, boy, I was a beat bunny. I had really pushed myself working all night with Iggy to weld that wheel. I had been gone for two days now and Ed had already sluiced all the ground I had pushed up, so he was anxious to get the bulldozer reassembled.

"Ed, that's a two-man job, but I am so tired I can barely stand up," I said. "We're just going to have to put it off until tomorrow."

"That's okay," Ed said. "I've got a lot of fine gold that needs to be panned out and separated from the sand. I will spend the rest of the day doing that while you rest."

I lay down in my bunk and do not even remember my head hitting the pillow—I guess I was already fast asleep. I got a full night's rest and woke up the next morning to Ed frying bacon and eggs. As soon as we finished breakfast we went straight to work, halfway rolling and halfway carrying the wheel from the helicopter to the bulldozer.

"I see you've changed my mounting poles!" Ed said, noticing the change in the way the wheel was fastened to the undercarriage. I told him how I had nearly lost the idler gear down by the river and that Heinz had helped me fix the boards to better secure the wheel.

"Well, it looks secure all right!" Ed said.

Reinstalling the wheel on the bulldozer was the easy part. It was putting the track back on that proved to be extremely difficult, especially without the right equipment. The whole track probably weighed a couple thousand pounds and we had it folded back on each side of the idler gear. I had a come-along winch that I hooked to both the edge of the track and the stanchions that stood up around the seat of the bulldozer. I winched the track up to where it was just hanging over the wheel and then I repeated the process at the back of the track. Then, I hooked the winch to each end of the track and used it to tug and compress the track back over the wheel. Finally, after getting the holes in the link to match up, I had to drive the master pin back into the track.

We fiddled with that master pin for a few hours, stopping only for some coffee and Katy's sweet rolls. The pin did not slide in the hole easily; it was a tight-friction fit, and only with our 16-pound sledgehammer could we drive it back in. As I worked the winch, Ed pounded the master pin with the sledgehammer and eventually we were able to get it in place. To tighten the track around the wheel we pumped hydraulic oil with a grease gun into a cylinder beneath the track. With the help of a push rod, the grease expanded the track and tightened it to the required tension. Finally, we had the track snuggly back on the bulldozer. We started the machine and drove it around to make sure the rollers were functioning properly. Everything was working correctly, and we were ready to start mining again!

Squaw Creek Gold

A few days after the equipment repair Earl came to visit us. Earl was taking care of our business matters in town while Ed and I mined on Squaw Creek. In addition to keeping the books, Earl was researching a piece of equipment called a magnetometer that could locate deposits of black sand as deep as 20 feet below the ground. Black sand is magnetic and is a good indicator of gold in the ground. In fact, all of the fine gold that we had recovered so far had been sifted out of black sand. Earl managed to borrow a magnetometer to try out on our claim and when he showed up with this tool we all got excited.

We crisscrossed our claim with the magnetometer, mapping out the entire area and recording the readings. We were trying to locate an old stream bed where black sand—and hopefully gold—would have settled thousands of years earlier. On a big piece of plywood, we created a chart that mapped the areas which yielded the highest readings for black sand. When we took a step back, we could actually trace a diagonal line from one corner of the board to another that indicated heavy concentrations of black sand in a winding path. We thought we might have located the underground stream.

With the data provided by the magnetometer we immediately moved over to start a new cut into the ground. As we excavated a section of our claim, if we found any pay dirt we crisscrossed the section in order to figure out the direction of the gold vein and then we continued to dig along that path. After five days sluicing the ground from our new cut we recovered hardly any pay dirt after clean up. We got no nuggets and only a few small batches of fine gold, so we moved to another area on our chart that indicated heavy deposits of black sand and started another cut.

Mining is like a game of hide-and-seek; if you manage to locate a pay streak, you do your darndest to follow it. After three days on the second cut we stopped for cleanup and, lo and behold, we had a lot of fine gold and even a few rice-sized nuggets! We were very encouraged so we kept going in the direction of this cut and sluiced for another five days. By the end of the week it looked like we were still recovering fine gold, so we kept sluicing a little bit longer than we normally would between cleanups. On our next cleanup, we had nearly a tub full of black sand saturated with flecks of gold. We were all excited because we had never recovered so much gold before. We decided that the magnetometer *did* work and could lead us to pay dirt.

After we finished the cleanup we sifted the sand through a pan to separate it from any dirt and gravel. What is left after panning is a concentrated mixture of black sand and fine gold. We spread the material out on a board and let it dry out in the sun. Then, with a piece of silk, which at some other time had probably been somebody's petticoat, we rubbed a magnet through the concentrate, lifting out all the black sand from the gold, which is not magnetic. Repeating this process many times, we separated all the fine gold from the black sand. When we were done we had a pint-sized mayonnaise jar about half-full of fine, flour-like gold.

Fine gold is deceptively heavy. It looks like dust and is so fine that it almost floats on water, but when I picked up that mayonnaise jar it felt like it was nailed to the table. This had been one of our best recoveries yet and it encouraged us considerably. We ended up with nearly 51 ounces of gold dust. It did not matter to us how big the flecks of gold were, it was the weight of the gold we were after. We continued on that cut for several more days and on our next cleanup we recovered about a third as much fine gold as we did on the first cleanup. This cut had been a real success.

We were learning more about mining every day. We were not old pros yet, but we did not feel like we were complete *Chichacos*, a term used up north for a tender foot or green horn, as we say in the states. We learned that the gold settled in pockets in the bedrock; you could mine all day without finding any pay dirt and then the next day wind up with a few nuggets from the same cut. At our peak we were mining between 400 and 500 yards of ground per day. On average, the dirt was only paying about $2.00 to $3.00 per yard in fine gold, but occasionally we got a good nugget, sending us jumping and dancing and shouting "Hallelujah!"

The gold mining process boils down to this: (1) dig a big hole in the ground down to the bedrock in the creek; (2) remove, wash, and sluice all the sand, gravel, and rock; and (3) put everything back in the hole. The process sounds simple enough, but it requires technique and skill. And the job is not done once your hole is refilled. A miner is required to dress up a hole after it has been worked in order to minimize the disturbance to the land. If we did not dress up our trenches the creek would end up looking like a cratered moonscape, and if we violated this regulation we were liable to get our permit pulled. Since I was not a native Canadian I was always careful to follow the rules because I did not want any bad marks against me.

We had to acquire a permit from the Canadian government to mine their land, and this could also be tricky. There was a lot of red tape to work through and it took a while before we were granted our mining permit. Then, once we received it, there were countless regulations to follow. For example, we had to build three settlement ponds with a bulldozer downstream from the area we were sluicing that would collect the water running out from our sluice box. The muddied water stirred up from our mining operation ran sequentially through the settlement ponds, and by the time it flowed out of the third pond, the water was almost completely clear again. Over the years, miners who let murky water flow out of their sluice boxes without letting the mud settle had damaged fisheries downstream.

Once we were finished sluicing an area on our claim we had to refill these settlement ponds, which was also an arduous task. Filling up the holes could be as hard as digging them out. We refilled these trenches with the rocks, or tailings as we called them, that had stacked up at the end of our sluice box. These tailings had to be removed from the box constantly so that they would not obstruct the flow of the water. We took the front-end loader, scooped up all the tailings, and dumped them back in the trenches to refill the holes. The ground was not quite as neat as it was before we started digging but it was much better than if we had just left it scooped away.

We managed to install a water system in our cabin out in the middle of the wilderness. It was our good fortune that many years earlier some miners on Squaw Creek had left a bunch of thin-walled pipe lying around their claim. This pipe was about 20 inches in diameter and close to 30 feet long. The old-time miners had brought in the pipe for a hydraulic water system. From a dam upstream, they ran the pipe down to their mining site and the pressure from the water was concentrated into a hose with a nozzle, washing the hillside down and rinsing out their sluice box. Now, we were scrounging up this old pipe to feed water into our own sluice box.

The next time we went into town for supplies we brought back a roll of plastic tubing hose about an inch in diameter and an old sink that we found at a junkyard. We then built a dam upstream, ran the pipe from beneath the dam down to our cabin, and attached the hose to the sink in our makeshift kitchen. Lo and behold, we had running water in our cabin! With an elevation change of nearly 40 feet down a steep hillside, the water pressure was quite strong. Ed, who had been doing most of the dishwashing, was especially excited about this cabin renovation.

One day Heinz and his two boys came by our claim from their site just below us on the creek. They saw our water system and were amazed—even envious.

"What if we brought our own hose out here, put a T into your line, and sent some water on down to our place?" Heinz asked.

"Feel free!" I answered. "Just bring us some hose and we'll hook you up."

A few days later Heinz was back with a bunch of his own vinyl hose. We connected their cabin to our water system, but they went a step further: Heinz built a lean-to on the back of his cabin and installed a commode and a shower! He even set up a propane heater to get hot water. We had some bargaining rights for furnishing their water, so occasionally we went down to their claim to take a hot shower. Heinz started calling us the Squaw Creek Water Works.

At another claim on Squaw Creek there was an old-timey prospector named Charlie Ross. Charlie must have been between 70 and 80 years old and he had so much beard you could hardly see his face. I do not think he had shaved in 40 years. Charlie was a real character who had started mining back in the days when prospectors just panned for gold. Later on, he hired a young man with some heavy equipment to help him mine down to bedrock. Charlie did very well on Squaw Creek; having been there first, he had several of the best claims and they paid him well. I really enjoyed visiting with Charlie. At first he was a little standoffish, but after he saw how hard we were working he accepted us and we got to be pretty good buddies.

One day I decided to have some fun with Charlie Ross. I guess all miners are jokesters, and I was not about to be left behind in that area. Charlie came down to my claim one day to ask us for help repairing a break in his steel sluice box. He was afraid he was loosing gold and wanted to know if we would weld his box back together. Naturally, I agreed to help and loaded up the welding rig. I also grabbed a can of gold spray paint. . .

Charlie's sluice box had quite a crack—the opening was nearly half an inch wide and was letting a lot of fine sand and gold flow out the bottom. Ed and I shut off his water, dried the sluice box, and went to work for a few hours welding the crack back together. At one point Charlie stepped away to fix us some sandwiches. I was always halfway afraid to eat anything Charlie cooked because you never knew what it could be. Anything that moved, wiggled, or lay still for a while, he would eat. While Charlie was gone I grabbed a stone that, were it gold, would probably have weighed 40–50 ounces. I spray painted the stone gold and, from a distance, it did look like an enormous gold nugget. Then, I dropped the rock in the nugget trap in Charlie's sluice box and waited for him to return.

A few minutes later Charlie returned with lunch.

"What is this?" I asked dubiously.

"Why, it's moose burger!"

I was hesitant to eat it, but the burger turned out to be pretty good. When we were done eating I packed up my equipment and prepared to leave, stalling just a little bit as I waited for Charlie to look inside his box. Finally, he walked toward the head of his sluice box and let out a holler. I knew he had found that rock! Charlie reached inside and grabbed the rock, then immediately started chuckling. He knew as soon as he picked it up that this was no gold nugget. We all laughed for a good while.

I got word a few years ago that Charlie Ross had passed away. I was sorry to hear that he was gone. Charlie was an original, one-of-a-kind, sourdough prospector.

I had heard stories about prospectors who stayed out in the wilderness together for so long that they would start fussing and fighting with each other. I always used to think it was just a joke, but it happened with Ed and me. Ed was doing most of the dishwashing and cabin cleaning while I was doing most of the cooking, and one day we got in an argument about where we were going to put our pots and pans. Ed had hammered some nails in the wall so that we could hang our pans up neatly, but they were so high on the wall that I had to strain to reach up and grab them. I fussed to Ed a little bit about this.

"Hey, let's put those pans back underneath the sink!" I said.

"Nah," he said, "let's keep them nice and orderly on the wall. This place looks bad enough already."

Of course, in retrospect, I can agree with him, but not at the time. Ed and I got in a heck of an argument over where to put a frying pan! Fortunately, it was just a minor skirmish, and it did not lead to any more serious disagreements. I still laugh about it today.

One day that season we found a 13-ounce nugget in the trap on our dump box. Oh boy, were we overjoyed! I thought, *we've really hit the pay dirt now!* But Squaw Creek was known for the occasional large nugget. Sooner or later, any miner on the creek would be rewarded with a big one.

The Lord only knows how long ago this gold nugget was deposited along the creek. As gold washes down a creek the heavier particles settle to the bottom first. As the water continues to rush over the gold throughout the years the smaller pieces wash farther downstream. Thus, the farther away you get from the original deposit upstream, the finer the gold becomes. The fact that we had already found a pretty good-sized nugget in the 13-ouncer encouraged us considerably and we believed that we were probably pretty close to the original gold deposit. Heinz and his two sons were working the claim just below ours and they were recovering some great nuggets as well, so we really believed we were in an area that would pay off.

Ed and I hardly slept the night we found the 13-ounce nugget. We sat at our kitchen table just ogling at the nugget lying in front of us. It turned out to be the best gold we would ever find on Squaw Creek. Any other nuggets we found weighed no more than half an ounce. While these were nothing compared to our 13-ounce nugget, we still prized them very much.

I was so anxious to know the exact weight of the big nugget I could hardly stand it. It felt pretty hefty and we all guessed that it weighed anywhere from 10–20 ounces. We had a small balance scale with us but it could only weigh up to one ounce, which this nugget more than surpassed. I was sitting in the cabin one day staring at the nugget when out of the corner of my eye I noticed a can of nails sitting on the other side of the room. Suddenly, I had an idea. I grabbed one of the nails and weighed it on our small balance scale. It weighed exactly half an ounce. Well, you can see where this is going. I decided I would make my own balance scale using the nails to equalize the weight of the nugget.

I found a foot-long steel rod and pulled the hand-drill from my toolbox. I drilled fine holes through the middle and each end of the rod. I then took an old piece of stranded copper wire, peeled off some finer strands, and tied them to three equidistant holes I had drilled in each of two mayonnaise lid rims. I brought the three wire ends from each lid together and strung them through the holes at the ends of the steel rod. Finally, I built a small wooden stand about a foot tall and stuck a pin through the middle hole of the steel rod into the wood. I now had a balance with two mayonnaise lids hanging down on each side. I put the nugget in one lid and one by one started placing nails into the other. The scale balanced at 27 nails. At a half-ounce per nail, that put the gold nugget at just over 13 ounces!

Later we took the nugget into Haines, Alaska for safekeeping at a bank. When we went in to deposit the nugget we asked if we could have it weighed. The nugget was just about a quarter-ounce over 13 ounces! I was amazed by the accuracy of my makeshift scale. I believe what made it work was the pin at the pivot point which removed any resistance from the balancing sides.

Around this time my wife Tracy came up to visit. She did not care much for the North Country—she had read too many stories about bears—so I was happy that she decided to come. I had her pose for a picture with my little balance scale on the steps of our cabin, and she was really excited when she saw that 13-ounce nugget of gold! I think for the first time she thought that we might just have a clue as to what we were doing out there on Squaw Creek. Years later, I left my homemade scale and can of nails in the cabin in case a miner should come along and want to weigh something.

It was sure nice to have Tracy around for that short period of time, and I know Ed enjoyed it too. For six weeks she did all the cooking and she did not mind washing the dishes either. Tracy was a big help to us during her visit and I think she got used to living out in the wilderness, but I know she sure missed having regular showers. Needless to say, Heinz' cabin became even more popular during Tracy's stay. She really took advantage of that amenity, and I do not blame her.

When it came time for Tracy to leave—I thought she was a really good sport to stay as long as she did—we went to Haines and caught a ferry to Juneau where Tracy would fly home on an airliner. I took a little vacation of my own from gold mining to see her off. We spent the night in Juneau and had a really good time visiting various sites that she did not have a chance to see on her way up to the cabin. The next day I dropped her off at the airport. I was ready to get back to Squaw Creek, but first I wanted to visit my friend Josephine Jurgeleit.

Jo Jurgeleit was a one-legged gold miner who lived in Haines. She'd had some health problems years earlier and was forced to have one leg removed. That gal was a really high-spirited go-getter. Jo had walking crutches that were fit for each arm, and I swear she could get around as good as, if not better than, anyone else. Jo drove an old Volkswagen Beetle that she rigged up with a hand clutch and she travelled all over the place—or at least where there was a road. Jo was still mining, as well. She had a claim on Porcupine Creek just south of the Alaskan-Canadian border and could

Ed takes a photo of Tracy with my homemade gold scale.

do just about everything on one leg. I never saw anything like it. She was also pretty salty, as far as her language was concerned. She is the only person I have ever met—including soldiers in the Marine Corps—who could cuss entire sentences.

Jo told me a tale about a young whippersnapper who had tried to run her off her claim. He kept harassing her and then showed up to her claim one day with a revolver. According to Jo, he kept putting his hand on that gun and waving it in front of her. She kept her eye on him, wondering what in the hell this young man had in mind, but I'll tell you for sure, that guy did not scare her. Jo told him in no uncertain terms to get off her claim. As she was talking she saw him put his hand back on his gun.

"Sonny, you got a sight on the front end of that gun?" she asked.

The man looked at her kind of funny and said, "Yeah, I sure do!"

"Well, you better file it off."

"Why would I want to do that?" he asked.

"Because it won't hurt near as bad when I stick it up your ass if you don't get off my property."

That was Jo Jurgeleit. She was something else.

Jo loved kids and often drove up to the Canadian border to give candy bars to the Native American children. She also knew Heinz and Katy Eckervogt quite well and frequently drove to Dezadeash Lake to visit with them. Everyone seemed to know each other up in that country. That was just the frontier way of life.

After visiting with Jo I bought some supplies that Ed and I needed back at our diggins' and then headed back up the highway to Squaw Creek. When I got to the Tatshenshini River, I ran into a problem: somebody had left the aluminum boat, which I had used to cross the water on my trip out, on the other side of the river. I thought, *well, what am I going to do now?* There was no way I could cross the heavy rapids of that river without the boat. *I'm just going to have to wait.* I went back to my truck, curled up in the back seat, and took a nap.

Around one o'clock in the morning (and still daylight out), I heard a noise and awoke to a couple of guys coming back across the creek in the boat. They had just gone over to the other side of the river on a lark. I was so thankful to get the boat back. I loaded up my things, crossed the river, and made the three-hour trek back up to my claim in the old four-wheel drive truck that we kept on the other side of the river.

Even though I had woken him up, Ed was sure glad to see me because he knew I would bring him something sugary to satisfy his sweet tooth. I handed over a box of candy bars that I bought in Haines. Ed's eyes were as big as saucers and he tore into them. I almost had to hide the candy bars so that he would not eat them all at once.

"Did you make us rich while I was gone?" I asked.

"I got a little gold, but things slowed down when I had to dig up the ground and dump it too. It made me appreciate what you're doing, Walt!"

We finally got to bed and started working late the next morning, and it was not long before we were in full swing again. That week we sluiced a different vein of ground and started finding pure copper nuggets the size of pigeon eggs! When I first saw them I thought they were gold, but as soon as I picked one up and felt the weight, I knew that they were not. It sure gave me a start, though. I kept some of them for souvenirs and later had a couple gold-plated to have some fun with friends back home.

Looking back, some of the happiest days of my life were spent mining on Squaw Creek with dreams of striking it rich. Plus, I just flat out enjoyed being outdoors and working with the land.

The 74.5-Ounce Nugget

One day, the Eckervogt's made a tremendous find while mining on Squaw Creek. After cleaning out their sluice box, Heinz' sons found a nugget that weighed 74.5 troy ounces. At the time it was the second largest gold nugget recorded in North America. The nugget was solid gold and had a nice shape to it. I had seen a lot of nuggets in my day, and a lot of pictures of nuggets that had been found in the North Country as well, but I never saw anything anywhere *near* the size of Heinz' nugget. From one side the nugget looked like a big potato, about the size of a knotted fist. It was very smooth with only a few dents in the surface. Turned over, the nugget looked almost like an ashtray, indented in the center and with a little depression on the side to place a cigarette. The nugget was about five inches long, two inches high, and very heavy.

The amazing thing about this nugget was that it was difficult to judge by looking at it just how heavy it would be to pick up, but it felt like you had a 10-pound sack of sugar in your hands!

Heinz first mined on Squaw Creek in 1981 at a site just above my claim. In the two years that he mined this claim he found a 33-ounce nugget, which at the time made quite a few waves around the world. If that nugget made waves, the 74.5-ounce nugget caused *tidal* waves—it made international news. Heinz had discovered a record-breaking nugget, but I truly believed that the largest nugget on Squaw Creek was yet to be found because Heinz had sluiced only a small area along the creek.

The day the nugget was discovered, Heinz' sons Thomas and Martin had been running the mine. They were working two shifts a day to take advantage of the long daylight hours and were running the equipment loader in a deep hole when they found the nugget. Needless to say, Heinz' boys were quite happy when they discovered what they had dug up. Later that day Thomas and Martin flew to the Eckervogt's home on Dezadeash Lake in a helicopter. They told Heinz that all the equipment had broken and that an inspector had shut down the mine. But Heinz was on to them—the boys were showered and dressed up, and something did not quite click. All of a sudden, they dropped the 74.5-ounce nugget into Katy Eckervogt's hands initiating a day-and-a-half long celebration at a Haines Junction bar. Those boys certainly deserved it.

The End of the First Season

As the first season faded out I began to notice a difference in Ed. It seemed to me that something was bothering him. He would sit there staring at the wall but his eyes were focused about 10 feet on the other side of it. It bothered me to see him this way, but I did not say anything for a while. Ed was normally such a happy-go-lucky guy, and he was a darn good guitar player. Often he would pull out his guitar and sing a few songs about Squaw Creek, but he was not doing that anymore. Finally, I decided one night that I ought to talk to Ed about it as we sat separating gold dust from black sand.

"Ed, what do you think about the whole situation?" I asked.

"What do you mean 'the whole situation'?"

"Well, our mining out here and how we're doing."

Ed was quiet for a minute before answering. "Walter, I don't know if I can come back next year. We're not finding much gold and I'm just not made for the frontier life, living out in the wilderness like this."

"Gosh, Ed, but we're really having lots of fun," I said.

"Yeah," Ed answered, "but I got involved in this primarily to make some money! I think I should probably do something else next year." Although we never got rich from gold that season, we earned enough to pay for what we were doing, included purchasing the heavy equipment.

"Well, I'm enjoying working out here with you," I said. "I hope you will come back. And we are going to have to shut down here pretty soon. It is getting colder every day and snow is beginning to fall—if we wait too long we may not be able to get out of here."

Ed almost jumped out if his chair. "I'm glad you brought that up!" he said. "I think we should get ready to shut it down and just close the season right now."

"Okay, if that's the way you feel, Ed, but think about the coming season and give it a lot of thought because I am definitely going to come back and try to do better next year."

"I'll give it a lot of thought," Ed said, "but don't count on me coming back."

We worked for about ten more days and slowly began buttoning things up. In that time we got four inches of snow, and that caught our attention.

"Walter, we are liable to get snowed in," Ed said. "If we can't get that four-wheel drive truck out of here, we'll have to hike out."

"You may be right. Let's take one more day to get everything stored away and then we'll leave."

We were approaching the month of October, and that was about as late as anybody should stay up there mining because at any moment the water would freeze. We loaded up all our equipment and personal gear, closed up the cabin, and started down the mountain. Boy, am I ever glad we left when we did. It snowed on us all the way down the mountain and it was difficult to keep the truck on the shelf along the steeper parts of the trail. On our left we could see over a cliff 500 feet down to the tops of the trees. It was not hard to visualize what would happen if we slid off that trail, but we slowly made it back down to the Tatshenshini River. We climbed in the little aluminum boat, poked the bow into the current, and were pulled right across the river. Once we reached the other side we dragged the boat onto the bank, turned it over, and secured it to the ground so that a strong wind would not blow it back into the river. It was not more than 15 minutes before Ed had started up his van and was on the road to Anchorage.

I took off in my Ford pickup toward the Eckervogt's home on Dezadeash Lake and spent the rest of the day visiting with Heinz and Katy. Katy fixed us a meal of moose burgers, and they were terrific. I am normally a small eater but I managed to get two of those burgers down. Moose meat is extremely low in fat. In my opinion it is not as tasty as beef, but if it was all I had to eat I would be happy to have it.

The next day we said our goodbyes. I felt like I was leaving family when I left the Eckervogt's home.

I took off and headed back home to Texas. I made it to Watson Lake in one day, and there I booked a motel room, had a nice meal, and got a good night's sleep. I must have slept soundly through the night because the next morning when I pulled the curtain back I could not believe my eyes—everything was white! I went out to the parking lot to check on my truck but all I could see were mounds of snow in front of the motel. All of the vehicles were covered in at least 18 inches of snow. I had to borrow a broom from the motel to brush the snow off of all the cars in order to find my truck! We were caught in a hellacious snowstorm.

When I finally got all the snow cleared off my truck and the engine was warmed up, I hit the road again and the snow did not stop until I was all the way to Edmonton, Alberta. Apparently, the snowstorm had swept ahead of me. I drove through Red Deer and headed for the border at Cut Bank, Montana where I would clear customs. From there, it was an easy three-day drive back to Texas. In total, the trip took six days to drive nearly 4,000 miles from Haines Junction to Austin.

I was happy to be home again and to see my wife and kids. I am sure they were glad to see me too because they never knew what could happen to me up there in the North Country. My family and friends were always relieved when I came out of it. I spent most of that winter at home trying to decide what I was going to do for the upcoming season, but one thing I knew for sure, I was going to continue mining. After some serious discussions with my partners back in Anchorage, both Ed Spencer and Earl Foster decided they were going to try their luck at prospecting a little closer to home. Everything at Squaw Creek was turned over to me and they told me to do what I wanted with the claim.

The Second Season on Squaw Creek

I decided to take a step back, regroup, and plan my life out to determine what I really wanted to do on Squaw Creek. Although I was chomping at the bit to try, I really did not know if I could be successful mining by myself. I still had a lot to learn about the mining business, so I spent the year studying different techniques and strategies and learned how to better recognize ground that might be pay dirt. I also spent a lot of time with other miners who worked on Squaw Creek. They were very helpful and answered my many questions about mining, advising me what I should and should not do. Most of them gave me good advice, but some of it was worth no more than what they were charging me for it—nothing.

Despite my relative inexperience, I was bound and determined to keep mining. I became acquainted with a number of people who had really hit it big. One friend of mine, after several years of barely making ends meet, wound up with 1,500 ounces of gold on one cleanup. I thought, *if I just stick with it, perhaps I could do the same thing.* The lure of gold was strong on all of us, but once you got a taste of it, it grew even stronger.

That spring I loaded up the trailer with my helicopter and gear and got ready to go. After careful consideration, I decided I would attempt to prospect alone on Squaw Creek that season. I drove to Seattle and reserved a spot on a ferry that would leave for Juneau, Alaska the next day. I spent the night at a motel in Seattle and thought about how large the city felt to me—it was a whole new world for a country boy like me.

The next morning I woke up early, got in line for the ferry, and drove into the belly of the ship. I then took an elevator up to the passenger level and parked myself on a comfy crank-back sofa in the lounge. I had declared my homestead for the next three days and two nights. After a one-night layover in Juneau, Alaska I made it to Haines. I spent a few days around town visiting friends I had become acquainted with, in particular Jo Jurgeleit. I really treasured every minute I spent with that gal because she was just so unusual and historical. Anytime she opened her mouth I knew I would hear some wild story that I had never heard before. In fact, Jo was such a character that National Geographic published a story on her in the 1970s.

Jo was full of advice for me as a new miner. Her late husband Arthur had mined on Squaw Creek so she was quite familiar with the area around my claim. Jo taught me about the four or five different types of gold that had been discovered in the area, and she could identify gold from Squaw Creek just by looking. This impressed me quite a bit.

When I left Haines, I made the 40-mile drive to Canada and stopped at the customs station. By now I had become pretty well-acquainted with the Canadian customs agent at this station, but I could tell he was a little leery of me bringing a helicopter into Canada because he was afraid I might have it with me for commercial use. For a time there I thought I was going to be turned away, but I finally convinced the agent that I was not bringing in the helicopter for commercial use. He knew I was just a miner so he signed me off and let me go.

I hauled the trailer up the highway and once again made my way to Heinz and Katy's house on Dezadeash Lake. Heinz was happy to see that I had made it with the helicopter.

"Maybe we can fly out and visit some new prospects," Heinz suggested.

"We can do that, but we're going to have to be careful because I am limited to personal use of the helicopter while I'm in Canada."

Heinz laughed and said, "I think mining is about as personal as you can get."

"You have a good point there."

My first trip in the helicopter that season was to my mining site on Squaw Creek. I wanted to investigate how the site had made the winter. Quite a difference it was flying there in a helicopter rather than negotiating up that trail in an old truck! I landed near the cabin and everything seemed to be in order. I could tell from the scratch marks on the door that some bears had been prowling around, but they had not broken into the cabin. Since everything looked good and I had nothing else to do I got back in the helicopter and explored up the creek. At various sites along the river I saw the remains of drill bits and small piles of tailings—evidence of last season's mining on Squaw Creek. Within a few days, I was prospecting again.

One day Heinz and I flew over to Jade Creek to visit some miners Heinz knew. They were finding some good nuggets and Heinz wanted to do some informal prospecting. That visit reminded me of the perils and pitfalls that miners faced. The day before we arrived those guys were hit by a tremendous burst of rain that flooded the river. In addition to damaging their sluice box, the water had completely flooded an old pickup truck parked on the riverbank that they had not had time to move before the storm hit. They showed Heinz and me the pickup and I had never seen anything like it before in my life. The truck was buried above the seats with sand. The windows had been rolled down and literally tons of sand and gravel poured into the cab of the truck. For all practical purposes the truck was ruined, but as we were leaving the guys were talking about checking out the sand that had been deposited in the truck in case any gold had been washed in during the flood. Fortunately, their camp was built back a ways from the river and was not in the path of the flood, but anything within the flood plane was either ruined or gone.

Heinz had another claim downstream on Squaw Creek that he was not planning on working, and since I was not having much luck on the claim that I leased the year before, he offered to transfer my lease to this new site so that I could give it a shot there. I looked the site over closely and found no evidence of heavy-machine mining on this claim in the past. I knew Heinz was finding pretty good gold on his claim below it, and everything pointed to a logical expectation that this site would also pay, so I agreed to lease another claim from Heinz.

I disassembled my sluice box and spent quite a few days moving my equipment. I had to make many trips back and forth to get everything to the new claim. Needless to say, I was spending a lot of time on foot as I moved between the two sites, so I carried my public defender 12-gauge shotgun in case I should cross paths with a bear. I used to always carry a .357 Magnum pistol, but everyone kept telling me that it would not be a good defense against a grizzly. "I agree," I would say, "but it's better than a pocket knife."

One day I got a little careless and was moving back and forth between sites without my shotgun. There was a lot of activity on the creek that day and as I was walking back to the old cabin from the new claim, a huge bear standing on the corner of the riverbank appeared out of nowhere. Right away I saw that it was a brown bear and not a grizzly, but I still stopped short to decide what to do. To my relief, when the bear saw me it simply ambled off and disappeared, but it did give me a start to come face to face with a beast I would have to look up to see. I never again forgot my shotgun if I moved any more than 100 feet from my cabin. Fortunately, I never had to use it.

Once I selected a location on the new claim where I wanted to prospect I reassembled the sluice box and got back to work, but it was slow-going doing everything by myself. Every once in a while one of Heinz' boys came by to visit and check to see if I needed any immediate help. Thomas was a really amiable, friendly young man and he knew I was prone to having a stash of candy bars at my camp. I would always pass one or two out to him. One day,

Thomas came by and helped me with some heavy lifting as I got all my equipment and gear in place. I was not expecting to do any real mining that season, but he helped me get everything prepared for the following year. I did a little more panning just to whet my appetite and on one of those pans I found a nugget. I was excited to see what would turn up next season.

Dan Johnson was one of my Canadian mining friends on the creek. Dan also knew Jo Jurgeleit, and she called him Danny. I tried calling him Danny a few times but it really bugged him, and he informed me in no uncertain terms that he did not like anyone to call him that.

"Your name is Walter. What if people started calling you Walterine? Would you like that?" Well, he had a point there. I was only calling him Danny because Jo did, but I did not call him Danny anymore after that.

Dan Johnson got as much gold as anybody out of Squaw Creek. He showed me his production one day and I could not believe my eyes. In addition to all his fine gold and "ordinary" nuggets, he had about half a dozen larger nuggets that weighed anywhere from 25–50 ounces. They just made my mouth water.

"You understand, I didn't find all these at once," he said. "I have accumulated them over several years of mining Squaw Creek. But it's true, I've always had great luck finding large nuggets."

I was returning to my cabin on Squaw Creek one afternoon after a fishing trip with Heinz when I thought, *I'll take Dan and his wife a nice trout.* They had a cabin about half a mile up the creek from mine, so I grabbed two really nice trout, put them in a sack, and walked over to their house. When I got there I saw that they weren't home, but their Rottweiler *was.* This dog watched their cabin while Dan and his wife were out and it did a heck of a job. I'd had some close encounters with bears before, but that dog scared me more than any other bear I had ever run into. He came roaring at me like he was on the attack and vicious sounds came out from between his horrendously sharp teeth. *This dog is going to grab me*

Hands full of Squaw Creek gold!

now! I thought to myself. I had the fish in a bag, which I quickly stuck out in front of me for the dog to smell. He sniffed the fish and must have decided that I was not a threat because he stopped growling and backed away. I started to make my way out of there, but the dog followed, and he did not stop until I was a couple hundred yards away. Finally, he turned around and went back to the cabin. I decided I would just wait until later to give Dan those fish.

That evening I heard Dan and his wife coming up the mountain in their truck so I walked back to their camp. As soon as I got within hearing distance of their cabin I yelled out to Dan.

"Call that dog! Call that dog!" I hollered.

Dan came out of his cabin. "What's your problem, Walter?" he asked.

"That dog of yours nearly ate me up today! I'm just trying to bring you some fish!"

"Well, I'm glad he didn't get the fish," Dan chuckled. He was quite a character. Dan was already pulling out his knife to clean the fish as he walked back to his cabin.

Dan later taught me a delicious way to smoke those fish using apple wood.

"We don't have oak or mesquite up here like you Yanks do, but we *do* have apple trees," Dan said.

Years later, if I could acquire any apple wood, I used it for my barbecuing. That was another good thing about making friends with the locals—they did not mind sharing their secrets. I dearly loved the people living in the North Country.

The Golden Zone Lost Mine

That season that I prospected alone on Squaw Creek I went on many exploratory trips in my helicopter. We have all used the term "off the beaten trail." I really experienced some "off the beaten trail" adventures prospecting in Alaska and Canada. Because I had my helicopter, I was able to explore areas of the wilderness nearly impossible to reach on foot.

On one of my exploring trips in the helicopter, I found a lost and abandoned gold mine called "The Golden Zone." Over the years I came across a number of old-timers who knew about the mine, even one man who used to work there, but it had not been charted on any maps or accounted for in any books. The Golden Zone was the name given to this mine when gold was first discovered there in 1903, and the founder of the operation realized he had discovered something better than most of the other gold strikes occurring around 1900.

The man who founded this mining operation was named Dunkel. I found his house, still standing, down the way from the old ghost town that was built around the Golden Zone mine. Dunkel lived in this house with his wife and three boys. In the attic of their house there was what appeared to be a schoolroom. It is possible that Dunkel and his wife taught his three boys and other children from the town in that attic. Study materials were still sitting on desks. As I heard later, one of Dunkel's sons became a lawyer and another a doctor. This just goes to show that not all the feats that were accomplished out in the wilderness concerned mining or other resource recoveries. These people seriously taught their children, and I thought that was an amazing thing.

This mine stayed in operation until World War II. At that time, all the miners throughout the country, particularly up in Alaska, were called in to mine coal, which I suppose we needed for the war effort. When this happened, almost all of the mining operations in Alaska were shut down, and in most cases the mines were never reopened. That is what happened to the Golden Zone. It just never got started again. By the time I visited the site in the early 1980s, the tunnel shaft had crumbled in several places.

As I explored further into the area I met an old-timer who used to work the Golden Zone mine. This fellow, named Harold Smith, was still hard-rock mining at age 72, healthy and strong as an ox. He was really a character. When I first met him I was a little bit taken aback. He immediately dropped his pants and said "I want to show you this scar on my leg." It turned out that he'd had surgery a few years earlier for a very serious injury to his leg from a bear attack. The doctors had to graft some skin from his thigh and he wanted to show me his big scar. Harold and a couple other fellows reclaimed the Golden Zone mine after it was abandoned to work it by hand, trying to rebuild that tunnel back into the ore body. I wished them luck, but it was some kind of tough job.

I do not know what type of ore body the miners discovered at the Golden Zone, but it was located some distance above the shaft they dug back into the mountain. They could not follow the vein straight down so they dug into the mountainside below it and built a tunnel to intercept the vein. That is what Harold Smith and the others were still attempting to do. It looked to me like they had a Herculean task ahead of them, but they were hardy fellows and if anyone could do it, it was them. They were the kind of people who built the North Country.

The ghost town was hidden deep in the mountains. It took tough, strong people to carry in everything necessary to build a town and establish a mining operation over an old mule trail that led into the middle of the wilderness. At that time, there were no railroads anywhere nearby. Around 1924 a railroad was built in the general vicinity, but it was still nowhere near the Golden Zone mine. There was an old dirt road that went from Anchorage to Fairbanks, but it too was a long ways away from this mine. At one location along their route the miners had a jumping-off point from that old dirt road and their mule teams forged a new path. The miners continued winding up through canyons and mountainsides, all the while building unbelievable roads and bridges to get their equipment up to their claim. The old trail that they built is now the Parks Highway, which extends up past Mount McKinley and Denali Park.

The miners transported enough equipment and supplies to build a community of more than a hundred people, most of whom were miners themselves. The town consisted of 16 buildings, 11 of which were still standing when I visited the Golden Zone, and 4 of which were two-stories tall. Just think about that for a minute: this town was so deep in the wilderness that I could only reach it by helicopter. It was amazing. All but one of the two-story buildings served as living quarters, and one had partially collapsed. Examining this crumbling building, I went up to the second floor and saw a very interesting room at the other end of the hallway from where I stood. I could see pictures and various articles of clothing still hanging on the walls. I thought, *I'll just go take a look at that room,* but when I started to walk across the hall I felt the floor creaking beneath my feet. The floor had already sagged about three feet on the other side of the building, which was right next door to a building that had already completely collapsed, so I gave up that idea. I will never know what was in that room because that building certainly would not withstand another 10 feet of snow, which it was bound to get the following winter.

One of the two-story buildings, constructed a short distance away from all the others, was the mill where the ore was processed. The building was constructed on the side of a very steep hill below the tunnel dug into the mountain, so the miners built a trestle from just below the mine opening to the top floor of the mill. They also installed an ore car that moved on rail tracks to transport the ore from the mine to the mill.

Each level of the building had a different operation. On the top floor (the first in the succession of operations), the ore was dumped into a huge crusher and broken up. The crumbled ore then dropped to the next floor and went through another crushing process, breaking the ore into even smaller pieces. Eventually, the ore ended up on the ground level where it went through a ball mill and was further crushed and concentrated into high-grade ore. By this time, the ore was powdered up like dust. All of this old equipment was still there when I visited the mine and I did not think it would take too much effort to get the mill running again. It was an amazing site to explore.

There was quite a bit of settlement, concentrated dust, and crushed ore in the bottom of these old tumblers where they crushed the rock. With my son Jay, who was with me on one of my visits to the Golden Zone, I managed to reach into one of the tumblers and scrape up nearly a coffee cup full of powdery residue, just for the heck of it. We tried to pan the material like we would pan for gold but the concentrate was so heavy that it did not work. It was all mineral, and it had a lot of color in it. Later, we brought the sample into town and had it assayed, and would you believe that it was over 40% gold and 30% silver? Altogether it was no more than a pound of mineral, but we recovered some gold out of that old mill just by scraping up the dust that had been left when the mine was shut down.

The mining operation was run by electric motors at an astonishing 440 volts. Here this mine was, dccp within the wilderness, and they were using electric power to run their mill. When I visited the mine, all these electric motors were strewn about on the ground and some of them looked large enough to weigh a ton. It was not too hard to imagine hearing the rock crusher running and miners yelling. It gave me an eerie feeling to wander through an old, abandoned mining mill like the Golden Zone.

Everything was still there, as if the town had been abandoned yesterday. There were old books and journals, and chemicals used for the mining operation. There was an old coat hanging on the wall in one of the buildings and I noticed something sticking out of the pocket. I pulled it out and it was a Christmas card. The card was still in the envelope and had been sent from somewhere in Minnesota, postmarked in 1932. I took that card with me as a souvenir. It was touching to find that old Christmas card there in the abandoned ghost town, and it made me wonder who this man was and where his loved ones were who had sent him the card. This man was living in the remotest wilderness of Alaska, almost to the end of creation, and was still receiving correspondence from his family.

There were tools of all description lying around the camp, and most of them were hand-forged. The mining town had a large, fully-equipped blacksmith shop, and the forge and all its equipment were still intact.

Another building, which I assumed was probably used as a warehouse, housed many crates containing various types of mining equipment. Some of the crates, still unopened after all these years, contained brand new motors for the mill. Next door to the warehouse was a complete assay laboratory. Most of its tools were also still intact, including electric ovens that were used to perform fire assays on the ore, in which gold and silver were melted in small ceramic crucibles.

Perhaps the most incredible part of the whole operation was the huge metal lathe, over 20 feet long, which was used by the miners to machine their own parts for the mill. If one of their machines broke they could not afford to shut down the mining operation and wait three months for new parts to be retrieved from the Lower Forty-eight. The miners simply had to make them. This lathe was probably the largest that I have ever seen, and it must have weighed at least 10 tons. What was so astounding was that this lathe was brought into the wilderness by mules. They could not have brought it in parts, either, because it was all one solid piece of metal. Mule teams had carried it up through the canyons, crossing several rivers, and eventually climbing to an elevation of 4,000 feet. You can just imagine a bunch of poor souls transporting something that heavy so far into the wilderness. I thought the accomplishment was fantastic and I stood there looking at the lathe in disbelief at what I was seeing. I had come across a city deep in the mountains, with no conceivable way for it to have gotten there.

I believe what helped preserve this old ghost town in the condition that it stood was its inaccessibility. Most modern day scroungers that go around collecting souvenirs from sites like this will just not attempt to get to a place as deep into the wilderness as the Golden Zone because the old trail has long since been overgrown by the thick forest of spruce, birch, and alders. I could just barely see from the air where the old trail used to be. Not too many people would want to backpack 40 or 50 miles back into a mountain, especially while carrying heavy equipment. You would have to be pretty loaded with support equipment to get that deep into the mountains; consequently, it would be nearly impossible to carry anything new back out. People like myself who have flown to the site have also not disturbed the remains of the Golden Zone. Except for a Christmas card, an old pot, and photographs that I took with my camera, I took nothing from the Golden Zone.

I wonder if people today could build something like the Golden Zone in the way that these miners built it. It is not that we haven't got the ability to do it; we are still human beings and strong and healthy, but it takes more than that. It takes that will power and hope and drive that the pioneer people had when they built this country. Since this country has been built, we do not seem to need that drive as much as we did back then and I think most people have lost it. I, myself, was flying through the North Country in a helicopter, so I better not be knocking anybody. Perhaps I am selling ourselves short. We could do it again if we *had* to. The pioneers of this country *had* to. There was no other way to go.

A typical ghost town in the North Country.

In a nearby canyon, about three miles away from the Golden Zone, I found another complete ghost town. Dunkel, the same fellow who established the Golden Zone mine, also founded this community. It was not quite as large as the Golden Zone but it was still a marvel to consider what they did. This ghost town had eight buildings onsite and they were all still standing. I found an old cache of black powder canisters in crates that I assumed were used for blasting. Other than where the bears had torn into them—apparently, a bear will bite into anything—the crates were still intact. The black powder canisters were about 6 inches in diameter and nearly 30 inches long. They looked like giant sticks of dynamite and they were packaged six to a crate. One of those canisters was probably not as powerful as a stick or two of dynamite, but they were still mighty explosive.

Strewn about the site were ore samples that had been dropped, and in these I could see outcroppings of gold carrying ore. In those days gold went for $35 per ounce, if not less. At the time I visited this site, however, gold was valued at well over $300 per ounce, so the cast aside ore samples sure looked good to me.

It was truly exciting to go into one of these abandoned mining sites realizing that no one had been there for many years. However, these sites were not forgotten by the wildlife. Every camp I explored had sustained some damage from bears. Apparently, these bears realized long ago that if there is a manmade structure in the woods it is going to have food in it, and one way or another they will get inside. I found one old camp with a building that had been weatherproofed with several rolls of heavy asphalted roofing material, and several rolls of this material were still lying on the ground. Later, a bear came along and found these rolls and must have thought it was chocolate candy because it bit and chewed into every one of them. Huge teeth marks punctured each layer of those rolls of roofing and they were completely ruined. Seeing those teeth marks gave me a better idea of the size of a bear's jaws. They are huge, and I want you to know, I am afraid of them! Of course, fear of bears should not keep anyone from enjoying the wilderness, but you do want to be alert.

I have been using the terms "ghost town" and "lost mine," but they are by no means lost. They are simply abandoned mining camps. There were dozens of ghost towns all over Alaska and you could purchase books that listed most of them from any Alaskan bookstore. The book I read, *Ghost Towns of Alaska* by Mary G. Balcom, listed many old ghost towns and deserted mining camps with their location marked by longitude and latitude. This book made it relatively easy for me to find these old ghost towns, but the deserted mining camps that I have described, the Golden Zone and the other Dunkel mine, were not listed in that book. Because I so thoroughly read through this book for the purpose of locating "lost" mining sites and found no account of those two towns, I am led to believe that there must be many, many more of these camps. Talking to some of the old miners, they informed me that these sites are scattered all over the state, just waiting to be discovered.

Grizzly Hostage

Sitting at my cabin window on my mining site on Squaw Creek one morning in June, enjoying that first cup of coffee, I took in the view of the snow-covered Noisy Range. Although the mountains were snow-covered year-round, there now appeared streaks of brown as some of the snow began to melt. This mountain range rises over 10,000 feet in some places and lies about 10 miles southwest of my mining cabin. I never tired of the view.

That morning I was also enjoying watching the little ground squirrels munching on a piece of my sourdough biscuits. There was a family of six, including four little ones. When I first returned to my cabin earlier that Spring I heard the squirrels' shrill whistle—their danger signal—but after one biscuit, they were tame as kittens under my feet. I do not know the true name of these fuzzy little balls of fur. In Alaska they are called parka squirrels; some call them gophers. They are similar to the little prairie dogs of West Texas. At any rate, they knew their handout would be ready every morning while I was there. Never late, they were waiting by my door everyday by 7:00 a.m.

This morning, all but one had grabbed their loot and scampered back to their den. This remaining one I called "Ace" since he was always the first to locate a tidbit I had placed in an obscure place. Suddenly, Ace let out a shrill whistle, dropped the biscuit, and darted under the cabin. I looked up and there was the raven, the mortal enemy of the little rodents. The bird dove in, missed Ace, but took his biscuit. Ace continued to whistle, safely hiding under the cabin. In a matter of split seconds, life-impacting decisions are rewarded or penalized in the wild.

My claim on the creek was on the Yukon border with British Columbia. I had been working Squaw Creek with moderate success, but the truth of the matter was that I loved the wilderness oasis. The mining was just an excuse to justify being there.

I had lived in peace there with the moose, grizzly bears, timber wolves, and other wild things about five months out of each year since I started mining. Most of my family did not care for what they called the lonely wilderness. I was many times alone up north, but never lonely. My wife Tracy spent a little time with me in the North Country, but as she put it, she "never made peace with the grizzly bears."

On Saturday, June 26th, I drove my old truck down the trail to the Tatshenshini river to pick up Ian McPhie from Haines Junction. By radio phone, we had arranged the evening before to meet at 9:00 a.m. Ian was a diesel mechanic who had recently overhauled the engine on my backhoe, but the engine needed some final adjustments and he was coming in to take care of them. Getting this kind of work done deep in the wilderness was not easy and I was feeling good that Ian had agreed to come help.

Ian arrived on time and we made the trip back up the trail. The repairs were uneventful and after I fixed some lunch I took him back to the river. He had a sack of oranges that had been left in his truck, and these he presented to me. I was happy to have the fresh fruit.

Now, for the trip back to the cabin. Fortunately, as it turned out later, it was a nice day, about 65° and mostly sunny. The old truck's engine sounded great, humming right along. I thought of the many trips I had made up this mountain in it. It seemed like an old friend. About halfway up the trail (and that's all it was), I crossed Six Mile Creek and began to climb a winding three-mile stretch that had been carved out of the mountainside. This stretch was always the toughest part of the journey as it was very steep and had to be made in low gear and four-wheel drive. I was just getting into the steepest and straightest part and I could see about 200 yards ahead. Coming down, it looked like a ski jump.

Suddenly, with no warning or sputter, the engine stopped dead. My first feeling was relief because I had recently repaired the brakes. I was able to slowly roll back down the hill until I had the rear wheels against the bank. After several attempts to restart the engine, I knew it was not going to happen. I had some tools with me but after a few minutes I determined that there was no spark and that the ignition coil must have gone out.

I would have to walk the remaining three or four miles to my cabin. I had not been carrying a gun on these trips because the old truck had been so dependable. Needless to say, I was somewhat apprehensive about walking that far in bear country with no protection. But there was no other choice. It would be several days before Doug Busat and his crew who were mining on the creek above me would be back after a few days off. Since I was blocking the trail with my truck I left him a note explaining my problem. Heavy on my mind was the fact that in the past few weeks hardly a day went by without seeing a grizzly, or at least a fresh sign of one.

I started up the trail with the sack of oranges in a small backpack and my nerves on a fine edge. *God! Was the hill always this steep?* My neck was swiveling like an owl as I kept a constant 360° sweep of the thick forest of spruce and underbrush. My throat and lungs were on fire as I tried to suck in more of the thin mountain air. In this situation, you must control your imagination, for every sound is expected to be a bear. A spruce hen flushed up almost under my feet sending my heart into overdrive! After that, I was convinced that I did not have a heart problem.

I stopped for a moment and then continued my hike. I rounded a sharp curve in the mountain trail and ran into a muddy area where several springs ran down the trail until they merged at a low spot and spilled over the edge of a cliff to begin a 500 foot descent to the creek below. The walk in the mud was difficult and very tiring so I stopped to drink some of the cool, clear spring water. I was half standing and half leaning against the bank when I felt the hair stand up on the back of my neck. I glanced up the trail and froze: there, about 100 yards ahead, was a big mama grizzly with her three cubs. *So this was the way it would happen* was the thought that flashed across my mind.

There is always a chance that a grizzly will attack, but often they just leave the scene. Unless it is a mother bear with cubs. Ninety-nine times out of one hundred she will attack to protect her young. I did not think she had seen me yet. She was eating high-bush cranberries and the cubs, which were about the size of a half-grown

Chow dog, were romping around and playing like little puppies. I had to get control of my thoughts and do something quick. *But what? Go back down the trail?* No, the bears liked to travel on the trail as it was easier to traverse than the thick brush, and I might encounter *other* bears because at this time of year they travel down to the river to feed on salmon.

Since I had not seen her tracks in the mud earlier, it was obvious the bears were on their way down the trail. *Could I sneak into the brush and wait for them to pass?* No, she would hear the noise. She had to see me any second now. I was sure she could hear my heart beating, my whole body vibrated to its beat. I carefully scanned the immediate area. *Maybe I could get up a tree,* but alas, all the trees were spruce with thick branches, and there would not be enough time to get up one before she got to me. No way. Then, just above me, I spotted a huge rock about 12 feet high, free standing. *If only I could get up on that rock.* I studied the rock carefully. I could not climb the sides! But there, a small spruce sapling grew alongside of it. I could climb up the tree and swing over to the rock.

It was my only chance. Time had run out as the big grizzly was now standing on her hind legs and sniffing the air! She had caught my scent! I think you could have heard my heart pounding a mile away. I very slowly turned around, faced uphill, and reached for a small tree root sticking out of the bank. I slowly pulled myself up the bank and into the brush. *If only I could do this without a stick or a limb breaking,* I thought, just as one did! Horrified now, I knew the mama grizzly must have heard me. Throwing caution to the wind, I raced for the big rock. I shot up the little tree, backpack and all, and swung over on top of the rock. I just lay there trying to still my heart and catch my breath. Then, I heard the horrible sound as the grizzly crashed through the brush, coming right at me! I could see her clearly now and she was looking straight into my eyes. The huge animal sounded like a bulldozer tearing through the brush with its engine turned off.

I quickly examined my position. The rock was free-standing on all sides; perhaps she would not be able to get up. But the little tree? Could she pull herself up on that? I could see when she stood that she was at least eight feet tall. She might reach me with a swipe of her paw. I had an area on top of the rock about five feet by seven feet. It sloped downhill and was uneven. I had to be careful as I moved about so that I would not slip off.

Feeling that I at least had a chance, I watched as the huge grizzly came closer, the cubs trailing along behind. She stopped about 20 feet away and stood up. I heard the blood-curdling growl deep inside her chest and throat, a sound like one you might hear from a mean dog when he is warning you to stay away, only a hundred times greater in volume. But I could not get away! Surely she could see that I was no threat to her cubs! But do animals reason? I have read and heard that they do not.

She dropped to all fours and smashed her way through the brush to the rock. Standing erect again, she began lunging at the rock, her long claws scraping over the edge just inches below me. I moved as far back as I dared. She then came around to the opposite side. Horrors! On the uphill side she could almost get her claws over the edge. She caught the edge of an outcropping at the top. *My God! She is coming up!* No, the rock was loose and she crashed back down. She roared again, mad now, as the piece of rock fell on her nose.

She bounded around to the other side. I again moved back. *This cannot go on, I have to do something to divert her attention from me.* I shot a quick glance at the cubs and I could not believe it! They were romping and playing. I shouted at her, "You dummy, don't you see I am not hurting your cubs?"

My voice seemed to make things worse. Hearing the limbs of the sapling tree start to shake, I thought this was the end: *she is coming up the tree!* Her head appeared at the edge of the rock. *Those teeth!* I could almost feel them tearing me apart. Needless to say, I'd had a marathon prayer going since this whole ordeal started. My prayer, to some extent, was answered as the small tree went crashing to the ground under the weight of the 700–800 pound bear. Shaken by the fall, she now stood just below the rock and continued her deep growl. I looked at the sack of oranges. A bow of the little tree had almost knocked them off. I pulled them over to the center of the rock. *Hey! The oranges, maybe I can distract her with them.* Tearing a hole in the net sack, I took an orange and tossed it to the cubs. They rolled it around a few times and then one of them bit into it. They discovered it was food and that it was sweet! I tossed another. Now two of the cubs had an orange. The other one was fussing and trying to get a bite. I tossed another. The cub that had gotten the first one grabbed this one too. Another fuss. I glanced back at the mother bear. She saw that something was amiss with the cubs and went to investigate. My prayer continued with thanks for a reprieve, if only for a minute or two.

Just as she reached the cubs I tossed some more oranges. Now *she* ate one. I tossed another. They were disappearing like peanuts. I looked at the sack. I only had about half a dozen left. I thought, *if I have to stay on this rock I should save a couple for myself.* I stuck two in my pockets and then proceeded to toss the remainder of the oranges to the bears. The mother bear did not seem as aggressive as she had been before. Maybe it got through her thick head that I was not a threat. It appeared that the cubs wanted to nurse, but mama did not seem to want them to.

I was afraid to relax but maybe, just maybe, I would make it out of this alive. The big bear finally lay down and let the cubs nurse. I began to realize how tired and weary I was. I very carefully lowered myself to a sitting position, but crouched to where I could keep my eye on the bear. God, I was tired. But I had to keep awake. If I dozed, I might fall right off the rock!

I noticed that the cubs were curling up to nap. *How long was this going to go on?* After a glance at my watch I found it had been almost two hours since I started my walk up the trail. I continued to watch the bears. The mother bear looked like she too was napping. But no! Now she was getting up and coming back to check on me. She circled the rock a couple of times growling and gnashing her teeth, and then she went back to lie down with the cubs. *How long will they sleep? Maybe I can get down and slip away.* No, now the little tree was gone. I would have to jump down with no way to get back up on the rock if she heard me. I would just have to wait it out and hope the bears eventually went away.

Sitting with my arms around my knees and my head in my lap, I must have dozed from exhaustion. Some sound brought me back. The cubs were playing around in the trail again. I did not see the mother. The hair on the back of my neck stood up. There she was, just below my feet, looking at me like I was fresh meat! *Will she ever give up and leave?* She seemed less aggressive but determined, nonetheless, as she again circled the rock. After two or three circles she returned to her cubs. They jumped all over her and played as though they did not have a care in the world. They did not, as far as I was concerned. After a while they all lay down again and were quiet.

I knew that when grizzlies found a kill or an animal carcass they would eat their fill and then cover the leftovers with sticks and mud, remaining nearby until it was all consumed. Was she treating me like a food cache? Planning to stay until they had me? I am sure there are many who live in, or have ventured into, the bush who have had an experience with a bear. Those of you who have will understand the predicament I was now in. A prisoner now, food later.

The bears all seemed to be sleeping again. I put my head back down on my knees and tried to rest. I dozed off again. Sometime later I woke up. I was stiff and sore and freezing cold. Although it had been a warm day for this area of the Yukon, nighttime was a different story. I looked at my watch, 11:05 p.m. That didn't make sense. *Let's see,* I thought, *I left the river at 2:00 p.m.* I had to concentrate. *Hell! That's nine hours!* I must have slept two or three hours, at least.

The grizzly. Where was she? I could not see her or the cubs. There was still plenty of light but the sun would shortly sink behind the mountains. I stood up, a spell of dizziness swept through my head, and I almost lost my balance. The shock of possibly falling off the rock snapped me back to full alertness. But still no sign of the bears. Was she just out of sight, waiting for me to come down?

A lifetime of agony. One wrong move now could be my last. I sat down to think. *I must have a plan.* I still had at least two miles separating me from my cabin. Although it would not get completely dark this time of year, after 1:00 a.m. it would be a kind of twilight. The thought of walking up the trail in dim light was not an option I wanted to consider.

I had to determine if the bears were still nearby. I pried a small piece of the boulder loose and held it in my hand, planning to toss it into the nearby brush and see if it brought any response. *Or should I? If she is still here, she might be ready to give up and leave.* The noise I would make could start the whole process over again! I hope no one ever has to face the decision I had to make. I decided to make some noise. I did not think I could last all night without rolling over and falling off the rock, perhaps sustaining a broken leg, or worse. Okay, I would make the noise.

I threw the piece of stone hard into the underbrush and listened. I strained my ears. Nothing. I would throw another rock if I could break off a piece. I grabbed a crack in the boulder but nothing broke off. I took out my buck knife and inserted it into the crack. A big chunk popped off. I let it fly. It glanced off a nearby tree and crashed through the brush. Plenty of racket! I waited. I waited some more. Not a sound, and my spirits climbed. I waited about 30 more minutes. I had almost one hour of good daylight yet.

I studied the ground below the rock. The bear had disturbed a patch of tundra moss just below the uphill side. It looked soft and I would try to jump and land there. If I sprained an ankle or broke a bone I would be in serious trouble. This was it! Without further delay, I hung my feet over the edge just above the moss, slid as far as I could to shorten my distance to the ground, and let go. I landed in the mossy area but tumbled back. My head struck the rock and almost knocked me out.

I was bleeding, but a quick check revealed only a small cut. *What else could happen?* I thought, but I was okay. I stood and listened for about five minutes. No sound. The grizzly bears were gone!

I started up the trail, almost walking backwards to watch my back. Moving at a near-jog I walked like the devil was behind me. I tried to ignore the burning in my throat and lungs as I gasped for air, hiking uphill. I kept going. Distance was safety for me now.

I reached my cabin at 1:30 a.m. that morning. The whole ordeal had lasted 11 ½ hours. This was an event in my life that I would never forget. I vowed never to be caught in bear country again without some protection. I spent a long time right there on the cabin floor on my knees thanking God again for my life.

I later discovered that it *was* the ignition coil that had quit. After replacing the coil, the engine purred back to life. Later, I sat again in my cabin looking out the window at the old truck. A warm feeling came over me because I again had my old friend, ready to go. I thought, *will I ever leave this place of beauty and peace? What about the little ground squirrels sitting on the doorstep waiting for a handout? The huge bull moose that passes within 50 feet of my cabin several times a week?* I did not know.

Colleen Kennedy's Claim

Before the end of the season that I spent prospecting alone, I got word of a lady named Colleen Kennedy who had a claim about a mile from me down the creek. Her claim had belonged to her husband but he had passed away and she was not doing anything with it. I worked her claim with a gold pan and got some pretty good color and a few little nuggets, so I looked this lady up in the phonebook, drove to her house in Whitehorse, and told her that I was interested in buying her claim on Squaw Creek. I asked her if she would consider selling it to me.

"I have thought about selling before," she said. "It's obvious that I'm not going to be able to do anything with it and I don't have anyone else in the family that has any mining experience."

"Well," I said, "I've been mining up there on one of Heinz Eckervogt's claims and I haven't done so well, but I've done enough to keep me interested. I would like to have a claim of my own, so if we could agree on a price, I would like to make you an offer on your claim."

"What are you willing to offer?" she asked.

I thought it over for a bit. There was a small log cabin that her husband had built on this claim that I could use as my base of operation, and the claim had an open space on a nearby gravel bar where I could land a helicopter. We bandied around on the price for a while and I waited a few weeks before I checked back in with her.

"Just tell me what your bottom dollar is and if I can afford it I'll buy it, if not I'll just go on," I told her.

"I want 15,000 American dollars," she said.

I was hoping to get the claim for much less than that and pick it up as a bargain, but I felt it was promising enough that it was worth the gamble. I bought her claim and agreed to let her retain a 5% interest on whatever I recovered, which would not be a problem if I recovered well. This purchase threw things for a little bit of a loop back home because I had to take money from the funds that Tracy needed while I was gone. I was sure betting on this claim. Colleen Kennedy and I went to the land office in Whitehorse and she transferred the claim over to my name. I now owned my very own mining claim in the Yukon Territory on Squaw Creek.

While I was back in Haines I made sure to visit again with Jo Jurgeleit. Jo was still mining on Porcupine Creek, and though she could not do much with one leg, she was sure trying. I told her that I bought a nearby claim from Colleen Kennedy and it turned out that Jo knew Colleen.

"She's a good person and whatever she told you, you can believe," Jo said.

"Well, so far it has been that way."

I spent a little time with Jo helping her get some things done around her house and I got to hear a few more of her wild tales. Her stories were all so unreal, but I believed that they really happened. Almost everyone I met in Haines confirmed her stories. It seemed to me that anybody in the mining business sooner or later would get to know Jo Jurgeleit.

Colleen Kennedy's claim on Squaw Creek was on the Yukon side of the border between the Yukon Territory and British Columbia. I was familiar with the land and I liked the idea of being in the Yukon Territory. It just seemed to have a romantic ring to it, and there was an allure that attracted me.

I decided to do a bit of exploratory mining on the claim for the remainder of the summer, so again I moved my bulldozer, this time from Heinz' claim down to the new claim that I had just bought. I dug a trench about 12–15 feet deep but did not hit bedrock. I stopped periodically to test the ground with a pan; I was getting color and the occasional rice-sized nugget, but still no bedrock. I checked the terrain and decided there must be a drop off above the claim that had filled with silt, sand, and gravel over thousands of years of water flowing down the mountain. I hoped that if I hit bedrock I would have a serious gold mine on my hands!

I shared my theory with a mining engineer I had become acquainted with in town, and to a certain extent he agreed with me.

"The problem is that if your theory is correct your gold is going to be very deep."

He suggested I move down the creek and dig another test hole to see if I could hit bedrock somewhere else, so I went to the very end of the claim and dug another trench with the bulldozer. Again, after digging nearly 15 feet below ground, I did not hit bedrock. At this point I began considering whether or not to go through the expense of having a drilling rig come out to my claim and dig some core samples. After some research I found that just the transport of the drilling rig into the canyon would cost more money than I could afford to spend. The only way I could justify the venture was to get some other miners to agree to have testing done on their claims as well so that we could divide up the cost. As time went by that season I got in touch with other miners in the area and made my proposition. Unfortunately, none of the miners could justify the expense either, especially since everyone above me could hit bedrock anywhere from 8–12 feet deep. I subsequently dropped the drilling rig idea and prepared to mine the claim the following year.

As summer wore on I decided I had probably done just about all I could to get ready for next year. I now had two promising claims to mine and I could not wait to return next summer. I found a storage barn in Haines, Alaska where I could keep my helicopter, saving me from having to haul it back home on the trailer. I could not believe the price to store the helicopter: just $50 for the winter. I shut everything down on my claim, spent a day or two visiting with Heinz and Katy, and then told them I would be back next year.

As soon as I got home I began working on plans for the following season, but while I was back in Texas I needed to produce more funds to support my mining operation. I also knew that I needed to do some of the things that Tracy wanted to do. Tracy was always understanding with me while I was gone on these projects and she helped me out with business while I was away. She also had a real estate license and kept business going successfully in my absence. In fairness, we discussed before we married that I was an avid explorer of the North Country and that I would periodically spend time away. At the same time, I wanted to be fair to her, so that winter I negotiated a few real estate deals and spent time doing some of the things that Tracy enjoyed. I carried on with my old routine—at least until the next mining season started.

The Mining Season with Tom Wolfe

One of my neighbors, Tom Wolfe, had for years now been interested in what I was doing up north, and he kept hinting that if I had any room for him he would also like to get involved in gold mining. We talked about it from time to time but had never come to any decisions.

While I was home that year, Tom Wolfe came by the house one day to talk more about mining. I could see the gleam in his eye—I recognized it as the same one I had when I first started mining.

"Well, let's think about this," I said. "We've got to acquire some kind of mountain goat type truck to get up and down the steep terrain. I have been seriously considering trying to locate a surplus army vehicle."

I was looking for a four-wheel drive M-37, which is really just an oversized pickup truck. Tom said he had seen an advertisement for a dealership up in Iowa that rebuilt and refurbished these kinds of trucks and he suggested that we check it out. It turned out that this dealership had several army vehicles to pick from at very reasonable prices.

Then Tom came to me with another idea.

"I've got this Dodge diesel pickup with duel wheels, and I also have a trailer that could haul an M-37. If you let me join you in your mining venture, we can take it up to Iowa and pick up one of those trucks." That was all it took to turn the tide and I made the decision that Tom would be a useful asset to the team. I looked forward to the next mining season with him.

Tom and I loaded up his pickup and we drove to the dealership in Iowa. We tried out three different surplus army vehicles, including the M-37, on some muddy, hilly terrain on the edge of town. We were both sold on the M-37 so we bought it, loaded it up on the trailer, and hauled it back to Texas.

I visited with Tom frequently to teach him how everything worked and what he needed to do to prepare for our summer on Squaw Creek. When the time came to get our gear together we rigged up a sign on our M-37 that Tom's wife Sharon had printed for us. "Alaska or Bust. Last of the Forty Niners," it said. We got a lot of comments about our sign on the drive to the North Country.

Tom and I left for Canada in mid-April. When we got to the Canadian border, the inspector looked at the sign on our truck.

"You Yanks are still at it, ay?" he said.

Tom's Dodge was just doing great hauling that trailer. We had a little bit of everything on it, including a four-wheeler that we would use to move up and down the creek. It took us about a week to reach Whitehorse and by the time we got there the snow had just about thawed completely. Finally, we arrived in Haines, Alaska. It had been a long trip on the highway, all of it hard driving.

Our first stop was Heinz and Katy's house, and they welcomed Tom just like they had always welcomed me. Tom was anxious to meet Heinz and was spellbound listening to the yarns he was spinning—and in Heinz' case, most of the yarns were actually true. Tom and I stayed in the guesthouse out back while we made the final preparations and repairs to our equipment.

After a few days of work we took Heinz out for a drive on the highway in the M-37. We were into May now and we decided to drive down to the Tatshenshini River to see how the ice was melting. Once we reached the river we got about half a mile up the road before we hit snow that was just too deep to negotiate. We managed to get the truck turned around and realized we would have to delay our departure to Squaw Creek considerably.

We spent a few more days working on our equipment. This year, I built a new sluice box and was trying out a slightly different system. I installed rollers supported by bearings that I hoped would speed up the sluicing process. When we were not working, Tom, Heinz, and I visited friends. Heinz' neighbor was named Art Papinou and he could tell stories faster than you could think them up. Art was a native French speaker but he spoke very good English—albeit with a heavy accent. We spent a lot of time with Art at the Dezadeash Lake Lodge, which was about the only place in the area where you could buy a meal, so many people gathered there to play pool or dominos and socialize.

We kept checking the trail but the snow was very slow to melt. Finally, in the first week of June, we checked the trail again and determined that we could make it through. We loaded everything onto the M-37 and headed back to the Tatshenshini River. Just like before, we broke through the surface layer of ice with our bulldozer and made our way across. Tom was like a kid in a candy store enjoying all the scenery and adventure. He was so happy he had joined us, and he was no slouch to get in there and do his part. Tom was a really big help and I was glad to have him along.

By mid-June Tom and I had everything set up and were sluicing on the new claim I had bought from Colleen Kennedy. Tom just worked like a Trojan. I do not know how he put up with me because when I get into the working mode I can sometimes drive people a little bit too hard. I really pushed Tom, and I think that if the positions had been switched I probably would have quit, but because it was my operation and I had the mining experience, Tom was really good about listening and taking my advice. He kept working away and understood that we were under pressure—I was starting a new claim and I really wanted it to produce.

Tom and I worked long and hard that season, but in the end, the claim was just not paying enough to be worth continuing to mine as hard as we were. We were running close to 300 yards of ground a day through our sluice box and it was paying only $1–2 per yard. That was just a drop in the bucket compared to what it was costing us to do it.

In the back of my mind I began thinking that this mining business was just not going to work. I had been mining on Squaw

Creek for several years now and still had not hit it big. Although there were a few seasons that I recovered some pretty good gold, the big pay dirt had eluded me thus far. I talked it over with Tom to see what he thought.

"I have enjoyed the heck out of being here, it's like a whole new vacation to do this, but based on what we've been able to produce, I'll probably have to bow out next season."

"Well, Tom, I don't blame you," I said. "You've worked real hard."

We worked late into October and then decided it was time to leave. As our luck would have it, just when Tom and I decided to shut down we began hitting some good gold and were finding more nuggets at cleanup. Over the course of the entire summer we had recovered about 7 or 8 ounces of gold, but in that last week alone we got nearly 12 ounces! It was hard to pack up the operation now that we were finally starting to see some success, but the weather was beginning to turn so I decided it was time to leave before the snow came in and the rivers froze.

Finally, Tom and I returned to Heinz and Katy's house. We had a good meal for dinner and the next morning Tom was on his way home. He was anxious to get back to Texas and I knew I could not keep up with him, so I stayed another day visiting with the Eckervogts. The next morning I loaded up all my equipment and began my own journey back to Austin. After a long drive home, Tom's family and my family went out to dinner to celebrate, even though we had come home with nothing. Tom insisted that it was all worth it because he had such an enjoyable time. Regardless of how it turned out, Tom thought it was a tremendous experience and I really enjoyed having his company.

The Return to Post River

In August of 1985 I returned to my cabin on Post River that I had built 10 years earlier. I was amazed at how well the cabin had held up; it looked just like I had left it nine years earlier. The only difference I noticed was that there were more traces of bears. The bears were never aggressive, but I could see their muddy paw tracks across my porch and on the windows—I guess they were just checking their reflection. I was amazed that they had not cracked any glass. Of course, if a window ever did break and a bear smelled food in the cabin, that would be the end of it. Bears never give up in the hunt for food!

In fact, I still had food left over—some of it 10 years old—from my previous visits to the cabin. There were canned blueberries that I had left in my food cellar which were still edible, and although I prefer the fresh variety, I used them to make another one of my special Walter Yates Post River Blueberry Cobblers. Only a grandma could beat my recipe! And my grandma taught me mine.

I brought a friend from Round Rock named Bert Hall with me on this trip. We were investigating a silver deposit on the side of the mountain that I climbed for my film *Breakaway* during the year I spent on Post River. About halfway up the side of the mountain was a huge outcropping of silver and we were researching the possibility of doing something with the deposit, but there were many problems facing us on this venture. There was no road to reach the site, it would be impossible to mine without heavy equipment, and the silver ore would be too heavy to fly out. I knew it was probably a hopeless cause, but we had a lot of fun examining the area.

A few days into our stay on Post River I got news of an arctic front moving into the area over my little portable broadcast radio. We cut our trip a few days short—I figured we had enjoyed just about all we could at Post River before the weather caught us. I cranked up the old Comanche and we flew out. Over the course of 10 years, both the river and my gravel-bar runway had changed. About one-third of the runway was now cut off and I decided I better not fly in there with the Comanche again. Next time, I would need a Super Cub or a Cessna 180—if not just a helicopter—because the gravel bar was just too short now. If the conditions weren't just right, and with more than one person in the plane, I might have some serious problems taking off.

After five days at Post River, Bert and I flew to the central Yukon to explore some gold country I had my eye on above Squaw Creek. Our plan was to hike about 30 miles up the mountain from my old claim to do some prospecting on a new creek. Our trip up the mountain lasted five days, and it turned out to be one of the most impressive prospecting trips that I had ever taken, but not for normal reasons.

Bert and I flew to Haines Junction from Post River and called Heinz Eckervogt. Always ready to help, Heinz came and picked us up from the airport. We unloaded our gear into his car and he took us back to his house where I told Heinz about the prospecting we wanted to do above Squaw Creek. I had flown over the area before and had my eye on a location that I felt would be well worth the trouble to prospect. The creek flowed out of a glacier bed and ran through a canyon between two mountains, eventually flowing into a large lake.

I could tell that Heinz was interested in the claim himself. He told me he had thought about prospecting in that area as well and knew exactly which creek I was talking about.

"It has all the promise of being really good ground," he said. "I don't know if anyone has ever prospected there before, but it is probably going to be worth your while. I wish I could go with you." At that time Heinz was not able to go with us, but he told us he would assist us however he could.

Bert and I got our packs together and enough supplies and food to sustain ourselves for a week in the wilderness (including a 30.6 rifle, just in case). Then, Heinz hauled us down to the Tatshenshini river. It was August when we made this trip and the river was running at its fullest from the melt off of the glaciers. It was too difficult to cross the river in a vehicle so we had to use the aluminum boat. Before we crossed the river, we made arrangements with Heinz to be picked up when we returned five days later.

Bert and I took the boat across the Tatshenshini and then started hiking up the mountain. I was fairly familiar with the route—particularly the first 12 miles—because I had travelled it so many times before to reach my claim on Squaw Creek. We stopped overnight at the mining camp and made a plan for our upcoming week of prospecting. We decided that we would climb the mountain over its steep and rough terrain rather than go around it via level valleys; although the trek over the mountain would be much more difficult, the route through the valleys would take four times longer.

We woke up early the next morning and it took us all day to get over that mountain. We then set up camp and hit the sack, but we did not sleep too well that night because we had spotted signs of bears and were a little bit fearful about one sneaking up on us. Fortunately, none turned up. The next morning, we loaded up again and made it to the creek by late afternoon.

We did not have the equipment to test the ground extensively, but we did carry with us a 5-gallon plastic bucket with holes drilled in the bottom that we could use to concentrate a few shovels of material by shaking it into a gold pan. Our first test yielded a lot of color and Bert and I were very encouraged. We stair-stepped our way up the creek, testing for color at different spots, and it seemed to me like it was increasing as we moved up the creek. We were five or six miles up the creek when we found our first rice-sized nuggets, one or two of them even pea-sized. We panned in areas where the creek swerved and swung out, depositing black sand and gold in the ground after years of erosion into the side of the mountain.

It was easy to see where the creek bed had once been before thousands of years of flowing water had altered its course.

On the third day we got within a mile of the head of the creek and the ground was yielding even better results. Our first test recovered a one-ounce nugget, something highly unusual to find just by panning. We worked late into the night because we still had daylight until 2:00 a.m., and by the time we quit panning we knew that we had really made a good strike. We must have recovered 12 ounces of nuggets from the tests alone! We congratulated each other and looked forward to getting back to Whitehorse to file for this claim.

On the morning of the fourth day Bert and I were having breakfast and discussing our good fortune when all of a sudden two grizzly-looking prospectors appeared from up above the creek. These guys looked as tough as nails and they wanted to know what in the hell we were doing on their claim.

"Wait a minute, mister," I said. "We're just prospecting and there are no posts on this claim. It's not yours."

"Well, we say it *is* our claim," one of them said. "We are not going to stand here and let some Yanks come in and take over what is ours."

"If it's your claim, how come it isn't posted?" I asked.

"We made this discovery about three months ago and we've been out in the country checking out some other ground. We haven't had time to stake our claim at the land office but we are on our way into town right now. We found it first and we are going to keep it."

By this time Bert and I were both getting nervous because these guys did not look too sanitary. One of them had a .357 Magnum slung on his hip and the other had a shotgun in his pack. The guy with the pistol put his hand on it and the other fellow looked like he was getting ready to do the same.

"I'll tell you what's going to happen," the more aggressive one said. "You fellas' are going to pack up and get the hell out of here. Forget your ever saw this piece of ground."

Then Bert cut in.

"Walter, that other creek we prospected last week looks as good as what we're seeing here. Why don't we just forget this thing and go back over there."

"What creek are you talking about now?" one of them asked.

"It's in the drainage out of the Noisy Range," I said.

"That don't concern us," he said. "But this is our claim, we've got control of it. If you know what's good for ya' you'll just get out of here." He still had his hand on that pistol.

I realized that our situation was not good. As deep into the wilderness as we were, it would not be hard for these men to rub us out, bury us under a rock, and never get caught—and they looked like they would do it. I knew these men were not going to back down, and as the saying goes, "I'm a lover, not a fighter." I looked at Bert and said, "I think you're probably right. If these guys say they found this claim first, even though they haven't filed for it, I guess we haven't got any right to contest them. The best thing for us to do is to pack up and leave."

The other fellow who hadn't said much chimed in at this. "That's the smartest words you ever said, mister." I think he meant it.

Discretion being the better part of valor, I decided we better get out of there. We put our packs on our backs, grabbed our pick and shovel, and started back down the creek. I kept an eye behind me, not sure whether they would really let us go or not. After we got away from them Bert began unloading on me. He said he thought he was going to have to change his drawers because he believed they were going to kill us.

By nightfall we had reached the camp on Squaw Creek and we stayed the night to get some much needed rest. Then, early on the morning of the fifth day, we hiked the 12 miles back down to the Tatshenshini River. When we got there, it sure was nice to see Heinz across the river with his truck, casting for salmon while he waited. He had three really nice silver salmon in the back of his truck that he had already caught. When he saw Bert and me, he came over in the aluminum boat and picked us up. With both of us trying to talk at the same time, Bert and I told Heinz what had happened.

"It sounds like two characters who are well-known around here for claim jumping," Heinz said. "It's possible we could get to Whitehorse before they do and file that claim."

"If you think it's worth it and that these guys won't look us up and try to shoot us later, then let's run on into Whitehorse!" I said.

"I am pretty sure I know who they are. We can file a complaint on them and get the Mounties to pick them up." The "Mounties" were the Royal Canadian Mounted Police.

The three of us jumped in the truck and beat it back to Heinz' house. There, we changed clothes and jumped in Heinz' Audi sedan that could really move. By the time we got to Whitehorse the land office was closed so we spent the night at a lodge. At 8 o'clock the next morning we were waiting at the door of the land office and as soon as it opened we went in to file the claim.

"Let's not just file one claim," Heinz suggested. "Let's file on the whole creek."

"Whatever you think is right," I said.

We filed the claim in all of our names so that we could decide later what to do with it. We had beat those guys to the land office, so that took care of that, but I was looking over my shoulder everywhere I went for the next few days that Bert and I were in Haines. We did not want to hang around.

About a month later I got a letter at home from Heinz telling me that after all that had happened at the creek he had gotten notice from the mining authority that the area we staked had been closed for a national park. The notice said we were to be advised that our claims had been revoked. I suppose it was for the best because the creek was so remote that it would have been very difficult to get bulldozers and front-end loaders into the area, but that is another piece of ground in the Yukon Territory that, in my opinion, is loaded with gold. And that gold is going to stay there.

On August 30th, after our 10-day trip to the North Country, Bert and I were back at Burwash Landing, approximately 200 miles east of the Alaskan border. It was time for Bert to return to Texas, but I was going to stay up north for a few days longer.

I flew to Fort Nelson to visit my friend Trevor Grimshaw. Trevor had many interesting experiences running his helicopter service, but I do not think any outdo the time he airlifted six horses out of a hunting camp in the mountains with a sling load. The horses were stranded on a mountain and would not have survived the severe weather that was headed their way. Trevor and his men rigged up a special saddle that would fit under the four legs of a horse, suspending it like a baby in a diaper. The special rig prevented the horse from kicking and falling out of its harness. Trevor had some truly exciting stories and it was always a pleasure to visit with him.

By the end of my visit with Trevor the arctic front had caught us and I decided it was time to return to Texas. With all the snow and ice I knew I would have to make my way south very carefully, but there was one important stop I needed to make on my journey home.

On September 2nd, 1985, the sixth anniversary of my helicopter crash in British Columbia, I flew over the crash site in a fixed-wing airplane. It took me a little while to find the exact spot, but once I did, I saw that the open clearing and the damaged trees were still there. The brush and the trees I had chopped down during my fall had grown up quite a bit, and I knew that in time the site would be completely hidden by the brush, berry vines, and ground growth that pervaded the muskeg tundra of British Columbia. I occasionally ran into someone at an airport or café in the North Country who remembered my crash, but as all things go, it was gradually forgotten. Of course, I would never forget the experience, but mine was just one of many crash stories in the North Country.

Exploring Adventures with Heinz

I spent most of the off-season exploring the North Country with Heinz from my helicopter. Heinz really loved to go flying and we often explored nearby glaciers. One day we got up the nerve to land on one, but we had to be very careful because glaciers are full of cracks and crevasses in the ice. The cracks will often bridge over with snow, so if you are not cautious while walking around on a glacier you might suddenly fall into one of the cracks. Aware of these dangers, Heinz and I carefully selected a point to set down the helicopter and we stayed just long enough to take a look around and shoot some photographs.

On another little side trip, Heinz and I flew the Bell 47 G4 northwest up the canyon to a hidden lake he had discovered years earlier. Heinz told me that this lake was just *loaded* with trout and that it was a great place to go fishing. At first I was a little leery of taking the trip because Heinz did not know exactly how far away the lake was and I did not want to burn up too much of the fuel that we would need to get back to Haines Junction, but Heinz assured me that it would not be a long flight.

We flew about 25 miles before we reached the lake. All of a sudden, the valley opened up in front of us and I saw a huge body of water stretched before me. I estimated that the lake spanned over 50 acres.

I hovered around looking for a place to set down the helicopter. After some searching, I found an outcropping of rock that had a level bench large enough to land on just a few hundred yards up a hill from the lake. We landed safely, got out our fishing rods, and started looking for a place to cast out.

"It won't make any difference where you fish," Heinz said. "I haven't been here in ten years but the whole lake is just loaded with trout."

We walked down to a firm peninsula-like formation in the swampy ground that surrounded the water. The lake had the most clear, beautiful water I had ever seen; you could throw a dime in it

10 feet away and be able to see whether it was heads or tails. I put an artificial lure on my line and cast out, and so help me, I thought the lake was going to explode! There were fish jumping all over the place, fighting for that lure. These trout were really spirited fish; they would leap up into the air and you could hear the line *zing zinging* as it was pulled through the water. I immediately hooked a trout, and at least half a dozen others followed as I reeled it in. I stood there catching one trout after another, and they were all about 18 inches long. I do not know if I have ever enjoyed a fishing trip so much. Most of the fish we caught and released, but we brought some back home with us as well. We had fish for breakfast, lunch, and dinner. Before the year was out I returned to that lake several times and I never had a problem catching a fish—it was just like ordering a fish from the market. This place was really a paradise, and I called it Trout Lake.

The Buried Ship

On one of my other exploring adventures I made yet another incredible discovery.

I found an old square rigger, a four-masted sailing ship, that apparently had run aground many, many years earlier. Four masts stuck up out of the sand marking the spot where the ship went down approximately a quarter-mile from the Gulf of Alaska. This gave me some indication as to what was happening to the terrain—the beach line had pushed outward, because the ship certainly had not beached so far inland. The ship as I found it was buried 25–30 feet deep into the sand with just the masts sticking out of the ground.

I was fascinated by this ship and wanted to find a way to excavate it out—who knew what could be found inside of it! After doing some research I discovered two other people who already knew about the ship, and I am sure many more knew about it as well. The men I spoke with believed the vessel was a Japanese trading ship that had run aground in 1897, perhaps en route to trade with the Russians. In the end, however, we were not able to dig out the ship. Both the U.S. and the Canadian environmental protection agencies were hard as horseradish and I was not able to get a permit to disturb the historical area. Highly protected sites like this were numerous all over the North Country, and the penalties for violating regulations were severe!

The German Soldier

Back during World War II there was a German foot soldier. This soldier carried a rifle, and if he met a member of the opposing enemy forces, it would have been his obligation and duty to his country to fire his weapon and attempt to take the other soldier's life. During the same war, in a different country, there was an American Marine. He was also a foot soldier and carried a rifle. Had he run into enemy forces, which he occasionally did, he too would have been obligated to shoot.

As you can probably guess, the former Marine was me. The German foot soldier was a mutual friend of the Eckervogt's who I met on one of my visits to their home in Haines Junction. Like me, the German's name was Walter, and we hit it off from the start. Walter and I spent a lot of time discussing our thoughts on life; he had an open mind and was easy to talk to. There was just one problem: Walter could barely speak English, and I was in even worse shape speaking German.

Heinz had planned a prospecting trip to an area one mountain range over from Squaw Creek. Heinz believed the area was really good ground for mining but he had never examined the land closely, so he invited Walter and I to go along with him. I immediately accepted the invitation because I saw it as just another adventure for me to take into a land where very few people had ever been. At the last minute, however, something came up and Heinz was unable to make the trip. Walter did not have a lot more time left on his visit to North America and he really wanted to go prospecting, so it was agreed that Walter and I would go ahead and take the trip together. What I learned on this trip would change my view on life.

Walter had served as a German soldier during World War II at the same time that I had served in the U.S. Marine Corps. Forty years later there we were, just by chance, thrown together on a prospecting trip—each of us using makeshift sign language to communicate. We planned to be gone about a week, which was about all the time Walter had left on his trip. We spent two days hiking and camping and about three days prospecting before we returned to Dezadeash Lake. In the end, we did not have much luck prospecting. We found one little creek that showed promise and yielded some color, but we got no nuggets.

Walter and I decided that the creek probably would not pay—of course, we could barely understand what the other was saying. Despite the language barrier we communicated pretty well and we certainly enjoyed ourselves. We had fun simply exploring the ground and being out there on our own in the wilderness. I even introduced Walter to the stick bread and stew that I invented during my year on Post River, and he was so excited to learn this technique. Walter often went camping back in Germany and he told me he could hardly wait to get back and introduce the recipe to his friends.

Walter and I were just two kindred souls that came together and clicked. I enjoyed the time I spent with Walter and I know he enjoyed it as well. I thought, *how unusual that we should end up together this way, sharing a rifle.* Forty years earlier, we would have been obligated to shoot one another had we met in battle.

"Here we are, two soldiers that could have once been fighting each other," Walter said, "but now we are exploring the wilderness together and really enjoying ourselves."

"That's true," I answered.

"It's a shame that the leaders of the countries that were at war back then could not get together and do the same thing we are doing now." I thought that was about as logical an idea that a man could come up with.

Our conversation made me look a little deeper into this person that I was sharing my time with out in the wilderness. We both remarked that we were fortunate that the two of us never met in battle. Most of Walter's service was in Russia fighting their army, while mine was in the South Pacific. This turned out to be one of the most moving experiences I had in the North Country.

We tried to teach each other some basics of the other's language. Walter was doing a lot better at English than I was at German, but I think he had been working on English for much longer. It is amazing how well we communicated. Of course, we did a lot of stick drawing in the ground and used our arms and other body language. I know Heinz' wife Katy was concerned about us going off together and not being able to communicate, but we both assured her that we could understand each other well enough to get by. And we did.

The ideas Walter and I discussed on that trip stay with me today. We fought because we were loyal to our countries and our countries were at war. We had to fight at wartime, but that did not mean we could not be civilized human beings in peacetime. Whether he be German, Russian, or Japanese, I realized that I could have had the same connection and friendship with any other former enemy soldier as I had with Walter. Regardless of nationality, when it comes right down to it, we all, as humans, tend to think along the same lines. With that in mind, I see no reason why we should ever have wars.

Walter and I carried a rifle with us on this trip just in case we needed protection from a bear. As we walked along through the wilderness we shared the duty of carrying the rifle. Walter would carry it for a while and I would carry it for a while. We got a chuckle out of that too.

Mining Season with Andy Andersen

An old bush pilot friend of mine named Harold Andersen—we all called him Andy—had retired to Sequim, Washington after years of running a flying service in Alaska, and I spent a few days visiting with him at least once a year. On one of those trips I told him about my mining operation on Squaw Creek in the Yukon Territory.

"What do you do down here during the summers?" I asked Andy. "Have you ever thought about mining?"

Andy's eyes lit up. "You know, as much time as I've spent in Alaska, I often thought I should try my hand at mining. If you have room for someone to help, I'd be happy to join you next season." It was decided that Andy would join me for the 1992 gold mining season.

Early that year I went to Seattle and spent a week with Andy to prepare our gear for the upcoming mining venture. Andy had acquired a surplus 2.5-ton army truck that could negotiate the mountains of the Yukon and we loaded everything you could imagine inside of it, including 20 sheets of plywood, containers of anti-freeze, and even a metal detector. Andy liked a drink that was a modified version of a martini, so he filled some gallon-jugs with gin and vodka and put them on the truck as well. We then shipped the truck to Juneau on a ferry. I met the ferry in Juneau, did some work on the truck, and then put it on another ferry from Juneau to Haines, Alaska

In mid-May, just before the trail opened to Squaw Creek, I took the truck into the Yukon Territory and met with Officer George, a Canadian customs agents I had become friends with over the years.

"You've got a lot of taxable merchandise on here to be bringing into the country," he said.

"Well, I expected to pay some kind of tax, but you understand that all of this equipment is for personal use. We are going to use it in our mining operation."

"It all fits in the same category as far as the Canadian government is concerned."

Officer George spent five hours going over the truck. I had to unload a lot of gear and I was getting pretty frustrated. After much negotiating he came up with a price and I wrote him a check for $400. I was really reluctant to pay this tax because the equipment had already cost me quite a bit of money, but this was the only way I was going to get the gear to my claim. I also reasoned that this price must be fair because if I had purchased the equipment in Canada it would have cost me much more. When I was finally cleared by customs I got back on the road, entered Canada, and eventually made it back at Heinz and Katy Eckervogt's home on Dezadeash Lake where I spent a few weeks waiting for Andy to arrive.

Andy was the kind of partner that I should have had all along. He was a terrific guy and could do just about anything. Andy arrived in June and we finally departed for the mountain. This time, we were taking in a Caterpillar 966 front-end loader that could sluice larger loads. As we made our way up the trail to Squaw Creek, Andy drove the old truck and I followed behind him in the front-end loader. It turned out to be quite fortunate that we had the front-loader because the truck got stuck several times and we had to pull it out with the Cat.

It was about a week before we got everything going, but when we finally did, we recovered some big nuggets! After three or four clean ups, however, it started slowing down so I decided to relocate. We were easily hitting bedrock and I wanted to find the same deposit we had hit before.

We moved a little up the creek to try to intercept this vein of pay dirt. Although Andy had not operated heavy equipment before, he picked up on it right away. It was a huge advantage not having to operate everything myself as I had in the past.

The transmission in the old army truck went out about mid-season. Andy said, "No problem," lifted the hood, and figured out what was broken. We got on the radio phone and ordered the necessary parts from a place in Seattle that Andy recommended. It took about two weeks to get the parts, and when they arrived, Andy rebuilt the transmission himself. That is what was so good about Andy. He could do just about anything. And that is what it takes to be a miner in the wilderness when you are so far from a repair shop. Andy and I took out a little over 50 oz. of gold that year. It was not a great success, but Andy was so happy to have shared in the gold mining experience. The memories from that summer were all Andy needed, and he went back to his retirement.

Mining Season with Bob Armstrong

A chance meeting I had back in Austin with an old friend, Bob Armstrong, whom I had not seen for several years, triggered a venture that both he and I will never forget. Bob was involved in politics and at one time ran for governor of Texas. He was a member of the Texas House of Representatives and served as the Assistant Secretary of the Interior under the Clinton administration. After hearing my stories of gold prospecting in the Yukon Territory, he too was bit by the gold bug! I invited Bob to come up to the Yukon and see a whole new world—the world of gold mining.

Bob's first trip up north will be long remembered. After spending a few days with me on Squaw Creek, Bob decided to join me in my next mining operation and returned home to prepare to join me next season. The following year, Bob flew up to Alaska via Alaska Airlines and landed in Juneau.

I had given Bob the names of some people he could call on if help was needed. One of my friends ran a shuttle service, Layton Flying Service, and he flew Bob to Haines, Alaska. There, he contacted my friend Jo Jurgeleit, the now 70 year old one-legged miner.

Bob and I had arranged a time for him to arrive at Squaw Creek, but we were using the "Caribou Network Calendar," which was more based on rumor than fact, so I was not sure exactly when Bob would arrive. I left my camp at Squaw Creek and stayed at Heinz and Katy's house while I waited for Bob's call announcing that he had arrived in Haines. Around 11:00 p.m. that night the call came, but Bob had a problem. He was calling from the U.S.-Canadian border, stuck between two customs offices. The U.S. customs office was about half a mile away from the Canadian customs office. The

Canadian office closed at 9:00 p.m. and Bob was told by the U.S. customs officer that he would not be able to enter Canada until 7:00 a.m. the next morning. Jo had driven Bob to the border in her VW Beetle and was sending him with a fresh 15-pound king salmon for the Eckervogt's to cook. She dropped Bob off at the U.S. customs office with his luggage and the fish and took off for home before Bob realized that he would not be able to enter Canada that night.

It turned out that Heinz and one of the Canadian customs officers were good friends. In the middle of the night, Heinz called this friend and explained our problem.

"Do you realize what time it is?" she asked Heinz.

"Well, yes, but Walter's friend is on foot, standing at the door of the U.S. customs office, and there is no place for him to stay. If you let him enter we will come down and pick him up."

After a few minutes of silence she asked Heinz what time we could be there and Heinz said we could make it by one o'clock. She reluctantly agreed to help us out.

Used to driving the German Autobahn with no speed limit, Heinz got us to the customs office 100 miles away on a gravel road in one hour. We arrived 10 minutes till one.

Heinz, the Canadian officer, and I were standing at the customs gate when Bob appeared. We all had to suppress a laugh at the sight of Bob struggling and half dragging his luggage and the 15-pound fish up the steep half-mile road in a night as dark as the inside of a black cow. Bob was cleared by the kind-hearted customs officer and we all promised not to mention her rule bending. I was proud of Bob for not using his government position in this difficult situation.

Bob spent one short season with me on squaw creek. He was enjoying the mining venture so much that he arranged for his wife Linda and eight-year old son Will to join us for a week. We all had a great time living the life as miners in such a primitive setting. Although our camp left a lot to be desired, Bob's family took everything in stride. I especially enjoyed the antics and true delight of little Will as, wild-eyed and enthusiastic, he stored memories of a once-in-a-lifetime experience—one in which he accidentally baptized himself by falling into Squaw Creek's 34° water. Linda's motherly love prepared him for his next adventure on Squaw Creek, but no swimming!

Only a few weeks into the season Heinz' two boys showed up at our claim and brought some horrible news. They had just gotten word that the Canadian government was going to convert all the land from Squaw Creek to the Yukon border into a national park. Of course, we were just now starting to hit some pay dirt, so it was a heck of a time to have to quit. Bob and I talked it over and decided we needed to get the whole story, so I hopped in the truck, went down the mountain, and headed to the Eckervogt's. Heinz confirmed what the boys had said. The good news was that we could continue mining and finish out the season, but no new permits would be issued for the following year. I told Heinz that I was going to go into Whitehorse to talk to the mining agency and get the whole scoop, but he said there was no need.

"We've heard everything. You have a year to finish up."

I returned to Squaw Creek and told Bob that our mining venture was going to be short-lived. He was disappointed, especially since we had started finding gold.

"Let's just get the best out of this season that we can," I told him. "We'll put in 12-hour work days and sluice as much as possible in the time we have."

As October approached, I told Bob that it would be best to go ahead and shut down rather than risk getting snowed in and stranded on the mountain. We packed up all our gear, parked our equipment on a lower claim, and left Squaw Creek.

It was obvious that our mining was over. I had been mining on and off now for over 12 years and had spent well over $200,000 on this venture. All together, I ended up recovering about 200 ounces of gold. That was quite a bit of gold, but for all the time and money I spent mining, it was a good thing I had enjoyed myself because it did not add up to what I had spent. Miners have a tendency to get together and swap stories, and those stories are what motivate you to keep going. I talked to one man who had hit some big pastries (large nuggets), and two seasons in a row had recovered over 1,500 ounces of gold. Those were the stories that drove me. I do not regret a penny or a day that I spent mining in the North Country because I loved every moment of it and those memories will stay with me for the rest of my life.

I stayed in touch with several other miners on Squaw Creek and three of us decided to hire an attorney and file for the reserves that we had more or less proven were sitting in the ground. The mining closure was preventing us from recovering the gold we had been working toward for so many years, and we felt we had a valid claim. A suit was filed in our names and we headed to Vancouver, British Columbia for the hearings.

The lawsuit dragged on for three years. In the first round the miners won and we were each awarded a little over a million Canadian dollars. I was quite satisfied with the result, but the government appealed the ruling and I had to return to Vancouver the following year to go through the hearings all over again. They really did not want to pay that money and grilled us hard. I was in Vancouver for six weeks and stood to testify nearly every day that I was there. It was sure getting old.

This time, the government won and the miners lost. The only thing we got paid were our legal fees, which were significant. I am sad to say that this was the end of my mining career. Those days will live with me forever, and I truly loved the seasons I spent hunting for gold. The one thing they could not take from us were the experiences of a lifetime that would stay with us always. How many kids will dream of the gold rush days but never actually experience the thrill of finding a gold nugget in their sluice box? I did it. There have been many grandchildren drifted off to sleep with visions of their granddads' stories lingering in their minds. The thought takes me back to those days in the Ozark Mountains when I dreamed as my uncle Jimmy told me similar stories. The tradition goes on.

Part VI
Later Life

Looking Back on a Flying Career

In a period of about 40 years I flew over a hundred different airplanes and owned 15 different aircraft. I flew just about every model in the Bell 47 series, including the 47 J2A, 47 G3, 47 G4, 47 G4A, 47 G, 47 G5, and best of all, a Bell 206 Jet Ranger. Boy, I am telling you, that is the aircraft. The Jet Ranger had an extra 100 horsepower that you would never use except in dire emergencies. I kept that Jet Ranger for five years and I used it in my real estate business buying and selling ranches. I could take out a prospective buyer to hover over a property and show all the fence corners. It really gave me a leg up on making a sale. Mostly, however, I flew the helicopter for fun. I absolutely loved flying helicopters, even though it was in a helicopter that I went down in British Columbia and nearly lost my life.

The economic crash we had in the eighties just about broke me and everybody else—particularly those of us involved in real estate—and I was forced to sell the Jet Ranger. I just could not justify owning it any longer with the way the economy had turned for the worse. The only time I ever saw that Jet Ranger in the air with me on the ground was the day its new owner flew it away. It was a sad day for me.

I bought and traded six different Piper Comanche's, including a 1971 turbo-charged Comanche that cruised at 230 MPH. I had to have oxygen to fly that plane. I also had two Cessna 150s that were converted to 150-horsepower engines, and in one of them I installed a constant speed propeller. That plane was great for flying up and down the coast and landing on the beach—it could take off in only a couple hundred feet.

In Alaska I had the opportunity to get in some really good flying times. I flew a Beaver (the workhorse plane of the north), a Cessna 185 on floats, and a J3 Cub on wheels, floats, and skis. I have flown just about every plane that Cessna makes, except for the 310. I also had co-pilot time in a Beech D-18 and an H-21, a double-rotor helicopter.

I built and flew three different aircraft, including a single-seater mini 500, a two-place Baby Bell helicopter, and a Zenith 701 two-place airplane. I will tell you for sure, it is an exciting thing taking off for the first time in an aircraft you built yourself, but it is far less nerve-wracking building and test flying an airplane than it is a helicopter. What you have, as the saying goes, are 5,000 rapidly moving parts traveling in loose formation. The day I finally finished building my helicopter and rolled it out on the tarmac I thought, *do I really want to start this engine?* But I did, and it ran just like it was supposed to. I played with the helicopter at first by pulling the collective and getting it light on the skids but not fully picking it up off the ground until I felt confident that I could control the aircraft. For me, it was about as exciting as staring down a bear, but when I look back on it, I often wonder if I knew what I was doing.

The Birth of Breakaway Park

Throughout the long winter months living in my cabin in Alaska from 1975–76, I spent many hours deep in thought conceiving and planning a fly-in subdivision. My dream was to live in a neighborhood with other people who dearly loved flying, and where we could keep our airplanes in our backyards. I gave considerable thought to how the airport would be laid out and designed the neighborhood in as much detail as I could without actually having a track of land to plan around. I would have to locate a property later, but I felt certain that I would be able to find a suitable site in Austin. I also wanted to be able to guarantee anyone who bought a property in the subdivision that the airport would not close up beneath them after they built their home, so I had to give serious thought as to how the airport would be managed. There was much to be planned and I thought day after day about this future neighborhood for pilots.

When I returned home from my yearlong stay in Alaska, the first thing I did was start searching for a track of land that would be suitable for this project, but also a property that I could afford. It was not easy. I spent nearly two years looking at land and I do not believe there was a real estate broker in Austin who did not at one time or another try to help me locate a site. The reason it was so difficult to find the right property was that there were so many facets of the project that had to be considered: I had to find a neighborhood where nearby property owners would not object to having an airport built close by; I had to come up with a logical explanation as to why this project would not be a threat to nearby property; and I had to find a track of land where it was physically possible to construct an airstrip. Luckily, I could argue that in *most* cases an airstrip would improve the value of any adjoining properties.

One day a friend of mine named Isom Shefield who was also a real estate agent called me on the telephone.

"Walter, I think I found your property," he said.

I was excited to hear this, but at the same time, I tried to contain my emotions because I had been disappointed so many times before.

"Where is it and how soon can we look at it?" I asked. We ended up looking at the property that very day.

The property was a little over 100 acres with some adjoining property that might also become available at a later date. The site was located about 15 miles northwest of the city of Austin and within three miles of the community of Cedar Park, which at that time was just a wide place in the road.

The first thing I did upon arriving to the site was to determine whether or not I could build a 3,000 foot runway on the property that oriented in the right direction. After a couple of hours walking the entire property and looking under every bush, I came to the conclusion that this property *was* in fact a very viable prospect for my fly-in subdivision. I decided to make an offer to buy the land.

"The owner of this property is by no means an amateur," Isom told me. "He has investments and he knows what his land is worth. He hasn't put a price on the property yet, he has just indicated that he would sell it."

It was 1976 and land prices in close proximity to the city of Austin had not yet escalated to the extremes that they would a few years later. Still, for a man who could barely afford to take on a project like this, the price was all-important. I researched other property sales in the area and finally decided on a price that I would offer.

"Let's offer him $1,000 per acre," I told Isom.

"I doubt if he'll take it, but it's a starting point."

Isom drew up the contract with an offer to buy the land and I signed it. I wrote an escrow check, crossed my fingers, and gave it Isom.

It did not take the owner of the property long to consider my offer—he rejected it that same day but said he would consider $1,500 per acre. I really wanted this land but I knew I was going to have trouble financing this. I had a few close friends who had indicated to me that they would help me come up with some of the money in return for a percentage of what the land would eventually earn, so I felt I had a little room to bargain. I countered his offer with $1,100 per acre, but this too was rejected. The owner stood fast at $1,500 per acre.

It turned out that I was dealing with Will Wilson, a pretty well-off and publicly known political figure who had once been the Assistant Attorney General of the United States under President Nixon. He was known to be a very wise and prudent lawyer. We went back and forth for several days until I ended up making my third offer.

"Just make it clear to Mr. Wilson that this is all the money I have and I can't obligate myself any further," I told Isom. "Tell him what I want to do with the property and if he has any objections I won't be able to buy the land." I then made an offer of $1,300 per acre.

For a few days Mr. Wilson left me hanging. Finally, the doorbell rang and there stood Isom with a contract in his hands.

"You just bought yourself a ranch," he said.

I began planning right away. Before I closed the deal and signed the contract I notified any neighbors who lived within a reasonable distance of the property what my plans were. I told them that I would be building a private airstrip and that there would be no big, noisy, commercial planes landing there, but I wanted to know if there were any objections before I bought the property. I got no objections.

The next condition I had to meet before signing the contract was to get approval from the FAA (Federal Aviation Administration) to build an airport. I submitted an application with my proposal to the FAA in Fort Worth, not expecting the long, agonizing waiting period to come. Eventually, Mr. Wilson got in touch with me.

"If you don't agree to close pretty soon, I'm going to have to withdraw my offer to sell."

I was really getting nervous and started contacting the FAA once a week. They must have gotten tired of me bothering them because, lo and behold, I got a letter in the mail signed by the FAA stating that they approved my site for a landing strip barring no objections that the area was impractical. That was all I needed—the next day I met with Mr. Wilson at the attorney's office and we closed the deal. I paid 20% down, which was all the cash I could raise, even with the help from my friends. My contract stipulated that I would pay 8% interest and that I had up to 10 years to pay off the rest of what I owed, but I could pay it off sooner. All the papers were signed and I now owned 134 acres of land and was deeply in debt.

The first thing I did was to purchase a bulldozer and begin clearing the airstrip. At that time, zoning and development regulations had not gotten so strict and I had practically no limitations on what I could do. I used common sense: when I could save a big tree I would, but I had to remove anything that would interfere with the safety of the airstrip. I'd had a fair amount of experience operating a bulldozer developing subdivisions in the past, so I had no trouble clearing the land myself. In fact, this whole undertaking was truly a do-it-yourself project, and it took me about six weeks to clear the area and measure out the space for a 3,000-foot airstrip.

With the help of an engineer friend of mine named Jim Watson, I laid out 20 lots on the land west of the airstrip. I wanted people to have room to live in the country, so the smallest lot was two acres and the largest was four acres. Each lot backed up to the airstrip, and when word of this subdivision got out to pilots in the area, I immediately started selling properties and had several people waiting in line. My first sell was to Glen Kirby, a retired U.S. Air Force colonel who owned a fixed-base operation in Georgetown. We had become friends over the years and, other than the lot I picked out for myself, he had first choice of the properties. Glen picked a lot just over two acres in size and began planning his new home. Robert McBride, another retired Air Force colonel and friend of Glen, came along and bought the next property.

In just one year I sold all 20 of the lots. *Now* I think I was selling them too cheap, but at the time I felt I was getting a heck of a price. I could sell a two-acre lot for anywhere from $12,000–$15,000, and this went a long way toward paying off the land.

Although I was getting down payments on the lots, I could not close on the sales until I got the plats approved. This was another lesson learned about developing land. When I started development of the subdivision I was under the jurisdiction of the city of Austin, but in the middle of the project jurisdiction changed to Cedar Park. I made countless trips to Cedar Park's City Hall and, believe me, it is no fun planning a subdivision in a small community. I just could not make the town council happy. I ended up with pretty close to what I wanted, but I had to give in on a few points. For example, I had to donate seven acres of my property for a future park, increasing my development costs.

When I finally got my plats approved I filed for record with Williamson County and went to work building streets. These, too, I constructed all by myself. I had built a few suburban developments in the past but I had never built one so elaborate and with so many streets. My engineer surveyed the land, marked the road's centerline, and staked a red flag every 100 yards for me to follow with my bulldozer. I then began cutting down trees. The land was about 80% covered with cedar and had an occasional oak and elm tree. As much as I loved trees, the only thing that allowed me to take them down was the fact that I was putting in an airstrip that people were really going to enjoy. For this, I had to sacrifice some trees. I accumulated tremendous piles of brush and on rainy days, when there was no danger of fire spreading, I would stack the brush in the center of the right-of-way of the road and ignite it with a gallon of diesel fuel. While the brush was burning I cleared the road behind the fire, and it was not long before I had all the right-of-ways for the streets completely cleared.

I then used the bulldozer to excavate the topsoil. To build a good base for a street I had to remove about a foot-deep of topsoil then fill the space back in with crushed rock and gravel, which we called road base. I then purchased a huge Caterpillar 12 road grader at an auction in Houston. The grader had a 14-foot blade that could move a lot of rock and I began grading off the streets. There was a draw on the south end of the runway that I filled in with the excavated topsoil, hauling it with a dump truck. I kept adding to the draw until it was filled and then I graded out the top and smoothed it over, making it level with the rest of the land. To this day, no one would ever know that there was a draw below ground.

As I closed on the properties I used the proceeds to retire my debt. About half of all funds coming in from my sales were put toward paying my note on the original land purchase. As I paid Mr. Wilson for a portion of the acreage, he signed a release of his lien and I was clear to sell that property to someone else. I also paid the percentage that I owed to my friends who had loaned me money—it was a real pay-as-you-go project. Any leftover money I put toward further development of the land.

At the completion of Section I, I had the airport constructed and the 20 properties closed. We formed an informal association of members to maintain the airstrip and bought a surplus mowing machine from the state to take turns cutting the grass. Best of all, I had finally sold enough of the land to pay off my note to Mr. Wilson. It was a great day.

Although I had set aside a lot for myself, I had not started construction of my own home yet. It was not till 1977 that I cut out four acres of land for myself and started to build our new home at the north end of the runway. After Glen Kirby, I was the second person to finish a house. Then, I started Section II of the project in which I helped the new property owners get their homes started.

The houses started popping up like mushrooms and I had a bunch of happy neighbors in the community that I decided to name Breakaway Park.

As time went by it became obvious that this project was going to be successful, so I stuck my neck out and got options for more land from Mr. Wilson. I had to pay considerably more money per acre now, but I had caused this price increase by my own development. I knew I could make it work so I did not squabble over the price. I bought an additional 30 acres of land from Mr. Wilson for $2,000 per acre. A few years later I bought 50 acres more at $3,000 per acre, all that was left of Mr. Wilson's available land. The price per acre had by now more than doubled since my original purchase, but I was getting good returns on my investment.

We all realized that we were living in a thriving neighborhood so we formed the official Breakaway Airport Association in order to have some control over future development. I came up with the conditions that assured homeowners in the neighborhood that I would not sell the airport out from under them later on. I have kept my word on those conditions and as a result we have a lot of happy people living in Breakaway Park today.

Section III included development of 30 additional tracks of land. I realized that I did not have to make the lots as large as those in Section I because most people were used to city zoning, which stuffed four or five lots into an acre. Still, I restricted the lots to sizes no less than one acre, most averaging around two acres per lot. Because I finally owned all of the land I could transfer titles immediately. With the help of my wife Tracy, we sold all of the properties and I was able to pay off all my debts. By the time Section III was complete, I started seeing my first profits.

I believe I was able to make the money I did, and as *soon* as I did, for the simple reason that I did so much of the development work myself, rather than hiring work crews to bulldoze the land and lay the roads. The feeling of pride that I got out of this project was more than worth the many hours I spent working the heavy equipment and building those streets.

I flew nearly every day and was thoroughly enjoying the new airport. I never will forget my first landing on that runway. I set down my Piper Comanche on the dirt strip (the grass had not grown in yet) and parked it in my own backyard. The dream I had conceived in my cabin on Post River had finally come true.

In Section IV of the project I had to negotiate with another property owner for a development contract in which he would furnish the land and I would develop it. Our water supply had come from individual wells that I had dug, but I was concerned about the number of wells I could punch into the ground and expect to keep getting water in the future. Eventually, I decided to negotiate with the city to bring in a water line; the only stipulation was that the water line had to be part of the city of Cedar Park. We wanted to enjoy the type of ownership we had under Williamson County but in order to get the water we had to move into Cedar Park's jurisdiction. In the end, Section IV did become part of the city of Cedar Park, and it has turned out to be the most elite section of the subdivision with its paved streets, curb and gutter, and sidewalks—jobs I had to contract out because I did not have any paving experience. Because Section IV had city water, a sewer system, and utilities, the cost of development skyrocketed; consequently, the lots were priced much higher. In fact, the lots were so expensive I was embarrassed to quote the prices to prospective buyers.

All lots in Section IV were sold by 2003, and the people who could afford to buy the lots could also afford to build really nice homes, many priced over $1,000,000. The homes are beautiful and I am proud to drive through Breakaway Park and realize that I am the one who hatched this thing. As the song goes, I did it my way (with the occasional concession to City Hall).

The Stagecoach

By 2003, when development of Breakaway Park was finally complete, I suppose I had worked my poor old body too hard. My body began protesting and I had some heart problems, eventually leading to open-heart surgery. While the surgeons were operating they discovered problems in my intestines and I ended up undergoing four major surgeries in the span of six months. All my friends and a few of my family members figured my do-it-yourself days were over, but they were wrong. I came out of those surgeries fighting mad after lying in a hospital bed for half a year. I am the ultimate do-it-yourselfer. I did everything the doctors told me I needed to do to recuperate and then I did it some more. It was not long before I was taking on new projects and working in my shop again.

Before all my health problems hit me I started a project that I had wanted to take on my whole life: building an authentic 1800s stagecoach. Over the years I collected different wagon parts, wheel hubs, and hardware, some of which ended up in my stagecoach, but most of which I used as patterns to make new parts. After my surgeries I could only work a couple of hours a day, but I gradually built up my strength and pretty soon my wife had to come out to my shop and pry me out of there to get me to eat supper. I also travelled around the country to different museums in Colorado, New Mexico, and Oregon taking photographs and measuring the dimensions of existing stagecoaches so that I could build the most authentic replica possible. After all my research I decided to copy the 1854 model stagecoach that Wells Fargo made famous in their bank logo. There were no construction plans that I could find so I had to make my own, and after crawling over various stagecoaches in museums and drawing design sketches, I believe I had a plan for a stagecoach that even John Wayne could not tell from an original.

I built the stagecoach from oak wood that I had cut from logs while clearing the land as I developed Breakaway Park. I installed lamps from a shop that remanufactured old lanterns on the sides

My stagecoach in a Fourth of July parade.

of the coach, just like the originals. I also installed a seat up front with a boot underneath to hold the strong box, which I built out of heavy steel. When showing the stagecoach in parades I would dress up in 1800s cowboy garb and throw the strongbox on top of the coach with the railing extending around the sides. I would even put on a sheriff's badge and carry a shotgun while a team of horses pulled me down the road. Of all the things I have built in my life, the stagecoach received the most praise from all around the country, and I believe it was my best project.

I made a deal with a man in West Texas named Bill Winston who had a small museum exhibiting several old horse-drawn wagons. Bill wanted to have a stagecoach, and I wanted my stagecoach to be available for all to see (and maybe even take a ride). Bill agreed to see to it that my stagecoach was kept in good shape and accessible to visitors. Today, it is still available for me to use in parades and festivals.

The Fugitive

On one midsummer morning, Tracy and I were relaxing reading the local newspaper and spending an easy Saturday at home when we started hearing police sirens. It sounded like the sounds were coming from the direction of Cedar Park. Shortly thereafter, I thought I heard a helicopter so I walked out on the back porch to take a look and saw a helicopter flying in circles over the area, obviously looking for somebody. Tracy was kind of nervous and I noticed her frequently looking out the back door.

"Just relax," I said. "Whoever it is, he's not coming here."

"Well, he might," she said.

I continued to read the paper when all of a sudden Tracy screamed.

"I think that's him coming! He's coming to the house! There's a man walking up the path!"

I have a workshop on the backside of our lot where I do all my projects and there was a pretty prominent path beat into the ground between the back porch and the shop. I got up and looked out the window—sure enough, there was a man walking along the path toward the house. Tracy ran to the back bedroom and locked herself inside, and I walked to the handy place in my house where I kept my .45 automatic. I stuck the gun in the back of my belt, just in case, and went to the back door just as the man got there. I opened the door.

"Could I have a glass of water?" he asked.

It was obvious this man was in bad shape: it was a hot day, he was sweaty, and his hair was all disheveled.

"You are the man the police are looking for, aren't you?" I asked.

"Yes sir, I am." He was very polite.

"I'll get you a glass of water," I said.

I did not want to aggravate the guy at the sight of the .45 I had stuck in the back of my belt so I decided to back away from the door before turning to enter the kitchen. I closed the back door, but as I did the gun slipped out of my belt and fell down into my pants! I just barely managed to keep myself together until I got into the kitchen and retrieved it. I then got the man a glass of water, which he nearly drank in one gulp. He wanted to know if he could have another glass so I went and got him another.

"I'll give you a hundred dollars to drive me down the road a little ways," he said when I returned.

"I'm sorry, fella'," I said, "I can't do that. You better turn yourself in immediately because sooner or later they are going to find you and you are liable to get shot. I don't know what your problem is but you'll be a lot better off just giving yourself up. Why are they looking for you?"

"They just say they've got a warrant for my arrest," he said. "I don't know."

He would not say what he had done, or even that he had done something.

"I'll tell you what I'll do," I said. "You go back there in my shop and wait."

"Then what are you going to do?" he asked.

"Well, I am going to assist the officers in arresting you. I have to. You know the alternative to this—you stand a good chance of being shot and killed. The sheriffs are pretty rough around here."

"Let me think about it. In the meantime, I'll go back in your shop."

Tracy had the forethought to report to the police that the fugitive they were looking for was here at our house, and it was not long before police cars showed up out front. The officers started jumping out of their cars with their guns drawn, all converging on the house across the street! They got the address wrong and were about to enter my neighbor Leroy Blair's house. Of course, the police had not driven up quietly. They were letting the neighborhood know they were there and I was sure the fugitive knew they were there too. I thought he might get away so I went outside, ran across the street, and got the officers attention to let them know they had the wrong house. I told them the man was back in my workshop and that he was ready to surrender. The police turned, ran over to my house, and started searching my workshop. I stood there watching them from a distance and pretty soon they came back out, looking perplexed.

"He's not here!" they said.

"He's got to be," I answered. "There's only one entrance to my shop and you just went in and out of it. We better look again."

In the back of my shop I had a few sheets of plywood leaning against the wall. This man had crouched down behind the boards in a space that hardly looked big enough for a grown man to fit. When the police found the man they arrested him and put him in handcuffs. As they walked by me I could see he was devastated.

"I'm sorry fella'," I said as he passed. "For your own good, we had to call the police to come get you." He did not say anything but just kept walking and the police took him into custody.

Sheriff Jim Boutwell used to live next door to me and we had become good friends. When I finally got a chance to talk to Jim later I asked him about the fugitive.

"Jim, what's the story on this man?" I asked. "What'd he do?"

"To begin with, he was an escaped prisoner and was being transferred when he got away. He is now being charged with aggravated rape and assault of a woman."

The police had been moving him from the city jail to the county jail, but he wanted to stop at his house to tell his wife what was happening. The police agreed, pulled up to his house, and watched as the convict went in the front door. After two or three minutes of waiting they realized he was not coming out quickly enough. It should not have taken him that long to tell his wife goodbye. The police officers went inside the house to get the man when a neighbor who had seen the whole thing hollered out to them.

"That man just came out of the house and ran into the woods!" he yelled.

The fugitive had used this ruse as a chance to get away. While the police were parked and waiting out front, he went in the front door and out the back and just started running. He escaped into some undeveloped ranch land heavily treed with oak and cedar. It was a little over three miles from where he had escaped to my house and he made his way through all that heavy brush to our subdivision, picking the Yates' house to ask for help. After everything was sorted out he was arrested and extradited to Georgia where the offence had occurred, and that was the last I heard of that.

The Smuggler

I had another law enforcement encounter that involved Sheriff Jim Boutwell when we were still neighbors in Georgetown, Texas. Before developing the Breakaway Park subdivision I lived just north of the Georgetown airport. Being an avid pilot, I liked to live as close as I could to the nearest runway. One day while I was out in my workshop I heard an airplane flying overhead that just did not sound right. I stepped outside to take a look and saw that it was a Cessna 172. The pilot made a pass at the runway but could not make his landing and I thought, *maybe he is a student.* I was closely observing him now and his flight behavior seemed so peculiar that I walked closer to the runway where I could see what was going on a little better. Naturally, being a pilot, I was watchful for any situation where another pilot might have a problem.

The pilot was attempting to land downwind, something any experienced pilot knows you are not supposed to do. The winds were about 15 MPH and he was coming in fast. Finally, the pilot managed to touch down and make his landing. He got all the way to the end of the runway and just barely stopped before hitting a fence.

What is going on here? I walked over to the airport which was only four blocks from my house and I talked to the man briefly. He told me he was a student pilot and that he was practicing his landings, but he was a wreck. I never saw a guy look so frustrated. I knew something was wrong.

"You don't have anyone with you in the plane?" I asked.

"No," he said.

"I thought maybe you might have been overloaded. With a downwind landing like that you are going to have a problem. What's your plan?"

"I've got a friend who lives in Georgetown," he said. "I'm going to go visit him and I just want to park the plane here for a few hours."

I helped him tie down the airplane, but while I was doing that I noticed in the back seat (a Cessna 172 is a four-place airplane) several large barracks bags stacked to the top of the plane that looked just like the ones we used in the military when moving around our gear. The plane was clearly overloaded and when I got a littler closer I could smell marijuana. I acted like I did not notice anything. Then, this guy got on the telephone and in less than five minutes another man picked him up from the airport and they drove off.

In the meantime, I went over to Sheriff Boutwell's house.

"Jim, I think we've got a marijuana smuggler who just landed out at the airport."

"What caused you to think that?" he asked.

"The guy made several attempts to land downwind and when I went to help tie down his airplane I noticed something in the backseat that looks suspicious as heck to me."

Jim and I went back to the airplane and examined it closely.

"I can smell it myself," he said. "That is marijuana."

"He told me he and his friend are just going for a cup of coffee," I told Jim. "Supposedly they are going to be right back."

"Well, we'll just wait them out," Jim said.

I stayed with the sheriff about 100 yards from the airplane. About 30 minutes later the two men drove up to the airplane and began loading the bags full of marijuana into the car. Jim would not let me go with him, but he casually walked over to the two men and placed them under arrest. And that is all there was to it. This experience just goes to show that if you keep your eyes open, an average citizen can help stop crime. If I had not recognized the way that airplane was being poorly operated this smuggler would have gotten away with his crime.

After this incident with the marijuana smuggler Jim and I got to be pretty good friends and I went with him on several stake-outs. One day, Jim asked me if I would consider becoming a reserve officer.

"We need people like you," he said. "It'll take about five or six weeks of training, but after that you will legally be a reserve deputy. We were just looking for someone like that, and you sure fit the bill."

I thought it over and said, "Jim, let me think about this and discuss it with my wife."

I really appreciated that Jim had considered me a candidate for a job like that. Of course, he knew I was an ex-marine and was well skilled in firearms. I talked it over with my wife and she was totally against me even thinking about anything like that. Although I wanted to help, I decided to decline the offer.

Seven or eight years later Jim came down with cancer and we lost him. He was a great law enforcement officer, a good friend, and an all around good guy. We all miss him very much.

The Family

As time goes by, I suppose we all look back with fond memories of when our children were growing up and some of the crazy antics they pulled. I was a fairly strict father and during the most formative years of the kids' lives things were pretty rough. I was trying to find my notch in the business world and it seemed like 12-hour workdays were the norm. We were doing okay, but I could not spend as much time with the kids as I would have liked. Nevertheless, I have many wonderful memories of times we spent together and I get a kick out of thinking about the crazy ways some things have turned out.

My oldest daughter Sharolyn called home one day after graduating from the University of Texas. Sharolyn had moved into her own living quarters and was doing great, and she told us she would be coming by to introduce us to her boyfriend.

"Great, we look forward to meeting him," I said.

Sharolyn showed up with this tall, slim fellow named Steve. She him-hawed around a little bit—I could see she wanted to tell me something but I couldn't tell what it was. Then, all of a sudden she said, "Dad, how would you like to have Steve for a son in law?"

"I'm sure it'd be fine if you are happy," I answered.

"Well, you got him—we're married."

She had done the same thing her Mom and Daddy did when they were young—she eloped. I do not know whether her parent's story had anything to do with her own decision to elope, but I guess she reasoned that if we had done it, it would not be so bad if she did as well. The first thing that scared the heck out of me was the thought that there might be some impelling reason why they did what they did. She assured me that I had nothing to worry about; they had just fallen in love and decided to get married. Sharolyn and Steve rented a nice home not too far from ours where we could visit often, but for a while—and I guess this is normal when young folks go off on their own—we did not hear from her too often. That is when you start missing someone: when they are there but you are not hearing from them.

It was about a year and a half later that she informed us we had a grandchild on the way, which turned out to be a boy named Shane. Shortly thereafter she gave us warning that another one was on the way! That turned out to be my granddaughter Erin. Both Shane and Erin have a special place in my heart because they were my first grandkids. I probably spent more time with my grandkids as they grew up than I did with their parents.

I am very proud of what Sharolyn has accomplished. She is the scholar of the family and was the first to go to college and get a degree—from the University of Texas, no less. She studied accounting and has done really well in the field. She has a job with a big company in Houston that has oil field interests, and she takes care of all the books in one of those tall buildings sticking up downtown.

Sharolyn was the more serious type. On the other hand, my daughter Susan was like a loose cannon. Boy, was she independent! She had a mind of her own. It was not too long after Sharolyn married that Susan got serious with a young man named Jim. It was obvious that she was moving too fast—at least *I* thought she was—but when they decided to get married she didn't run off, she let us have a really nice wedding. I guess I just missed Sharolyn having a wedding, but it turned out that I really liked the young man she picked and I felt sure that Susan had picked a good one too. Susan got married at Crestview Baptist Church in Georgetown, Texas.

Susan was more of a tomboy than Sharolyn. Growing up, she often went with me on short trips in my airplane. She really loved flying. I took her on one of my trips down to the coast, just she and I, and I introduced her to fishing, which she really picked up quickly. I taught her how to cast with a simple Zebco reel that would not snarl up too badly and she would throw that line out there and her eyes just flashed. She was on the edge, like she was ready to jump off a diving board. I thoroughly enjoyed watching her on the water.

After that first trip I took Susan fishing with me several more times. Once, the whole family went up to the Pedernales River about 30–40 miles west of where we lived to a good fishing spot with pleasant level grounds and big pecan trees. It was a good place to fish and have a picnic. I believe Susan was the first one to catch a bass that day, and the one she caught was the biggest fish that she had ever caught. I had not caught many better than that myself. While she reeled it in I told her to keep a tight line, and she was getting coaching from all sides.

"Don't rush it!"

"Hold on!"

Finally, she landed the nice big bass on the bank of the river. I will always remember those days the family spent together.

As time went on, we all seemed to start going in different directions and we did not see much of each other, but we kept the phone running hot all the time and stayed in constant contact.

One day while I was barbecuing in the back yard, Susan came up to me and said, "Dad, I've got a new hobby." Her life was already full of hobbies—she took a whole lot after her Dad.

"What are you doing now?" I asked.

Susan pulled out a bound booklet and handed it to me. I opened it up and I was horrified! There on the front page was a photograph of her first parachute jump. She had taken up skydiving! I was really worried about it and we talked it over quite a bit.

"I wish you'd have told me this before you did it," I said.

"Well, I would have done it anyway, Dad." That's Susan. She would have.

Susan stayed with parachuting for a long time but she quit when she started having kids. By that time, she had logged over

500 jumps! I was proud of her for what she was doing, and she knew it. I considered her a chip off the old block because she was out to enjoy all the adventures that were available to her. I don't want to say that I set a bad example, but I did not set a good one either by the things that I did, and a lot of it rubbed off on Susan. When I finally realized that's just the way she is, I encouraged her to do more, and she did.

I used to tell Susan stories about the way she was as a little girl. One day in 1990, long after she had grown up, I decided to write down some of those stories. I thought it would make her happy to know her Dad was always thinking about her. One of those stories I named "The Purple People Eater," and it went like this:

Once there was a little girl. Not just any little girl, but one even at that young age (she did not give much thought to such things at that time, but she was about five years old) dreamed of great things. She had a little friend that dreamed with her—they knew of movie stars and great actresses. The world was theirs to do with as they would.

This kid was pretty smart. She was pretty too. One day her Daddy came home from work (he worked a lot in those days and was sorry not to be able to spend more time with her) and she ran up to him and said "Daddy, flip me!"

Now, let me tell you, to "flip her" as she requested, with eyes flashing, was no easy chore, but her Daddy loved to do it and it was one of their fun things. So how does one "flip me"? First, you must have one trusting little girl. It is best if she only weighs 48 pounds, but it can be done if she weighs more than that (just add a little more love!). So the Daddy takes the little girl gently by the ankles and holds her upside-down. Now, he starts to swing her back and forth like a pendulum on a clock (but faster). He holds her so that her hair (quite long) just sweeps the floor. Higher and higher she goes from one side to the other, all the time squealing with delight. If you imagine the face of a clock, she is swinging in an arc from about 11 o'clock on the left to 1 o'clock on the right.

Now (and you have to be quick), just as she reaches 12 o'clock, he gives her a little "up" flip and turns her loose. She does a complete flip in the air and is coming down headfirst! This is where Daddy grabs her ankles again, throws on the breaks, and gently lowers her to the floor for a "soft landing."

One day this little girl's Mommy and Daddy had some friends visiting that had just been married. They were drinking champagne to celebrate. Now, anyone knows when you remove a cork from a bottle of champagne it swells up and will not go back in the bottle. So Bill (that was her Daddy's friend's name) being quite a devil with a keen sense of humor, called this little girl over.

"Honey, if you can put this cork back in the bottle, I will give you a quarter."

Now, in those days, a quarter was a lot of cash for a little girl like her. She had her little friend with her and both their eyes were flashing with excitement. Her friend said, "Can I have a quarter too?"

Bill laughed. "Of course, honey," and he winked at us, as if to say, "my fifty cents are safe."

Out the door they went. The four friends continued to visit and for a little while the cork was forgotten.

Suddenly, the little girls burst back into the room, proudly holding up the champagne bottle, which was very well corked! Bill looked at it in great wonder. The little girl's Daddy was somewhat taken aback too. Her Mommy looked proudly at the other lady and winked her eye. Bill reached in his pocket and gave each of the little girls a 25-cent piece, at which time there was an urgent request that they be allowed to go up to the corner store in order to enjoy their good fortune. It was decided that her older sister Sharolyn would go along, and away they went—smarter and a little richer.

Bill and the little girl's Daddy began to examine the "cork job." Then they both laughed and laughed and almost rolled on the floor!

"You know, you got a real smart kid here," Bill said.

I sure agreed with that. She had taken the cork and very carefully with a kitchen knife whittled it down until it was small enough to fit easily into the bottle.

This little girl's big event came when she and her friend decided to enter a talent contest held in Austin at the Capitol Theatre. Now, this was not a case where she came to Mommy and Daddy and asked to try this. This was a case of "we are going to do this!" I was so surprised that all I could say was, "Great, I hope you win." As she walked away, she looked back over her shoulder and said matter-of-factly, "We will."

The next several days were spent trying to come up with an act to suit their talents. The big event was almost upon them. Daddy came home one day and asked, "Well, what's the big act going to be?"

You know these silly songs that go around sometimes—well, it just so happened that there was one at that time called "The Purple People Eater." This little girl says, "We are going to sing the 'Purple People Eater' song." Now, her Daddy wanting to maintain his dignity did not want to let on that he even knew such a silly song.

"That's good you picked something new," he said.

"No, Daddy, everybody knows it!" I guess in her little world that was true.

She practiced every day, and her daddy reached a point where the day for this contest had better come soon or he may be forced to leave the country (who knows to this day if that song is what caused him to start travelling).

Finally, the big day came. She and her friend proudly stepped on stage and sang their rendition of the Purple People Eater song loud and clear. It soon became clear as people were laughing and calling out in the aisles that they were either going to be thrown out of the theatre or win a prize.

They won a prize.

Her Mommy and Daddy were very proud of their smart little girl. They call her Susan.

At the time when my serious health problems began and I had open-heart surgery and intestines removed that I wish I still had, Susan and her husband were living in South Carolina. She got word of what was happening and came home to be with me. Susan has a heart so big there is always room for another's comfort. The way the doctors were talking, she thought she was getting ready to lose her Dad. I was in pretty bad shape. When I got discharged to go home, Susan and Tracy rigged up a hospital bed in the den and Susan moved into the guest room to wait on me hand and foot (I've got to hand it to her husband for letting her doing this). For three months I was immobile, but Susan stayed with me and nursed me back to health. She would have made a wonderful nurse—she just has a talent for it. She understood the intravenous feeding that I had to have and was even able to give me the shots that I needed. I loved having her around and I do not know what I would have done without her because I needed someone to take care of me 24 hours a day. Tracy was also working so hard taking care of my needs; she was exhausted and sure needed the help.

With all the time she spent away from her husband I began to be concerned about Susan's home life. One day, her husband arrived and I think his intention was to bring Susan back home. He missed his wife, and I don't blame him. I felt guilty for having kept her so long, but she would not have had it any other way. I was getting to where I could move around on a walker, so she and her husband decided it was time to go home. That is a time in my life that has a special place in my heart for the way Susan gave her full self to helping me get well. It is one of my fondest memories of her.

I am about as proud a parent, and grandparent, as any can be. I always encouraged my children to be their best, and they have done it. My son Jay is one of the best A&P mechanics in the country, servicing helicopters in Oregon. Now that Greg was in real estate, I let him market the lots I was developing in Breakaway Park to help him get started. Breakaway Park was very successful and this gave him a good start in the real estate industry. Among the four of my kids, I now have nine grandkids! Mine is a happy and full family.

Do-It-Yourself Projects

I have built an airplane and two helicopters, and it is surprising how many home-built airplanes are operating in the skies today. I dare say that the majority of them are every bit as good as commercially-built aircraft. When you build your own airplane or helicopter, you know that your life, or somebody else's life, will be at stake when you are flying it, so you do not cut any corners. Fortunately, I seemed to be gifted with a mechanical aptitude, so I saw no reason not to build my own airplane.

When you decide to build your own airplane you must sift through hundreds of available kits and packages that are available on the market. You can buy an equipment-filled kit or you can go completely from scratch using only the plans, but there are many options available. I decided to build a Zenith 701, a two-place airplane with a STOL kit. I went to the Zenith factory in Mexico, Missouri, about 100 miles west of St. Louis, to fly one of their aircraft before I made the decision to build their model. I wanted an airplane that I could use in the bush and that could make landings off airports. The Zenith 701 could land in 300–400 feet and take off in only 100 feet, and that opened up new opportunities for a pilot like me.

The Zenith factory had a program where you could visit their factory and build a part of the plane in their shop to get acquainted with the aircraft and see whether or not it was what you really wanted to buy. Along with my friend Leroy Blair, I travelled to the factory and built a vertical stabilizer. We stayed in that shop for two days with guys leaning over our shoulders all day long advising us what to do. Finally, we mastered the correct technique for riveting and fitting aluminum metal together.

My first flight in the Mini-500 helicopter that I built.

I put a deposit on a kit and when it was ready, Leroy and I drove it back home on a boat trailer. All the parts were packaged in a large crate. The first thing I did was inventory all the parts—if something is missing from the kit, it is best to find out right away. The instruction manual starts from the very beginning: how to lay out your parts and assemble the most basic structures. I worked atop a table I had built while waiting for the parts to come in that was made out of heavy timber 4 feet wide and 12 feet long, providing me a level platform.

I started on the fuselage first. When you get started, it can be confusing to follow the intricate, detailed directions, but with Leroy's help, and after studying the plans closely, we were able to figure it all out. When we needed help from the factory we just called them up on the phone—they were available all day long.

After building the fuselage I constructed the plane's tail section and the wings. Whenever I did not have a tool necessary to complete a step, I just borrowed it from a neighbor. That's the beauty of living in a fly-in subdivision where 30–40% of the residents are pilots—someone always had the right tool. After finishing each of the main component parts I then had to put them all together. I installed the tricycle gear, with the two main gears and the nose gear in the fuselage, and then I mounted the engine. I selected a

The first flight in my Zenith 701 airplane.

100-horsepower Rotax 912S motor, which turned out to work very well for my airplane. I set the attaching bolts to the motor at a certain torque pressure and recorded all my settings and calibrations as I worked to make sure that the final product was exactly to the specifications of the manual.

By the time I assembled all the components into one piece, I installed the tail feathers, horizontal stabilizer, vertical rudder, and wing struts. The model I built had a cuff directing the airflow to curve over the leading edge of the wing, which added to its slow-speed and short-field take-off capabilities.

Once all the pieces were in place I had to find a good painter. Some pilots get professional paint jobs, but my neighbor Mark Lazar was talented with a paint gun so he helped me out. Painting an airplane is a tremendous job so I really appreciated Mark's help. I did a little spray painting myself, but I could never do the job that Mark did. I chose the different colorations and stripes that I wanted and then Mark masked off the plane to apply the base coat. One of my neighbors, Bob McBride, had assembled a "paint booth" in his hangar and let us use it to do our paint job because if the least little speck of dirt or a flying insect get into the area, the fumes will engulf the particle or bug and it will fall into the paint.

With Leroy's help, I had the plane ready to fly in seven months. I could not work on it everyday, but it took me about 600 hours to complete. This is the kind of project that you just do not want to rush. The machine is going to hold you up in the sky someday, so you do not want to take any shortcuts.

♒

The Helicopter Platform

When I started flying helicopters I found it to be a big strain moving them in and out of the hangar. One day, I got the idea that I would construct something to make the process easier. At the end of the runway—my lot sits right at the end—I built a helicopter hangar about 15 feet wide and 40 feet long. I laid a track from the front of the hangar to about 50 feet out from the entrance and poured two long, narrow concrete bases. I then took strips of two-inch angle iron with welded bolts and laid them down in the wet concrete, using a gauge to measure the width in order to ensure that the iron was laid parallel. When the concrete set, I had a good, solid track on which to lay down a platform on wheels. I welded a large dolly about 10 feet wide and 12 feet long out of channel and angle iron. I then covered the dolly with two-by-six pieces of lumber with cross braces for support and installed wheels that fit the track. When it was all finished, I had a platform that rolled on the track without resistance. I could land the helicopter on the platform and with just one hand push it back into the hangar.

The only difficulty was learning how to land the helicopter in such a confined area. To practice, I put a couple of two-by-twelve boards on the ground separated by the same width as the skids of my helicopter and I exercised picking up and setting down the helicopter on top of the boards. I practiced hour after hour until I was satisfied I could accurately and precisely land on the platform. Over time, I had people from all over the country come by my hangar to look at my dolly, and many of them adopted the structure for their own hangars. I was quite proud of this fact, and it sure made the job of parking my helicopter much easier.

The Pontoon Boat

I built several boats over the years, but the one I am most proud of is the perfect boat for an outdoor-type person who loves fishing and camping. I built the boat entirely from scratch and even drew up my own design plans. I constructed a combination camper and fishing boat that you could even ski behind if you wanted to.

The boat is a pontoon-type craft. I made the two pontoons out of marine plywood approximately 2 feet wide, 2 feet tall, and 20 feet long. I placed bulkheads at intervals down the length of the pontoons to straighten them and then I applied fiberglass to the interior and exterior of the vessel, sealing it completely with fiberglass resin and cloth. I wanted to add some protection to the boat in case it was moving quickly down a river and punctured a hole on a log or rock, so I filled the pontoons with foam making the boat unsinkable. After much computation and comparison to other pontoon boats I decided to install a 50-horsepower Johnson motor that could easily run in shallow water. As large as it was, the boat was quite buoyant and I could drive it through water only eight inches deep.

One of the things I still love to do at the coast is go floundering at night. I rigged up lights at the front of the boat and railing along the sides so that I could support myself as I cruised around in shallow water. With the help of my lights, I can spot the flounder in the sand while cruising in the water at a very slow speed—almost as if I was walking. When I spot a flounder I gig it right from my boat. I enjoy floundering more than any other type of fishing. Even with my boat, I used to walk for hours at night just carrying my lantern and wading in the water.

I built uprights on my boat to hang a canopy. With a light canvass material normally used for sails, I mounted flaps that hung down over all four sides of the boat. I added zippers on the corners and during the day I could roll them up and tie them with strings at the top. At night when I got tired of fishing, I anchored the boat, rolled down the flaps, zipped up the corners, and camped out. I had myself a floating camper! I even built a modified trailer to haul the pontoon boat around. I got more use out of that boat than any other I have owned because it was so utile. I designed the boat with speed in mind, and with my 50-horsepower motor, I could cruise at about 22 MPH—*pretty good for a pontoon boat,* I thought.

I installed a fish finder that located fish swimming in the water below the boat. Whenever I took a trip I brought along my Coleman stove and fixed whatever fish I caught right there in my camper. In the mornings I made coffee and fried more fish for breakfast. That was the kind of life I enjoyed. I still enjoy floundering today, but at my age I've had to stop going on solo trips in the interest of common sense (and my wife). In fact, Tracy loves to go out on the boat. We can fit as many as 12 people on the pontoon and she thoroughly enjoys going out on Lake Travis with our friends, cruising up and down the water.

Building an Electric Truck

Around my 85th birthday I started running out of projects. I had not built anything for several months and was anxious to start something new. One day I was glancing through a catalog called Lindsey's Technical Books that advertised instruction manuals for just about everything you could want to build. The catalog includes instructional books for anything from 1800s-style vehicles to modern equipment, but the one that caught my eye was called "Build Your Own Electric Vehicle." I thought, *that's a good plan.* Without much further consideration I hauled off and ordered that book.

The converted electric truck.

The manual was very descriptive, listing different types of vehicles that are better for conversion, and I decided a small pickup like the Ford Ranger or the Chevrolet S-10 was the most suitable considering the weight of all the batteries required to operate an electric vehicle. I started looking for trucks that I could buy at a good bargain and found a 1998 Mazda pickup with a similar body to the Ford Ranger. The truck had been wrecked but the repairs weren't anything I could not take care of myself, so I bought it for a cheap price and went to work.

The amount of work required to remove a gasoline engine from a truck was beyond the ability of an 85 year old man, so I got a little help. I located somebody interested in purchasing the original motor—it was still in good shape—and made a deal with him: if he would remove the engine and all the other heavy parts I would just give him the engine for free. He immediately accepted the offer.

The instruction manual mentioned a company in Wolfeboro, New Hampshire called Electric Vehicles of America that sold electric conversion packages. They provide all the parts necessary for converting a vehicle and prepare a package that fits your specific make and model. The package is a little bit expensive but I liked their sales pitch and decided to go with their company. To save a little money I ordered the basic kit rather than the complete kit, which provided me with the motor, controller, charger, and all the schematic diagrams needed to assemble the vehicle. By the time the parts arrived I had my truck emptied and ready to go.

First, I went to work building the brackets underneath the bed that would hold the batteries. I put lifting struts on the pickup so that I could raise it up myself later on; the batteries would have to be serviced regularly. I made the brackets out of two-by-two angle iron because they had to support quite a bit of weight. Then, I installed 20 six-volt golf cart batteries that weighed 60 pounds each, placing 16 of the batteries on the brackets beneath the truck bed and 4 batteries under the hood to equalize the weight lost by removing the gasoline engine. I had the same axel weight all around the truck and in the same proportion as the original truck design.

My neighbor Leroy Blair who often helps me with my projects, as well as Mark Lazar who helped me build my helicopter, assisted me with the wiring and electricity in the truck. With the help from my friends, I had the truck conversion completed inside of three months. The job could easily be completed in one month, but I am not in as good of health as I used to be and I could only work on the truck for two or three hours per day.

The truck needed to be repainted after all the repairs I made. Since I am an avid Texas Longhorns fan I decided to paint the truck a very patriotic color: burnt orange. Just below the dashboard I installed an instrument that is like a fuel gauge only it calculates how many volts of energy are left in the batteries.

Finally, I rolled out the truck to take it for a test drive. Believe me, driving an electric truck is entirely different than driving a gasoline-engine vehicle; you have to learn how to drive carefully and efficiently. With a full charge on my batteries I can drive on average 70 miles, which takes care of running around town on errands and visiting friends within a few miles radius of my home. Sometimes I even drive the 25 miles to Georgetown, and a full charge easily gets me there and back. In fact, the more I operate the vehicle the better it gets. The battery range increases the more they are recharged, actually becoming more efficient.

There is no use for a clutch driving an electric vehicle, so it is best to select a car with standard transmission. My Mazda pickup had a five-speed transmission so I removed the clutch and sent it to Electric Vehicles of America. Their company offers a service at a very reasonable price that exchanges your clutch for an adaptor plate. With the adaptor plate you do not need to depress the pedal to shift gears, you can shift on the go. With this technique I "hesitate" in neutral while shifting gears and I operate around town in second or third gear. The truck can reach the same speeds it could with its standard gasoline engine, but the faster I go the more I deplete my batteries so I had to learn how to operate the vehicle in such a way that I didn't burn rubber on take-offs. I generally cruise around 45 to 50 MPH, which is ample speed for local travelling.

When I take off from a red light or a stop sign, sometimes I aggravate the people behind me because the truck starts off slow. Everybody seems to be in a hurry to get somewhere and they are burning rubber trying to get around me. In order to let people know why I was taking off so slowly, I had the word "Electric" printed across the tailgate and a lightning bolt painted on each side of the truck. This interests people when they see the truck and they realize what I am working with. Now, instead of getting aggravated, they slow down and take a look.

I do not drive the truck everyday, but when I do drive it I charge the truck with 220 volts. Mark Lazar rigged up an outlet in the corner of my garage that fits the plug on my charger and I let the batteries charge overnight. A full charge only takes four hours and the charger shuts off automatically once it is complete. In the morning, the truck is ready to go. I have calculated that with the cost of the electricity required to charge the truck I can operate the vehicle at 1.5 to 2 cents per mile! That sure beats those $40 fill-ups at the gas station. The batteries have to be replaced every three to four years, but the expenses are still less than those for gasoline-operated vehicles. What I did was a trade off: the truck is not good for long-distance trips, but driving around town is very cheap, especially after training myself to drive the truck in the most efficient way.

Although they are still somewhat of an oddity, I see more and more electric cars on the road each day and I do not think it will be long before there are charging stations at every corner to increase range of travel. One of my neighbors has now converted his own electric vehicle, a Ford Ranger pickup, and he takes it to the golf course everyday. What's more, electric vehicles like mine are not polluting the atmosphere—there is absolutely *no* discharge from my truck. Knowing this gives me a little fuzzy feeling that I am doing my part. Plus, the truck is just fun to drive. I have to use my horn more often because sometimes people do not hear my quiet truck coming down the road, but I think in time we are going to see electric cars all over the highway.

Sunset

My destiny was set during the Great Depression years. I was born in 1924 and was six years old when it started. As I write these memoirs in 2010 we are experiencing another economic downturn. I am here to tell you that what we are going through now, compared to that of the 1930s, is like comparing a mashed toe to a broken leg!

At a time of such widespread hardship, when we really had to survive off of the land, I learned all the skills and knowledge I would need in order to one day experience the stories I have related here. It is my fervent hope that all who read these adventure stories are able to travel back in time and enjoy them as I have, and that what I have written will encourage others to better enjoy what God has put here on earth. Although fate has cancelled my travel card, my destiny has served me well and my memories are with me always.

Growing up in the Great Depression era really shaped my life. Of course, I was not aware of it at the time. There were no kids for me to play or roam around with in the forest on Burny Mountain, so I did it alone. Everybody was poor at that time and it made a person try harder. I think that was ingrained in me—to always give it my best—and it has affected me throughout my life. Growing up in Arkansas and Texas, my family was always pretty poor while many of our neighbors were pretty well off—not rich, but certainly better off than we were. We did not have any extras in life, and you can imagine how that would hang over a young kid like me. Especially at school, I felt inferior to the other kids, and because of that, it was always on my mind in whatever I did to prove myself to others. I grew up trying to do everything a little better than the next guy, and I believe this drive has a lot to do with all the risks I have taken and projects I have taken on in my life. I always tell myself, *I could have done that better,* and that is what drives me on.

For most of my life I was completely oblivious to this compelling urge to work harder and take greater risks than others. In fact, I did not recognize it until I started recording all these stories and experiences. Everything I have done has been a personal challenge, and, apparently, I subconsciously started doing things that would make me stand out to others. I did not openly look at it this way, but I think I have been trying to prove myself to others and to *myself* my entire life. When I got my pilot's license, I decided I was going to be the best and I practiced everyday. There was not a maneuver or technique that satisfied me until I felt I had perfected it. I studied navigation, weather, cartography, engine performance—everything. I spent many hours—days, really—practicing off-airport landings and I got to be a pretty good bush pilot before I ever went to the North Country. Always in the back of my mind was this dream of flying and exploring in Alaska and I spent my life preparing for it.

My days becoming skilled flying in the North Country were enhanced by advice I sought from the local bush pilots. They taught me every trick in the book and those not in the book, too. If I did something risky, it was after I had learned it from them. I must have looked like I really needed the help because some of those guys went out of their way to teach me. Their lessons included flying on floats, skis, and large tundra tires, the weather, the mountain winds, and, in general, just flying in sub-zero temperatures and maintaining an aircraft in such harsh conditions. I learned something new everyday and I practiced until those teaching me would be completely satisfied that I could do it. Most of all, I have lived my life trying to convince Walter Yates that he could do it.

When we come into this world, we are probably born under a certain star that guides us through life and helps us obtain and use knowledge. Along the way we pick up idiosyncrasies and our own philosophies on life. These are just a few notes and facts on being me: it is wrong to go along with a way of life that you do not believe in just because it pleases another. I prize the privilege to be alone. In the long run, it does not help to act as though I am something I am not. I am an imperfect person. I by no means function at all times in the way that I would like to function. I have found it of enormous value when I can permit myself to understand another person. Most of all, I can trust my experience, although I depend on that which I do not yet know, and upon that which I have not yet done. Evaluation by others is not a guide for me; experience is the highest authority. The facts are friendly. My life, at its best, is a flowing, changing process in which nothing is fixed. I try to live by my interpretation of the current meaning of my experience. And finally, yesterday is a cancelled check, tomorrow is a promissory note, but today is cash.

As I look back on my life, I have not always been the person that many thought I was. It would appear that I am rich—that is true as far as what I have learned about life and the world around me. I have discovered and enjoyed all that God has put on this earth.

As a young boy growing up with a loving family as poor as a church mouse, I realized that most of the treasures of the world had to be worked for. The people around me who seemed better off than the rest were those who had some kind of business of their own, and money seemed to be worth more when I earned it myself. I started off with a paper route. After one year in high school, I was self-educated. Later, after I was discharged from the Marine Corps, I went into business for myself—small at first, but then it grew—in electro-plating, floor covering, and finally, real estate. I learned to fly airplanes and helicopters and made the world *my* world. I would set my goals and work to make them happen. If I planned a project or an adventure, I worked harder to be able to afford it. I did not save much money—I spent it as I made it, paying for my adventures as I went along. I thought I would surely live forever!

All my activities would make it appear that I had lots of money. I should have been saving my money for "old age." My advantage was that I did not mind hard work, and I was rewarded for it. Due to old age, along with my injuries from World War II and the helicopter crash in British Columbia, I am now 100% disabled, but still not retired at 86 years old.

My system and style of work provided me with what I needed to spend a lifetime exploring Alaska and the Yukon Territory and to fly up and down the coast, including the Yucatan Peninsula. I made a lot of money, but I used it for what it was for: enjoying life and raising a family. I have a loving family that has put up with me for all these years, even though I spent a lot of time away. They have always supported me.

I could have had several million dollars tucked away by now; instead, I have a million memories.

Now, in my waning years, I have the satisfaction of looking back on the things that I have done, the adventures I have taken, and the places of beauty I have seen. The majestic snow-covered mountains I have flown over surely no eagle has seen more than I, and the inner peace I gained from the time I broke away has never been lost. Do you have that urge calling you? I say, answer it!

About the Author

Walter Yates spent his early years on Burny Mountain (now called Yates Mountain) in Arkansas, living in a log house built by his father. He went to school in a one-room building in Loy, Arkansas, four miles from home. Loy is long gone now but lives on in memory for all the hardy souls that gathered there and told tall tales.

At age ten his family moved off the mountain and later moved to Texas. Walter loved to read adventure stories and dreamed of the day he would live some of his own. He joined the U.S. Marine Corps at age 17, one week before Pearl Harbor thrust the U.S. into World War II. He served in the South Pacific and was wounded on the island of Guadalcanal.

After learning to fly, Walter's adventures led him all over the world. His love of the wilderness drew him to the North Country where he built a log cabin 100 miles from the nearest neighbor and lived off the land while filming the documentary *Breakaway*.

Tragedy nearly ended his adventurous life when his helicopter crashed and burned in British Columbia. Badly injured, he lay there for 14 days before his rescue by the Royal Canadian Air Force.

After his recovery, Walter spent several years gold mining in the Yukon Territory. Most notable is the season he spent exploring ghost towns and deserted gold mines with his helicopter.

Walter Yates has built several boats, two helicopters, and an airplane. As a real estate developer he established many residential neighborhoods, including the fly-in subdivision called Breakaway Park in Cedar Park, Texas where residents keep their planes in their backyards. He lives there today with his wife Tracy.